Seen & Heard

What people are s
Max Atkinson's wri

"Knowledgeable, well-written and oc
expect from a professional communications consultant. Well laid-out ....
being visually stunning, Max wins points for plenty of functionality, links and
videos. He seems to be on something of a crusade against the heinous practise
of powerpoint presentations, which lends this blog a unique flavour. Not many
blogs out there focus so much on politician's presentation style, so this makes a
nice addition. Regular posting and decent opinion pieces round out what is a
thoroughly impressive piece of work."

— **Politics.co.uk review of the blog**

"For all those who are serious anout the art of making speeches... There was
scarcely a single major speech, in my eleven years as leader of the Liberal
Democrats, that I made without benefiting from Max's personal advice and help."

— **Paddy Ashdown, Leader of the Liberal Democrats, 1988-99**

"As a speechwriter for Ronald Reagan, I relied for rhetorical direction on the
great speakers from Demosthenes to Churchill, on the great guides from
Aristotle to the President himself, and on Max Atkinson. No one surpasses
Atkinson in the rigor and clarity with which he spells out how to move
audiences to applause, get quoted in the media and become known as the
most brilliant presence on any podium."

— **Clark Judge, Managing Director, White House Writers Group**

"Neither politicians nor business leaders can lead today without the ability to
communicate effectively with audiences of all sizes and compositions. They
have two choices: (1) be born with the ability, or (2) read Max Atkinson's
books and learn."

— **Michael Sheehan, Speech coach to President Bill Clinton**

"Over the last 30 years I have spoken in 28 countries, launching cars, opening
buildings and guest speaking at conferences. Throughout I have read any book
on oratory that I can lay my hands on and Max Atkinson's Lend Me You Ears is
by far the best. I had planned, in my retirement, to write the perfect book on
public speaking. I will now have to find something else to do."

— **Peter Hancock, Managing Director, Peter Hancock International Ltd.**

By the same author

Lend Me Your Ears: All you need to know about making speeches and presentations

Our Masters' Voices: The Language and Body Language of Politics

Conversations and commentary
on contemporary communication

Seen
& Heard

Max Atkinson

Author of the international bestseller
Lend Me Your Ears

Text ©2008-2014 Max Atkinson

Seen & **Heard**
Conversations and commentary on contemporary communication

Published by Sunmakers, a division of Eldamar Ltd,
157 Oxford Road, Cowley, Oxford, OX4 2ES, UK
www.sunmakers.co.uk
Tel +44(0)1865 779944

Version 1.0

ISBN: 978-1-908693-197-8

www.speaking.co.uk
maxatkinson.blogspot.co.uk

For Joey

maxatkinson.blogspot.co.uk

Foreword

The publication of this volume co-incidentally marks the 10th anniversary of *Lend Me Your Ears*, Max Atkinson's definitive and bestselling book on speech writing and delivery. The problem with writing a definitive book is that it leaves very little else to say on the subject. But since then, Max definitely has had more to say. His thoughts, opinions and analysis of speakers, speeches and all those in the business of communication have been diligently captured in detail on his blog, which he started in 2008.

The blog was received well. Politics.co.uk awarded it the same score (8/10) as Iain Dale's Diary, one of the country's top-rated political blogs. In their review, Politics.co.uk said of Max's blog, *"Not many blogs out there focus so much on politicians' presentation styles, so this makes a nice addition... decent opinion pieces round out what is a thoroughly impressive piece of work."*

It was positive comments like this that triggered the idea of turning the knowledge on the blog into a book. The logic for this move is fairly obvious. As everyone knows, reading from a book is very different from reading from a screen, and even though the blog in its entirety is fully and freely available, navigating a web resource is quite a time-consuming task. A book can serve a different purpose: it can complement the blog as well as opening it up to a broader and different type of readership. We made the decision not to simply print the lot, but to focus on key posts which showcase the timeless and valuable advice and analysis Max offers.

Many of the blog posts refer to videos. Of course we can't include those in a book. But if you navigate to the particular date on the blog, you'll find the links there.

What you will find here, presented in chronological order, are unusually insightful critiques of some major and influential recent political speeches (the arrival of Obama jumps out as particularly important). You'll find in-depth details on the approaches adopted by British political figures. Margaret Thatcher is there of course, and Tony Blair. Max charts the fall from grace of the Labour party and Gordon Brown's last hurrah, through to the formation of the 2010 coalition government that brought the Conservatives out of the wilderness and the Liberal Democrats into power.

There is something for everyone in Max's observational tour. We have insights and ideas to reflect on, while the links and references provide prompts for further explanation. It all adds up to an essential "communicator's almanac", and by publishing it in this format, the blog becomes a reference work that will stand the test of time.

– Ayd Instone
Publisher, Sunmakers
October 2014

Contents

27th September 2008

Tips for Gordon Brown's conference speech

David Cameron does it. Nick Clegg has tried it. But there is no need for Gordon Brown to bend to fashion by abandoning the traditional lectern for a no-notes, pacing the stage speech.

He tried it at Warwick in July, but the regular pacing – two or three steps from side to side – was distracting. Instead he should make the most of looking and sounding like the "elder statesman" he has become.

It also throws up other problems, such as what to do when the audience applauds. Do you walk aimlessly around, stand still, look down, look away? At a lectern, at least he can look down as if to check his script, turn a page or have a drink of water, all of which look a good deal more natural.

Maybe there's a lesson to be learned here from Neil Kinnock, who is reputed to have had a lectern made to measure to fit the width of his shoulders.

Secondly, he needs to appreciate the importance of pauses. Churchill, Thatcher, Reagan, Clinton, Blair and Cameron paused, on average, every five words. But, in some of Mr Brown's speeches, he is pausing only once every fifteen words. This needs to come down. When and where the pauses come make a huge difference to the meaning, feeling and emphasis.

Thirdly he needs to think about his hands. In the past, Brown has resorted to a small number of repetitive gestures that seemed contrived or robotic. This is another argument for using a lectern: at a podium, his hands tend to look after themselves and appear more "natural", whether clutching the sides or moving away occasionally to give emphasis.

Finally he should make his speeches simpler. He tries to pack far too much information into them, including long recitations of statistics and huge numbers. He cannot rely on everyone finding such things easy to understand.

Published in *The Times* before Gordon Brown's conference speech.

27th September 2008

More tips for Gordon Brown's speech

When it comes to party leaders' speeches in the television age, it's widely believed that the audience that really matters is the millions watching excerpts on news bulletins at home, rather than the hundreds who are actually there in the conference hall.

But for Gordon Brown this year, his live audience is arguably far more important than usual, consisting as it will of key Labour decision-makers and activists who will have to be won over if he's to succeed in reducing the heat in the kitchen. So here are three tips that could help to make or break his performance on Tuesday.

1. Make everyone in the audience feel included

It's quite common for speakers to look at one side of the audience more frequently than they look at the other. For example, during Mrs Thatcher's speeches, she used to look to the left three times more often than she looked to the right. But Gordon Brown suffers from by far the most serious case of "skewed eye-contact' I have ever seen, and spends the vast majority of his time looking towards his left. His glances to the right sometimes fall to as low as 5% of the time, as happened in his speech to the Labour Party Forum in July, during which he only looked to the right for just under two of the 37 minutes it took to deliver.

The trouble with this is that it's likely to make half the audience feel ignored or left out, as if he's not really speaking to them at all. And with a conference audience made up of so many doubters, dissidents and plotters, he really cannot afford to risk making a large proportion of them feel excluded or uninvolved. So he needs to remember to alternate his gaze to both sides (and straight ahead) for the duration of his speech.

2. Try to trigger as many bursts of applause as you can

Although observers and commentators are not equipped with clapometers, the fact is that they do notice how much applause there is and use this as a basis for assessing the success or otherwise of a speech. This means that the more bursts of applause there are and the longer the standing ovation at the end, the more favourably will the speech be reported by journalists. So the more positive the response Mr Brown gets, the more will it weaken the case of those who want to continue their campaign against him – and might even see them off for the foreseeable future.

Two key points need to be borne in mind when it comes to maximizing the frequency of applause. The first is that about 70% of the applause in political speeches comes after the speaker attacks, criticises or ridicules the opposition.

The second is that most bursts of applause come after the speaker has used one or other of a small range of very simple rhetorical techniques. This means that he should use these to package as many of his key messages as possible, because the more use he makes of them, the more applause will he get.

If he could equal or exceed Margaret Thatcher's 1981 conference speech, when she was applauded, on average, every three sentences, Mr Brown would surely be home and dry.

3. Don't lift lines from other politicians

In 1988, Senator Joe Biden's campaign for his party's presidential nomination collapsed when he was exposed for having borrowed verbatim from a Neil Kinnock speech during the 1987 general election – an indiscretion that has continued to haunt him since being selected as Barack Obama's vice-presidential running mate.

There was a strong echo of this in Gordon Brown's July speech to the Labour Party Policy Forum, when he said "There is nothing bad about Britain that cannot be corrected by what's good about Britain", which was suspiciously close to a line from Bill Clinton's inaugural address in 1993: "There is nothing wrong with America that cannot be cured by what's right with America."

Brown was lucky that it went unnoticed at the time. But the Labour Party Conference is a much bigger stage, and Mr Brown and his speechwriters should be aware that there is nothing to be gained by taking the risk of being accused of plagiarism.

27th September 2008

Did Gordon Brown take my advice?

Judging from his conference speech, Gordon Brown seems to have taken on board the three main points I recommended on these pages on Monday, and arguably gained from some of the benefits I had in mind.

The first was that he should stop trying to emulate the "unscripted" walkabout style favoured by Messrs. Cameron and Clegg and return to the lectern. By doing this, he looked much more comfortable than when he's tried walking about: his gestures looked much more "natural", he didn't have to worry about what to do during bursts of applause and, perhaps most important of all, he came across as a confident and experienced elder statesman.

My second concern was that, in some of his previous speeches, his average pause rate was only once every fifteen words – three times longer than in speeches by the likes of Churchill, Thatcher, Reagan, Clinton and Blair, who used to pause, on average, every five words. Not pausing often enough can cause two main problems. One is that it's much easier for audiences to follow if they can take in short chunks at a time. Another is that even slight pauses can transform the meaning, emphasis and mood of the point being made.

On this occasion, Mr. Brown made a startling improvement on some of his other efforts by matching, almost exactly, the one pause per five words of the famous leaders mentioned above.

The third thing that's worried me about his speeches is his past tendency to pack in long lists of statistical information that doesn't instantly mean very much to the average listener. On this too, he did particularly well. Certainly he had some big numbers, but there was a really nice sequence where he made them come to life with real life examples, such as "That's not just a number, that's the dad who lives to walk his daughter up the aisle" – a contrastive technique that he used four or five times in quick succession.

And the contrast, in its various forms, triggers about a third of the applause in political speeches. Before Mr Brown's speech, I'd said that if he could equal or exceed Mrs Thatcher's achievement at the 1981 Conservative conference (when things weren't going too well for her either), at which she was applauded, on average once every three sentences, he would be home and dry.

He came very close, with a rate of once every 3.5 sentences – so he might just be nearly there.

27th September 2008

Time for Cameron to surf applause?

When it comes to speech-making, David Cameron has enjoyed more success than most British politicians of his generation. His short unscripted pitch for the party leadership in 2005 was enough to transform him from rank outsider to eventual winner. And his speech at last year's conference was so effective that it was arguably one of the factors that helped to deter Gordon Brown from calling an election at a time when Labour were still safely ahead in the polls.

If Mr Cameron has already mastered most of the key techniques that set a good orator apart from an average one, the question arises as to whether there's anything else he could be doing to take the next step into the premier league? And one thing he might like to consider is the art of surfing applause, a technique that's only to be found among those at the top of their trade. Past maestros include

Martin Luther King and Tony Benn, and today's most prominent exponents are ç Sarkozy and Barack Obama.

Unlike most speakers, surfers don't just stop whenever the audience applauds and wait until they've finished. What surfers do is to carry on speaking after the applause has started, which creates a number of positive impressions. It makes it look as though you hadn't been seeking applause at all, and are really quite surprised that the audience has interrupted you with an unexpected display of approval.

Then, if you keep trying to go on while the audience is still clapping, it's as if you're telling them that, unlike less passionate politicians, you're the kind of person who regards getting your message across as much more important than waiting around to savour the applause. If you're really lucky, and the broadcasters want to put this particular extract on prime time news programmes, the lack of any clean break between your speech and the applause makes it difficult for them to edit without including the adulation of the crowd as well – so that the various positive impressions are transmitted beyond the hall to the much bigger numbers viewing or listening at home.

On the plus side, Mr Cameron is already exhibiting the first signs of surfing in some of his speeches, but needs to carry through with it a bit further if he's to make the most of it. A sign that he was almost ready for fully-fledged surfing came in his 2005 conference speech, when he said:

> "That is a stain on this country and this government [applause starts] and what is – [applause stops] – and what is the government's answer?"

This was all right as far as it went, but he didn't have to stop after only a single attempt at carrying on and then wait for the applause to subside before speaking again. More experienced surfers don't just make one aborted attempt to speak during the applause, but do it several times in a row, as in this example from Barack Obama:

> ".. that threatens my civil liberties. [applause starts] It is that fundamental belief – [applause continues] – It is that fundamental belief – [applause starts to fade] It is that fundamental belief that I am my brother's keeper, I am my sister's keeper, that makes this country work."

The important thing is to make sure that you don't say anything that really matters while the noise of the applause might still drown it out, because there's no point in developing the message until you're sure it will be audible.

Repeating the first few words, as Obama did in the above example, is probably the easiest and safest way of doing it, but it's not the only option. Another is to keep adding a few more words each time until the applause has died down enough for people to be able to hear the fully formed sentence you want them to hear. Really experienced surfers develop a finely-tuned ear for the volume of applause that enables them to know exactly when it's become quiet enough for it to be safe to carry on.

Tony Benn often used to do this three or four times before carrying on with his point, as in this example from the 1980s:

> [Applause starts] "My resent – my resentment – my resentment about the – uh – [applause fades] my resentment about the exclusion of the House of Lords …"

Nearly 30 years later, he's still at it:

> "That's the [applause starts] real distinction that we have to face – and it's not just – actually – [applause stops] you can't even give Karl Marx the credit for that."

It might seem, of course that the Conservative Party's annual conference is far too important and exposed a platform for Mr Cameron to start having a go at surfing the applause. But he has already been showing a natural inclination to do it, and taking it a small step further might not be any bigger risk than his daring departure from the lectern in 2005 – which yielded such a handsome dividend.

27th September 2008

Wisdom of forethought?

Back in 2004, when Brownites were busy briefing against Tony Blair, I wrote an article questioning whether Gordon Brown would make a good or better leader. It was rejected by the various newspapers I sent it to, but, in the light of events since he became Prime Minister, I don't think it was too far off the mark, written in September, 2004:

Can Labour afford to back Brown?
1979 Revisited?

On the day after the 1979 general election, I remember being flabbergasted by a letter to *The Guardian* that seemed completely out of touch with reality. Signed by Tony Benn and a group of like-minded colleagues, it attributed Labour's defeat entirely to the fact that it had failed to pursue policies that were left-wing enough. The authors conveniently ignored the fact that the Callaghan government had only managed to stay in power because of a pact with the Liberals. And they were undaunted by the complete lack of evidence of any widespread support for left-wing policies from an electorate that had just voted Margaret Thatcher into office.

With the price of ignoring the preferences of the electorate as high as eighteen years in opposition, the party ought surely have learnt its lesson. But calls from Labour malcontents to replace Blair with Brown are beginning to sound like the first drum beats of a renewed retreat from political reality. It's not just that the anti-Blair agitators have apparently forgotten that bickering and division are a sure-fire recipe for damaging a party's fortunes. They also seem to be assuming that the electorate would be happier, or at least just as happy, with Brown at the helm as they are with Blair.

What harks back so resonantly to 1979 is the fact that the change being pressed for by the siren voices within the party once again seem to have more to do with internal party feuds than any rational assessment of Labour's wider electoral appeal. Unlike the last time the party turned in on itself, the present situation has little or nothing to do with policy. After all, Blair and Brown were co-architects of New Labour, even though Brown now seems obsessed with deleting the phrase from his vocabulary. Nor, as far as the average voter can see, does there seem to be much difference between them about current policies. So whether the malcontents like it or not, the issue actually boils down to personalities – or to be more precise to which of them has greater electoral appeal. And this is where I find myself almost as flabbergasted by the pro-Brown lobby as when I read the Benn letter 25 years ago. And there are at least three reasons why a Brown leadership could be one small step, and perhaps even a giant leap, towards electoral disaster.

Lawyer v. Lecturer?

Gordon Brown's first problem is that, when it comes to communication skills, the former lawyer has the former university lecturer beaten hands down. Blair knows how to craft and deliver a speech. He knows how to make the most of rhetoric, imagery and anecdotes to get his points across. And he has that rare and essential electoral asset of being able to attract respect, however grudging, from supporters of other parties. His "people's princess" speech on the death of the Princess of Wales caught the mood of the nation, regardless of party affiliation. And the impact of his speeches after 9/11 transcended national boundaries: such was the power of his oratory that, for a while at least, many Americans, Republicans and Democrats alike, looked on Blair, rather than Bush, as the world's leading spokesman against global terrorism.

By comparison, even the most casual research into audience reactions to Gordon Brown's speeches comes up with descriptions like "the quintessence of dour", "a finance geek in a grey suit", "serious", "sombre" or just plain "boring". However much he may be admired for his undoubted intelligence or competence as chancellor, he comes across as dull and uninspiring – except to a tiny minority of political commentators who delight in looking for the presence or absence of words and phrases that might be a coded hint about the current state of his relationship with Blair and/or the party at large.

In an age when coverage of speeches makes up an increasingly small proportion of broadcast political news, Brown's supporters might offer the defence that dourness on the podium doesn't matter as much as it did in the past. But even if there is some truth in this, the trouble is that their hero has a second, and arguably even bigger, handicap in the way he conducts himself in what has become the main cockpit of political debate on television and radio, namely the interview.

Not Answering Questions

For at least two decades, viewers and listeners have had put up with the sight and sound of politicians treating interviewers' questions as prompts to say anything they like, regardless of what they were asked, or as yet another opportunity to dodge an issue. As an exponent of how to carry this depressing art to its limits, Gordon Brown has no serious competitors among contemporary British politicians. When he was still shadow chancellor, one commentator noted that if you asked him what he had for breakfast, his most likely response would be "what the country needs is a prudent budget" – and that would merely be the preamble to a lecture about his latest thoughts on the matter. I recently asked one of the BBC's most experienced and best-known presenters what it was like to interview him. His answer was rather more outspoken than I'd expected:

"Brown answers his own questions, never the interviewer's, and is utterly shameless. He will say what he wants to say and that's it. And he'll say it fifty times in one interview without any embarrassment at all. I've never met anyone quite like him in that respect. I once spent 40 minutes on one narrow point and still failed to get him to make the smallest concession. He's extraordinary and is never anything but evasive and verbose."

If politicians like Brown think it clever or smart to get one over the interviewer with such tactics, they betray a staggering lack of sensitivity to two rather obvious and basic facts about the way people interpret verbal communication. The first is that viewers and listeners can tell instantly when interviewees are being evasive. And the second is that they don't much like it. Politicians may say that they're worried about their low esteem in the eyes of the public and growing voter apathy. But it never seems to occur to them that their relentless refusal to give straight answers to questions might have something to do with it.

The "drink tonight' Test

Finally, Gordon Brown fails a simple test that I've found to be an interesting barometer of charismatic potential. I first started using it during a stint as visiting professor at an American university which just happened to coincide with 1984 U.S. presidential election. Noting that all the bumper stickers on cars in the faculty parking lot were pro-Democrat, I took to asking colleagues a simple question: "If you could go out for a drink tonight with Reagan or Mondale, which one would you choose?" Without exception, they opted for Reagan, who was duly elected a few weeks later.

According to this test, the Tories have made a number of serious blunders since the demise of Margaret Thatcher: it pointed to Heseltine rather than Major, Clarke rather than Hague and Portillo rather than Duncan Smith. And, if the opportunity had arisen, David Davis might have come out ahead of Michael Howard

Applied to Labour's choice of leader after the death of John Smith, the test resulted in 100 percent of my respondents opting for a drink with Blair rather than Brown – a statistic that has remained unchanged to this day. Add to this the prime minister's greater effectiveness as an orator, the chancellor's dour image and continuing evasiveness in interviews, mix in the damaging effect of internal splits and squabbling, and the plan to ditch Blair in favour of Brown begins to look almost as far removed from electoral reality as the left-wing fantasies of Tony Benn and his cronies in the 1980s.

27th September 2008

Mediated speeches – whom do we really want to hear?

I've just been watching the first of the US presidential debates on the BBC's main evening news programme, as I wanted to see what the candidates had to say, how well they said it and how competent they seemed. But actually I had to watch and listen to far more from the BBC's correspondent in Washington than from Obama or McCain – the reporter was speaking for 2.4 minutes compared with 30 seconds each for the two candidates – i.e. the BBC forced its viewers to listen to more than twice as much media commentary as we were allowed to hear from the the candidates themselves.

Of course, I shouldn't really have been surprised because I know that things have been moving in this direction for a long time. Between 1968 and 1988, the length of excerpts from speeches shown on American television news programmes during presidential campaigns fell from an average of 42 seconds in 1968 to an average of only 9 seconds in 1988. In the UK, during the 1979 general election campaign, BBC 2 showed a nightly half-hour programme of excerpts from the day's speeches. It was not continued during the 1983 election, and, by 1997 (and all subsequent UK elections), viewers were much more likely to see shots of politicians speaking in the background, with the all important foreground being dominated by a TV reporter summarising what the speaker was saying – as also happened during parts of tonight's report on the Obama-McCain debate.

But does it matter? I think it does, because television has the capacity (which it used to exercise long ago) of allowing viewers/voters to hear arguments coming directly from the horses' mouths, from which they used to be able to draw their own conclusions about what they saw and heard – which strikes me as something that should be encouraged in a democracy.

But tonight, as usual, the BBC took it upon itself to tell us all what to think – i.e. "the debate was a tie with no clear winner." From the little they did let us hear, I'm not sure I agree. But, without seeing rather more than 30 seconds of Senators Obama and McCain arguing their cases, I'm not really in much of a position to come to a considered or definite conclusion of my own. And that's precisely why I find this ever-increasing occupation of the air time by media employees so unsatisfactory and and why I worry about the damage it might be doing to the democratic process itself.

30th September 2008

Cameron takes to the lectern in a crisis

One reason why I suggested last week that Gordon Brown should give up trying to emulate David Cameron's walkabout style of delivery and return to the lectern was that it would make the embattled P.M. look more statesmanlike.

So what does Cameron do when he wants to appear statesmanlike in the middle of today's financial mayhem? Well, it was back to the lectern, back to a script and hardly any movement at all, let alone any walking about.

And making this unscheduled emergency intervention at his party conference on the day before his big speech was probably a very smart move. Otherwise, the risk was that both he and the Conservative conference would have been completely wiped off the front pages and prime-time news programmes by all the reports of financial crisis. But doing what he did paid off and got him to the top of tonight's BBC 10 o'clock television news.

His dilemma now is how to play it tomorrow? Will we see another "unscripted" walkabout or a carefully scripted statesman speaking at a lectern?

1st October 2008

"Mature, grown-up and statesmanlike" Cameron at the lectern

So David Cameron did stay at the lectern for his big speech – and won the instant accolade of being "mature, grown-up and statesmanlike" in one of the interviews with the party faithful a few seconds after he'd finished.

But there's still some room for improvement in his delivery. There were quite a few mis-readings of the script that had to be corrected as he went along. If, as seems likely, this was because he hadn't had enough time to rehearse all the last-minute changes that were apparently made, the lesson is clear – late modifications are fine, but only if you leave enough time to rehearse the new lines.

He also did something I'd never noticed before, perhaps because it doesn't happen when he's doing a walkabout speech. In fact, it was a rather unusual form of "skewed" eye-contact. It wasn't that he excluded one half of the audience by hardly ever looking at them at all, as is likely to happen if you're sitting to Gordon Brown's right during a speech. What Cameron did was to alternate between one very long period looking one way and another very long period looking the other, with occasional glances straight ahead.

On average, it was about 20 seconds each way, which means that the rest of the audience was having to wait for about five sentences before they got another glance from their leader.

The most extreme case was one sequence when he spent nearly a minute and a half (about twenty sentences), looking continuously to one side, effectively excluding everyone on the other side (and in front of him) for a very long time indeed.

So my advice would be that, if he's going to carry on using a lectern, he needs to work on alternating his glances much more frequently than he did in this speech, so that no one in the audience can complain that he's ignoring them for unusually long periods of time.

10th November 2008

Rhetoric & imagery in Obama's victory speech

The *Independent on Sunday* asked me to annotate Barack Obama's victory speech last week, the results of which were published on 9th November. Here is my introduction followed by the speech with my commentary interwoven:

It's not often that a single speech launches a politician from obscurity on to the national stage. Ronald Reagan achieved it when he spoke in support of Barry Goldwater at the Republican Convention in 1964, and Obama achieved it with his keynote address to the Democratic Convention four years ago. Already he ranks highly in the league of all-time greats like Abraham Lincoln and Martin Luther King. He is particularly fond of contrasts, three-part lists and various combinations of the two. He also knows how to use imagery both to increase impact and to make his points evoke associations with great communicators of the past like Lincoln, King and Reagan. But one of the most interesting things about all this is that, even when you can see that Mr Obama is using the same simple techniques that every other inspiring speaker uses, the power and impact of his language remain undiminished.

The speech

"If there is anyone out there who still doubts that America is a place where all things are possible; who still wonders if the dream of our founders is alive in our time; who still questions the power of our democracy, tonight is your answer."

Obama kicks off by evoking the American Dream, implicitly linking to Martin Luther King's "I have a dream" speech – by addressing 3 groups of people out there.

"It's the answer told by lines that stretched around schools and churches in
numbers this nation has never seen; by people who waited three hours and
four hours, many for the very first time in their lives, because they believed
that this time must be different; that their voices could be that difference."

This is the first of 3 groups of people for whom "it's the answer". High turnout
depicted by images of voters in queues, etc.

"It's the answer spoken by young and old, rich and poor, Democrat and
Republican, black, white, (first groups depicted by series of contrasts)
Hispanic, Asian, Native American (group of 3), gay, straight, disabled and
not disabled (two more contrasting groups) – Americans who sent a
message to the world that we have never been just a collection of
individuals or a collection of Red States and Blue States: we are, and
always will be, the United States of America."

The 3rd item contrasts with the first two; and this "not red states-not blue states-
but United States" line harks back to Obama's speech at the 2004 Democratic
Convention, that first brought him to wider public notice, where he used it to
introduce the "politics of hope" theme that has become one of his trademarks.

"It's the answer that led those who have been told for so long by so many
to be cynical, and fearful, and doubtful of what we can achieve to put their
hands on the arc of history and bend it once more toward the hope of a
better day."

The "hope" theme again, plus the image of bending an arc towards a better future.

"It's been a long time coming, but tonight, because of what we did on
this day, in this election, at this defining moment, change has come
to America."

A contrast between "what's been coming" and "what's now come" – and it's come
at 3 moments ("this day", "this election", "this moment").

"A little bit earlier this evening I received an extraordinarily gracious call
from Senator McCain. He fought long and hard in this campaign, and he's
fought even longer and harder for the country he loves. He has endured
sacrifices for America that most of us cannot begin to imagine. We are
better off for the service rendered by this brave and selfless leader."

McCain has done 3 worthy things ("fought a campaign", "fought for the country", "endured sacrifices").

> "I congratulate him, I congratulate Governor Palin, for all they have achieved, and I look forward to working with them to renew this nation's promise in the months ahead.
>
> "I want to thank my partner in this journey, a man who campaigned from his heart and spoke for the men and women he grew up with on the streets of Scranton and rode with on that train home to Delaware, the vice-president-elect of the United States, Joe Biden."

Biden has also done 3 things ("campaigned", "spoken", "ridden on a train"). The train imagery personalises his praise for Biden, who started commuting daily from Delaware to Washington in 1972, after his two young sons had survived a road crash in which his wife and their daughter died.

> "And I would not be standing here tonight without the unyielding support of my best friend for the last 16 years, the rock of our family, the love of my life, the nation's next first lady, Michelle Obama. Sasha and Malia, I love you both more than you can imagine, and you have earned the new puppy that's coming with us to the White House."

Note that the invitations to the audience to applaud Biden and Michelle are perfectly executed – the person is identified, praised and finally named. Naming the person earlier tends to confuse audiences as to when and if they are supposed to applaud. Mention of the puppy for the children depicts him as a thoroughly "normal", kindly father and family man.

> "And while she's no longer with us, I know my grandmother is watching, along with the family that made me who I am. I miss them tonight, and know that my debt to them is beyond measure. To my sister Maya, my sister Auma, all my other brothers and sisters – thank you so much for all the support you have given me. I am grateful to them."

This sentence can be heard as an implicit reminder that he's a practising Christian who believes in life after death, followed by more "I'm a family man" references.

> "To my campaign manager David Plouffe, the unsung hero of this campaign, who built the best political campaign in the history of the United

States of America. My chief strategist David Axelrod, who has been a partner with me every step of the way, and to the best campaign team ever assembled in the history of politics – you made this happen, and I am forever grateful for what you've sacrificed to get it done.

"But above all, I will never forget who this victory truly belongs to – it belongs to you."

Puzzle-solution.

"I was never the likeliest candidate for this office. We didn't start with much money or many endorsements. Our campaign was not hatched in the halls of Washington – it began in the backyards of Des Moines and the living rooms of Concord and the front porches of Charleston."

This is the first of 3 points about his campaign ("started modestly", "built by working men", "grew strength from young people"). Then this first point uses a combined contrast and 3 part list, in which Washington is contrasted with 3 ordinary provincial cities. Adding to the impact of this contrast between Washington and the 3 other places are simple images that contrast the corridors of power in one ("halls of Washington") with everyday places in the others ("backyards", "living rooms" and "front porches").

"It was built by working men and women who dug into what little savings they had to give $5 and $10 and $20 to the cause."

Second point about campaign is that it was built by 3 types of drains on personal cash.

"It grew strength from the young people who rejected the myth of their generation's apathy; who left their homes and their families for jobs that offered little pay and less sleep; it grew strength from the not-so-young people who braved the bitter cold and scorching heat to knock on the doors of perfect strangers; from the millions of Americans who volunteered, and organised, and proved that more than two centuries later, a government of the people, by the people and for the people has not perished from the Earth."

Third point is that it grew strength from 3 groups of people ("the young", "not-so-young people", and "millions of Americans"). Sacrifice depicted by images of young people leaving homes and supporters braving contrasting climatic conditions – summed up as a proof that Abraham Lincoln's most famous line, also a 3 part list, still applies. He could have said it hasn't disappeared, vanished or died, but "perished" has the advantage of adding another alliterative word.

> "This is your victory. I know you didn't do this just to win an election and I know you didn't do it for me. You did it because you understand the enormity of the task that lies ahead."

The two reasons "why you didn't do it" are contrasted with the third reason "why you did".

> "For even as we celebrate tonight, we know the challenges that tomorrow will bring are the greatest of our lifetime – two wars, a planet in peril, the worst financial crisis in a century."

There are 3 challenges ahead, and the third one is longer than the first two. This is a feature of some of the most famous 3 part lists of all time, such as "life, liberty and the pursuit of happiness" and "father, son and holy ghost". "Tomorrow" obviously doesn't mean "Thursday" and is a simple metaphor for the future. The hazards to the planet can be described in many different ways, but "peril" has the "poetic" advantage of alliteration.

> "Even as we stand here tonight, we know there are brave Americans waking up in the deserts of Iraq and the mountains of Afghanistan to risk their lives for us."

Obama uses the "deserts" and "mountains" imagery to highlight the tough conditions American soldiers are facing.

> "There are mothers and fathers who will lie awake after their children fall asleep and wonder how they'll make the mortgage, or pay their doctor's bills, or save enough for their child's college education. There is new energy to harness and new jobs to be created; new schools to build and threats to meet and alliances to repair."

The contrast between brave Americans waking up to face difficulties in foreign places and American parents unable to sleep because of difficulties at home – of which there happen to be 3 (paying "mortgages", "medical expenses" and "college fees").

"The road ahead will be long. Our climb will be steep."

This simple image of the long road and steep climb was quite widely featured in the media as the main soundbite from the speech. It is also the first of 3 challenges that lie ahead ("it's going to take time", "there'll be opposition" and "we need to remake the nation").

"We may not get there in one year or even in one term, but America – I have never been more hopeful than I am tonight that we will get there. I promise you – we as a people will get there."

The mountain-climbing imagery, followed by "we as a people will get there" evokes the last speech made by Martin Luther King on the night before he was assassinated: "I've been up to the mountain, I've looked over and I've seen the promised land. I may not get there with you but I want you to know tonight that we as a people will get to the promised land."

"There will be setbacks and false starts. There are many who won't agree with every decision or policy I make as president, and we know that government can't solve every problem. But I will always be honest with you about the challenges we face. I will listen to you, especially when we disagree.

"And above all, I will ask you to join in the work of remaking this nation the only way it's been done in America for 221 years – block by block, brick by brick, calloused hand by calloused hand."

There are 3 alliterative building images, involving repetition of words, to characterize how this has always been done. It's also another example where the third one is the longest of the three.

"What began 21 months ago in the depths of winter cannot end on this autumn night."

A contrast between winter and autumn.

"This victory alone is not the change we seek – it is only the chance for us to make that change."

An alliterative contrast between the victory not being the "change" but the "chance to make the change".

"And that cannot happen if we go back to the way things were. It cannot happen without you, without a new spirit of service, a new spirit of sacrifice."

The 3 reasons why it can't happen, and alliteration with four words beginning with "S" (and more "S-" words at the start of the next sentence).

"So let us summon a new spirit of patriotism; of service and responsibility where each of us resolves to pitch in and work harder and look after not only ourselves, but each other. Let us remember that if this financial crisis taught us anything, it's that we cannot have a thriving Wall Street while Main Street suffers – in this country, we rise or fall as one nation; as one people."

A contrast between "ourselves" and "each other", followed by contrast between Wall Street and Main Street, where street names are simple metaphors depicting the worlds of high finance and ordinary everyday shopping.

"Let us resist the temptation to fall back on the same partisanship and pettiness and immaturity that has poisoned our politics for so long."

Lets not fall back into 3 errors ("partisanship", "pettiness" and "immaturity"). He could just as well said "harmed" or "damaged" politics, but "poisoned" has the advantage of alliteration with other "p" words close by.

"Let us remember that it was a man from this state who first carried the banner of the Republican Party to the White House - a party founded on the values of self-reliance, individual liberty, and national unity."

The Republican Party had 3 founding values, and Lincoln surfaces again, with a reminder that he, like Obama, started out in Illinois state politics.

"Those are values that we all share, and while the Democratic Party has won a great victory tonight, we do so with a measure of humility and determination to heal the divides that have held back our progress. As Lincoln said to a nation far more divided than ours: "We are not enemies, but friends … though passion may have strained it must not break our bonds of affection."

Another quote from Lincoln, which starts with a contrast between "enemies" and "friends".

"And to those Americans whose support I have yet to earn – I may not have won your vote tonight, but I hear your voices, I need your help, and I will be your president too."

A combination in which the second part of the contrast is a 3 part list ("you may not have voted for me", "but 3 things link us together").

"And to all those watching tonight from beyond our shores, from parliaments and palaces (alliteration) to those who are huddled around radios in the forgotten corners of the world – our stories are singular, but our destiny is shared (contrast), and a new dawn of American leadership is at hand."

This is addressed to 3 groups of people ("foreigners", "political leaders" and the "developing world"), with alliteration and image of people in "huddled in corners". The mood and imagery here is reminiscent of the way Kennedy addressed different parts of the world in his inaugural address in 1960: "To those peoples in the huts and villages across the globe ..." The image of a "new dawn of American leadership" also has echoes of another line in Kennedy's inaugural: "The torch has passed to a new generation of Americans ..."

"To those who would tear the world down – we will defeat you. To those who seek peace and security – we support you.

"And to all those who have wondered if America's beacon still burns as bright – tonight we proved once more that the true strength of our nation comes not from the might of our arms or the scale of our wealth, but from the enduring power of our ideals: democracy, liberty, opportunity and unyielding hope."

An alliterative image of a "beacon burning" echoes one of the first few lines of Martin Luther King's "I have a dream" speech: "This momentous decree came as a great beacon light of hope to millions of Negro slaves who had been seared in the flames of withering injustice." Then we have another contrast in which the third one, "power of our ideals", contrasts with the first two. The first three of these are commonly cited as American ideals, but "hope" resurfaces again, having been a central theme for Obama since he published his book *The Audacity of Hope*.

"For that is the true genius of America – that America can change. Our union can be perfected. And what we have already achieved gives us hope for what we can and must achieve tomorrow."

The genius of America has 3 components, "hope" again and "tomorrow" again used as metaphor for the future.

"This election had many firsts and many stories that will be told for generations. But one that's on my mind tonight is about a woman who cast her ballot in Atlanta. She's a lot like the millions of others who stood in line to make their voice heard in this election except for one thing – Ann Nixon Cooper is 106 years old."

This starts an extended anecdote to highlight a century of change, setting it up by contrasting this one with the many other stories that could be told. This woman just happens to come from the same place as Martin Luther King (Atlanta). And the fact that she's 106 enables him to talk about events from the past century, as MLK did at the start of "I have a dream". His reference point was the emancipation proclamation, in relation to which he produced a series of sentences starting with "One hundred years later ..." ("But one hundred years later, the Negro still is not free. One hundred years later, the life of the Negro is still sadly crippled by the manacles of segregation and the chains of discrimination ...").

"She was born just a generation past slavery; a time when there were no cars on the road or planes in the sky; when someone like her couldn't vote for two reasons – because she was a woman and because of the color of her skin.

Transport imagery is used to highlight technological change, and it now turns out that she is black as well as female and very old – which sets it up for him to say more about Martin Luther King's central themes of emancipation and discrimination.

"And tonight, I think about all that she's seen throughout her century in America – the heartache and the hope; the struggle and the progress; the times we were told that we can't, and the people who pressed on with that American creed: Yes, we can."

His thoughts about her are expressed in 3 contrasts ("heartache and hope", "struggle and progress", we can't versus we can). The repetitive sequence of "Yes, we can" that eventually results in the audience joining in as a chorus, harks back to Obama's speech after losing the New Hampshire primary, where he did exactly the same thing. The audience participation can be heard as a secular version of the regular crowd interjections ("Yeah Lord", "Holy, Holy Holy", "Amen", etc in Martin Luther King's speeches. "Yes, we can" has no religious connotations and carries no risk of making Jews and members of other religions feel excluded.

> "At a time when women's voices were silenced and their hopes dismissed, she lived to see them stand up and speak out and reach for the ballot. Yes, we can."

The first two negative things in the history of women's emancipation that she saw are contrasted with a victory in which they achieved 3 things.

> "When there was despair in the dust bowl and depression across the land, she saw a nation conquer fear itself with a New Deal, new jobs and a new sense of common purpose. Yes, we can."

An alliterative image referring to how a previous bad time in economic history was overcome by 3 new things.

> "When the bombs fell on our harbour and tyranny threatened the world, she was there to witness a generation rise to greatness and a democracy was saved. Yes, we can."

Two nasty things about war are contrasted with "salvation".

> "She was there for the buses in Montgomery, the hoses in Birmingham, a bridge in Selma, and a preacher from Atlanta who told a people that "we shall overcome". Yes, we can."

The 3 negative images of racial discrimination contrasted with a positive reference to Martin Luther King (again).

> "A man touched down on the Moon, a wall came down in Berlin, a world was connected by our own science and imagination. And this year, in this election, she touched her finger to a screen, and cast her vote, because after 106 years in America, through the best of times and the darkest of hours, she knows how America can change. Yes, we can."

The 3 images of advances she witnessed, followed by her being able to use modern technology to vote and a contrast between "best of times" and "darkest of hours".

"America, we have come so far. We have seen so much. But there is so much more to do."

A 3 part list with the third item longest and contrasting with the first two.

"So tonight, let us ask ourselves – if our children should live to see the next century; if my daughters should be so lucky to live as long as Ann Nixon Cooper, what change will they see? What progress will we have made?"

There are two rhetorical questions to lead into the peroration.

"This is our chance to answer that call. This is our moment."

This focus on "our moment", and "our time", developed further in the next sentence, again echoes Martin Luther King's "I have a dream" speech, in which his reference to "the fierce urgency of now" prefaced three sentences starting with "Now is the time …"

"This is our time – to put our people back to work and open doors of opportunity for our kids; to restore prosperity and promote the cause of peace; to reclaim the American dream and reaffirm that fundamental truth – that out of many, we are one; that while we breathe, we hope, and where we are met with cynicism and doubt, and those who tell us that we can't, we will respond with that timeless creed that sums up the spirit of a people: yes, we can."

The image of opening "doors of opportunity' brings us back to the American dream theme, harking back to the opening line of the speech. This simultaneously lets the audience know that he's nearly finished, continues to echo the spirit of Martin Luther King and gives a sense of overall structural unity.

"Thank you, God bless you, and may God bless the United States of America."

(P.S. A question I'm often asked by people attending my courses and/or who've read one of my books is: "how frequently can you can get away with using rhetorical techniques and imagery?" This speech in an impressive example of how they can be used to get across almost every single point you want to make – and, in this case, had the effect of moving many who heard it, both live in Chicago and around the world, to tears).

12th November 2008

The Queen's Speech: an exception that proves the ruler

At the State Opening of Parliament on 3rd December, the Queen, as she does every year, will be reading out her government's legislative plans for the months ahead. Most commentators will be listening to the Speech to find out what Gordon Brown is going to be putting on the statute book in 2009.

How not to speak inspiringly

But you can also listen to it as a model of how not to give an inspiring speech.

Public speaking at its best depends both on the language used to package the key messages and the way it is delivered. Using rhetoric, maintaining eye contact with the audience, pausing regularly and in particular places, stressing certain words and changing intonation are all essential ingredients in the cocktail for conveying passion and inspiring an audience. This is why it is so easy to "dehumanise" the speech of Daleks and other talking robots by the simple device of stripping out any hint of intonational variation and have them speak in a flat, regular and monotonous tone of voice.

When it comes to sounding unenthusiastic and uninterested in inspiring an audience, the Queen's Speech is an example with few serious competitors. She has no qualms about being seen to be wearing spectacles, which underline the fact that she is reading carefully from the script she holds so obviously in front of her. Nor is she in the least bit inhibited about fixing her eyes on the text rather than the audience. Then, as she enunciates the sentences, her tone is so disinterested as to make it abundantly clear that she is merely reciting words written by someone else and about which she has no personal feelings or opinions whatsoever.

Seen & Heard

This is, of course, how it has to be in a constitutional monarchy, where the head of state has to be publicly seen and heard as obsessively neutral about the policies of whatever political party happens to have ended up in power. The Queen knows, just as everyone else knows, that showing enthusiasm, or lack of it, about the law-making plans of her government would lead to a serious crisis that would be more than her job is worth. So, even when announcing plans to ban hunting with hounds, she managed not to convey the slightest hint of disappointment or irritation that a favorite pastime of her immediate family was about to be outlawed.

The Queen's Speech is therefore an interesting exception to the normal rules of effective public speaking, and her whole approach to is a fine example of how to deal with those rare occasions when you have to conceal what you really feel about the things you are talking about. Another master of this was Mr McGregor, an official spokesman for the foreign office during the Falklands war, who made regular appearances on television reading out progress reports in a flat, deadpan monotone – presumably because a vital part of his job was to give nothing away that might have encouraged or discouraged viewers, whether British or Argentinian, about how things were going in the South Atlantic.

How to prevent a civil war

A much more surprising case was Nelson Mandela's first speech after being released from prison in 1990. Here was a highly effective communicator, whose words at his trial 27 years earlier are to be found in most books of great speeches, and who had had the best part of three decades to prepare an inspiring and memorable text. But it was not to be. As if modeling his performance on the Queen's Speech, he buried his head in the script and spoke in a flat measured tone that came across as completely lacking in the kind of passion everyone was expecting from someone who had suffered so much and was held in such high regard by his audience.

Having waited for years for this historic event, anticipating something on a par with Martin Luther King's "I have a dream" speech, I remember being disappointed and surprised by what I saw and heard from the balcony of City Hall in Cape Town. It was only later that it dawned on me that this was another case where rousing rhetoric would have been completely counter-productive. The political situation in South Africa was poised on a knife-edge and his release from prison had only happened at all because the apartheid regime was crumbling. It was a moment when anything more inspiring from Mandela might have come across as a call to arms and could easily have prompted an immediate uprising or civil war. But the political understanding with the minority white government was that the African National Congress would keep the lid on things for long enough to enable a settlement to be negotiated. As when the Queen opens parliament, Mr Mandela knew exactly what he was doing, how to do it and that he could not have done otherwise.

Displaying neutrality

So as well as listening to the content of the Queen's Speech on 3rd December, it is also worth close inspection as an object lesson on how to address an audience if you're ever in a position of having to convey complete neutrality and detachment. Or, if you'd rather rise to the much more usual challenge of trying to inspire your audience, pay close attention to the way she delivers it – and then do exactly the opposite.

15th November 2008

Will there be any "rhetorical denial" from the Obama camp?

Effective speakers don't always like to see their technical ability being noticed and analysed by others.

I first became aware of this back in 1984, when I published a book on the rhetorical techniques used by politicians to trigger applause in speeches (*Our Masters' Voices: The Language and Body Language of Politics*).

It included a chapter on charisma, part of which used the rhetorical ability of Tony Benn, then at the forefront of the Labour Party's lurch towards the far left, as an example of how technical skill at oratory can get politicians into prominent positions. Apparently, he didn't like this at all, and went around telling people that audiences didn't applaud him because of how he said things but because they agreed so much with what he was saying.

Years later, both of us appeared on the same television programme, for which I had recorded a piece illustrating the main rhetorical techniques with video clips from political speeches. When asked what he thought of this, Mr Benn replied "Well, it's rubbish" and went on to elaborate as follows:

"I suppose you can analyse great speeches, but it's a bit like analysing a great painting in terms of the chemical composition of the pigments on the canvas."

If I'd been given a chance to respond, I'd have said "Yes, and how many other people could have come up with such a powerful simile (with alliteration bringing the image to a close) to make their point?"

At the start of the 1987 general election in Britain, David Owen, who was leader of the SDP (which had broken away from the Labour Party largely because the Bennite tendency had taken it so far to the left), announced that "Reason, not rhetoric will win this campaign." So here he was using an alliterative contrast, one of the most important of all rhetorical techniques, to tell us that there wouldn't be any rhetoric from the SDP.

This tendency of good communicators who use rhetoric effectively to deny that they are using it at all goes back at least as far as Shakespeare. Having started his Forum speech in Julius Caesar with a memorable three-part list with the third item the longest (Friends, Romans and countrymen) and two powerful contrasts (I come to bury Caesar, not to praise him. The evil that men do lives after them. The good is oft interred within their bones), Mark Antony later uses another contrast to inform the audience that he, unlike Brutus, is no good at public speaking ("I am no orator as Brutus is, but, as you know me all, a plain blunt man"), even though this is the most famous speech in one of the most famous plays in English literature.

Now that so many commentators, including me, are waxing lyrical about Mr Obama's technical mastery of rhetoric, imagery and alliteration, it will be interesting to see if any of his aides start trying to tell us that his success in communicating with mass audiences has had more to do with what he says than how he says it.

Why lists of three: mystery, magic or reason?

The fact that the three-part list is such a commonly used rhetorical technique often raises the question of what it is about the number 3 that's so special. It's sometimes suggested that there must be something magical or mystical about it. But there is, I think, a much more rational explanation.

Its most likely source is the commonest form of human communication, namely everyday conversation. In the research literature of conversation analysis, there is the idea of there being an implicit or tacit "economy rule" that works along the lines of "say things as briefly as you can unless you have a good reason for doing otherwise".

So when we complain that someone is "long-winded", "likes the sound of his own voice" or "is always hogging the conversation", we are in effect noticing and complaining that he's breaking the economy rule. And the fact that there are actually words in the English language, and probably in other languages too, for referring to such rule-breaking behaviour (e.g. "verbose" and "garrulous") means that it's something that happens (and is complained about) quite often.

We also know something about how three-part lists work in everyday conversation, thanks to a fascinating paper by one of the pioneers of conversation analysis, the late Gail Jefferson. Among other things, her detailed empirical studies showed how frequently they occur in conversation and how they are often treated by others as indicating that the person who produced the three-part list has finished and that someone else can now start speaking without fear of being accused of interrupting.*

As for why so many lists come in threes, the most likely explanation is that 3 conforms to the economy rule, because the arrival of a third item is the first point at which a possible connection implied by the first two is confirmed, and has the effect of turning a "possible list" into a "definite" or "complete enough list" of similar things.

For example, if my first two words are "Rose" and "Lily", I could be starting a list of flowers' names or a list of women's names – but you won't know for sure which of these it is until I add a third one.

If my third word is "Joanna", it becomes a list women's names; if it's "foxglove", it becomes a list of flowers' names (and, if it had been "Botham", cricket fans will hear it as a list of cricketer's names – Lily and Lillie, the famous Australian fast bowler, may be spelt differently, but they sound exactly the same).

The arrival of the third item in a list is therefore the first and earliest point at which a possible list can become an unequivocal and unambiguous list of similar items, and you don't need a fourth, fifth or sixth word to establish this. So, if you're following the economy rule, you wouldn't (and shouldn't) add any more after the third one.

This is not to say, of course, that we can never use longer lists in conversation without risking complaints. Sometimes we want to convey a sense of "muchness", as when we want to emphasise that something was much better or much worse than normal. "He went on and on and on" may be a fairly common way of complaining that someone was being "long-winded", but "He went on and on and on and on and on" is to make a more serious criticism by depicting the violation of the economy rule as having been far more extreme than usual.

*Gail Jefferson (1990) "List-construction as a task and a resource". In: George Psathas, eds. *Interaction Competence*. Washington, D.C.: University Press of America: 63-92.

2nd December 2008

"There's nothing wrong with PowerPoint – until there's an audience"

The other day, my wife went to a meeting that had been advertised as a social event, but which turned out to include a number of unscheduled PowerPoint presentations. On the way out, she said to the friend she was with that she would not have bothered to go if she'd known that they were going to have to listen to three speakers reading from PowerPoint slides.

A stranger overheard her complaint, turned round and sounded as though he was looking for an argument. "There's nothing wrong with PowerPoint" he asserted, but then added the profound words "until, that is, there's an audience."

And he does have a point. I've now asked hundreds of people how many PowerPoint presentations they've been to that were inspiring or memorable. It's a question that typically produces a deathly silence. Most people struggle to think of a single instance, and the biggest number anyone has ever managed to come up with is two.

Further investigation into these rare exceptions usually reveals two important facts: (1) the slides were mostly pictures illustrating what the speaker was talking about, and (2) there weren't very many of them.

However, the idea that slides are essential to the modern business presentation has become so entrenched that you sometimes have to be careful about questioning the dominant orthodoxy – and not just when you happen to be on your way out of a presentation. When I wrote about the (many) problems they create for audiences in *Lend Me Your Ears*, my publisher's lawyers tried to get me to tone down some of my comments in case Microsoft, purveyors of PowerPoint to the world, decided to sue.

I refused to change a word, on the grounds that I wasn't saying anything that couldn't be confirmed by even the most casual research into audience reactions to slide-dependent presentations – and you have a defence in English law, if you can show that what you are saying is true.

In any case, it's not actually Microsoft's fault that slide dependency has become the industry-standard model of presentation. There may be some fairly dubious assumptions built into PowerPoint (e.g. the first set of templates offered to users positively encourages them to produce lists of written words), but the global epidemic of presentational paralysis that we're up against was actually spawned much earlier by the misuse of overhead projectors – aided and abetted by a technological "advance" in photo-copying technology.

I say the "misuse of overhead projectors" because they were originally invented to solve a problem with writing and drawing on black boards and white boards (which has gone down well with audiences for generations) in large auditoriums, where people can't always see what's being written on the board.

That's why a key component of the first overhead projectors was a winding roll of acetate that enabled speakers to write and draw on it as they went along, and project their handiwork on to a big screen that everyone could see.

All was well for a while, but the rot set in during the 1970s (before anyone had thought of PCs, let alone PowerPoint) thanks to the invention of photo-copying machines that could print just as well on acetate as earlier models had done on paper.

The main casualty was the ancient (and very effective) art of "chalk and talk", through which many of us learnt much of what we learnt at school and university. It was replaced by the use of ready-made slides, consisting mainly of lists of written headings and sentences that were actually the speaker's notes.

So widespread and comprehensive did this practice become that overhead projector manufacturers were soon able to cut their production costs by discontinuing the winding rolls of acetate, and it wasn't long before machines that would only accept ready-made slides became the norm.

The advent of computer programs like PowerPoint may have made slides easier for audiences to read than in the days of acetates, but how many of us, when we're sitting in an audience, really want to read and listen at the same time? And how many of us, when speaking to an audience really want to supply our listeners with a continuing source of distraction?

As the stranger said to my wife the other day, "There's nothing wrong with PowerPoint – until there's an audience."

6th December 2008

The office Christmas party speech: roads to failure and success

One of the advantages of being self-employed is that I'm normally spared from the annual rigours of the office Christmas party. Sometimes, however, you simply can't escape from being dragged along to one as the spouse or partner of an employee.

Once when this happened to me, the boss came up to me during the pre-dinner aperitifs, apparently to ask my advice. "Ahh -" he said, "you're supposed to be an expert on public speaking, so how about a few tips for my speech."

At such short notice, all I could suggest was that he should make no more than three points, and stick to drinking water throughout the meal – making the obvious point that alcohol interferes with the very part of the brain that produces speech.

I also pointed out that, by the time he got up to speak, everyone else would be at different stages of intoxication and he would have the advantage of being one of the few people in the room with a clear head. "Then, once you've made your speech," I said generously, "feel free to hit the bottle as much as you like."

He made it pretty clear that he didn't think much of my advice by promptly ordering another gin and tonic and telling me that his wife had already agreed to drive him home. During the dinner, he drank one glass of wine after another, glancing at me occasionally with what looked suspiciously like a defiant grin.

Then, when the time came for him to speak, this normally articulate and entertaining communicator slurred his words, and rambled on for what everyone agreed afterwards was far too long. It was difficult to tell one point from another, let alone how many he was making – other than that there were far more than the three I'd recommended.

The safest way of avoiding such embarrassment is obviously not to make a speech at all. But people at office parties do expect someone to say something, even if it's only to wish them a happy Christmas. And there are always going to be people there to be welcomed and/or thanked. So, if you're the one on whom this burden falls, here are seven steps to see you safely through it.

Seven Steps to Success

1. Plan what you want to say in advance, jot some headings down on cards and don't be afraid to be seen using them on the day. Apart from giving you the added confidence that comes from knowing that you won't forget what to say, it will make you look conscientious and professional for having gone to the trouble of preparing a few words specially for the occasion.

2. Drink as little alcohol as possible, and preferably none at all, before making the speech.

3. Welcome and thank everyone for coming, with a special welcome to spouses, partners and any other guests from outside the office.

4. Thank everyone involved in organising the event, preparing food, booking the venue, etc.

5. If appropriate, mention any significant or amusing things that have happened since the last Christmas party, and perhaps speculate on what lies ahead in the coming year.

6. Wish everyone a merry Christmas and happy new year – and make sure you sound as though you mean it.

7. Be brief: five minutes is probably the absolute limit. After all, hardly anyone ever complains about a speech being too short, and the biggest compliment you can be paid is when people say they wish you'd gone on longer.

11th December 2008

Gordon Brown's gaffe shows what Gail Jefferson meant by a "sound formed error"

Yesterday, I was phoned by a BBC radio station and asked to comment on Gordon Brown's gaffe about how he had "saved the world" when he'd apparently meant to say "saved the banks". As this was the first I'd heard of it, they allowed me an hour or two to have a look at it before phoning back to do the interview.

News of this high profile slip of the tongue reminded me of a fascinating paper on the "Poetics of Ordinary Talk"* that I'd heard Gail Jefferson, one of the founders of conversation analysis, give at a conference in Boston in 1977. It included a discussion of what she called "sound formed errors", by which she meant cases where a speaker's choice of a "wrong" word seems to be triggered by sounds in the words that came just before it.

In one of her examples, the first syllable of "Wednesday" was abandoned and corrected to "Thursday": "I will be up that way Wed – uh –Thursday."

Gail's suggestion was that, as the mistaken initial selection of "Wednesday" came just after there had been two "wuh" noises in quick succession, it could have been the repetitive sounds that triggered the error.

This made me wonder whether there had been any "wuh" sounds in what Gordon Brown had said just before saying "world" when he'd meant to say "banks". So it was with considerable surprise and delight that I spotted no less than four of them in the sentence leading up to the error that's caused him so much embarrassment.

> GORDON BROWN: "The first point of recapitalisation was to save banks that would otherwise have collapsed and we've not only saved the world – erh – saved the banks."

The fact that there were so many "wuh" sounds before the error was a real gift to me because I could now say something in the interview that might be a bit different from the various speculations coming from other commentators since the gaffe had hit the airwaves.

I also said something else in the interview, but I can't remember whether it was in the original Jefferson paper, had came up in the discussion after it or was something I'd noticed or been told about some time since 1977. This is the idea that "sound formed errors" and "triggered puns" (also featured in her paper) are more likely to happen when a speaker is tired, because that's when the brain is most likely to take handy short cuts like selecting words that sound like others nearby. This led me to suggest that Gordon Brown's error might have happened because he was more tired than usual, a comment I now regret – as it enabled the interviewer to get away from what I thought was quite an interesting subject and go down the track they'd presumably been hoping their "expert" would take them along in the first place.

"So can we conclude from this" asked the interviewer, "that the stresses of the job are getting too much for him?"

Er, no. I just said that he might have been tired.

But I do think it qualifies as a prime example of exactly what Gail meant by "sound formed errors" – and how they can sometimes get you into trouble you could have well done without.

*Gail Jefferson, "On the Poetics of Ordinary Talk", *Text and Performance Quarterly*, 1996, 16(1), 1-6.

Obama's rhetoric renews UK media interest in the "lost art" of oratory

Judging from the number of approaches from the media I've had since the election of Barack Obama, his outstanding speaking ability seems to have made some in our media wake up to the fact that, with the notable exceptions of Tony Blair and David Cameron, there's been a shortage of good orators in recent British politics. Some radio journalists told me the other day that they couldn't think of any current members of parliament who stood out as effective speakers.

The irony is, as I've hinted in some earlier blog entries, that the media themselves have probably played a major part in this by deciding that speeches do not make "good television" and by giving ever greater priority to interviews as the main form of political communication – a process that seems to have begun during the late 1980s and has accelerated ever since.

It's something into which I hope to do some more research. Meanwhile, the fullest discussion of these issues I've written so far was an introductory chapter in the book *Great Liberal Speeches*, edited by Duncan Brack and Tony Little (Politicos, London, 2001).

17th December 2008

You don't have to be Barack Obama to use rhetoric and imagery to discuss the financial crisis

When I show clips of top politicians in action to illustrate the power of rhetoric and imagery, people sometimes react by saying that such techniques may be all very well in political speeches but wouldn't be much use in the kind of technical presentations they have to do.

It's alright for Barack Obama to say things like "The road ahead will be long. Our climb will be steep", as he did in his victory speech in Chicago, but conjuring up images of journeys and hills isn't the kind of thing that professionals like economists and bankers can do.

My usual reply to such reactions is that nothing could be further from the truth – because I've yet to come across any subject where rhetoric and imagery can't be used to make a point more clearly and/or effectively.

Rhetorical techniques (including contrasts, a puzzle-solution format and a three-part list) and imagery can be used to discuss the ongoing financial crisis. Complicated it may be, but here we have a Nobel prize-winning economist (Joseph Stiglitz) talking about an economy going into "a tailspin", using a contrast (between two points in time and two contrasting facts) followed by a medical metaphor ("the cure is worse than the disease").

The video (it can be viewed on my blog) then cuts to a segment from a prime-time (UK) television news broadcast (from ITN) in which the newsreader starts by using a puzzling headline that gets us wondering what the governor of the Bank of England's "most downbeat prediction yet about the economy" actually is and a solution that seems to be using an image ("the 'nice' decade is over") – though actually Mr King's use of "nice" is a reference to an acronym for "Non-

Inflationary Consistent Expansion", that's been used by economists to describe the sort of growth the UK has experienced since Labour came to power in 1997.

He then uses a three-part list and a metaphor ("travelling along a bumpy road") that's immediately picked up by a reporter, who continues the journey imagery ("en route") and sums the problem up with a simple contrast ("high inflation and low growth").

Seen & Heard

3rd January 2009

Margaret Thatcher and the evolution of charismatic woman: Part I Cultural and vocal challenges

When I wrote *Our Masters' Voices* (1984), Margaret Thatcher was prime minister and looked well set to win at least one more term of office (and actually won two more). The following is a somewhat revised version of what I wrote then, and will be followed in due course by some further blog entries about how she and her advisors sought to solve the problems she was up against as the UK's first woman head of government.

It was important for Martin Luther King's success as a communicator that there already existed a distinctive black religious tradition that could be readily adapted for speaking on behalf of the civil rights movement, because American political oratory before the 1960s had been dominated by white males. But, when Mrs Thatcher came to power in 1979 after winning the first of three UK general elections, there were no such obvious models for women. For thousands of years before that, politics and speech-making had been almost exclusively male preserves.

There are no records of any famous female orators in classical Greece or Rome, where the early texts on rhetoric assumed that the practitioners would all be male. This was very evident in the opening pages of Quintilian's classic work *The Education of an Orator*, where he had this to say about the aim of the book:

> "We are to form, then, the perfect orator, who cannot exist unless as a good **man**; and we require in **him**, therefore, not only consummate ability in speaking, but every excellence of mind ... since the **man** who can duly sustain **his** character as a citizen, who is qualified for the management of public and private affairs, and who can govern communities by **his** counsels, settle them by means of law, and improve them by judicial enactments, can certainly be nothing else but an orator." (Quintilian, *Institutes of Oratory, or The Education of an Orator*, p. 4, emphases added)

In the years before Mrs Thatcher became prime minister of the UK, a number of women had become heads of government in other countries – Mrs Bandaranaike in Sri Lanka, Mrs Peron in Argentina, Mrs Gandhi in India and Mrs Meir in Israel – success stories that might seem to suggest that the male-dominated political mould had already been broken and that women in the future would in be able to enjoy equal opportunities in the pursuit of political careers.

Even then, however, there were two reasons for caution in drawing any such conclusion. The first was that three of the women who'd achieved high political office also had close family ties with male national heroes who had recently died, with Golda Meir and Margaret Thatcher being the only ones who had reached the top entirely by their own individual efforts.

A second reason for caution is that women faced and still face cultural and physical obstacles with which men never have to contend. In the absence of any established tradition like that in which black American leaders Martin Luther King and Jesse Jackson were able to operate, female politicians still have to develop new ways of surviving and thriving in such a male-dominated profession. This raises the question of whether the solutions found by Mrs Thatcher established any ground-rules that might benefit aspiring women politicians of the present and future.

Some of the problems faced by women in politics are obviously much the same as those faced by women in any other male-dominated profession – aptly summed up by the adage that "they're damned if they behave like men, and damned if they don't." If a woman acts in a tough, decisive or ruthless manner, she risks having her femininity being called into question. But if she appears gentle, indecisive or conciliatory, her male colleagues may conclude that she's simply not up to the job.

This is a dilemma familiar to most professional women, but female politicians face another disadvantage because public speaking is such an important part of the job – not just because the techniques of oratory and debate have been monopolised by men for so long, but also because of the difference in length of male and female vocal cords that affect the pitch of the human voice.

Pitch can be a problem for all public speakers, whatever their sex, because it tends to rise when someone is nervous or is speaking louder than usual – both of which are likely to happen in speeches. For women the problem is more acute because the natural pitch of their voices has a higher starting point than is the case for men, with the result that it cannot rise as far before reaching a level at which it sounds "shrill".

This might not matter but for the fact that high pitch tends to be strongly associated with emotional or irrational outbursts – a deeply rooted cultural assumption that probably derives from (and is sustained by) the screams of each new generation of infants. The fact that the sound of a woman raising her voice is more likely to be negatively evaluated as "shrill" or "screeching" is probably at the heart of a source of irritation that's familiar to many professional women, namely the tendency of male colleagues to accuse them of "overreacting" whenever they become involved in arguments.

Nor is it just a matter of there being negative associations with high pitched voices, as there are positive associations between lower-pitched female voices and attractiveness, "huskiness" and "sexiness". Shakespeare's positive evaluation of low pitch has long been enshrined in the dictionaries of quotations:

"Her voice was ever soft, gentle and low, an excellent thing in woman"
(King Lear, V, iii).

So the fact that Mrs Thatcher took positive steps to lower the pitch of her voice was a perfectly rational response to a real problem. Under the guidance of the

National Theatre, she underwent training that included humming exercises aimed at lowering her previously natural pitch. Comparing recordings of speeches she made before and after tuition reveals a clearly audible difference. When played through a pitch and intensity analyser, the reduction in pitch came out at 46 Hz – a figure that's almost half the average difference in pitch between male and female voices.

This significant decrease was all the more remarkable because it was achieved after Mrs Thatcher had already passed the age at which the pitch of women's voices tends naturally to rise: generally speaking, it falls up to the age of about forty-five, after which the it gradually starts to rise.

The lowering of her voice had other consequences that probably contributed both to the greater clarity of her talk and to its "statesmanlike" character. For example, the human voice-production system works in such a way that a reduction in pitch tends to slow down the speed at which we speak, and the tutored Mrs Thatcher spoke noticeably more slowly than she did before having any voice coaching.

You can inspect the change in her style of speaking in the clips on my blog showing her in one interview just after she became leader of the opposition in 1975 and another about ten years later after she'd spent two terms as prime minister.

5th January 2009

Margaret Thatcher and the evolution of charismatic woman Part II The "Iron Lady"

The problem of pitch (see part I) was only one aspect of public speaking that Mrs Thatcher took seriously after becoming leader of the Conservative Party in 1975. She also took advice from professionals in the theatre, television and even evangelism. One of her main speechwriters was Ronald Millar, a playwright about whose influence Mrs Thatcher's biographers have noted as follows:

"She ... turned out to be an amenable pupil to Millar's methods, which included advice on delivery as well as script. Millar has become known as the author of the jokes (he was responsible for "U-turn if you want to – the lady's not for turning"), but his principal skill was and is playing director to the leading lady, a combination of firm steering mixed with reassurance." (Wapshott and Brock, *Thatcher*, p. 161)

"The lady's not for turning" is but one of many contrastive punch lines supplied to Mrs Thatcher by Millar, and it was at his suggestion that she quoted the following four contrasts from St Francis of Assisi as she entered Downing Street after winning the 1979 general election (see video with blog entry on 1st January 2009):

"Where there is discord, may we bring harmony.
Where there is error, may we bring truth.
Where there is doubt, may we bring faith.
Where there is despair, may we bring hope."

Since before the 1979 election, television producer Gordon Reece had provided Mrs Thatcher with extensive and detailed guidance on how to perform effectively on the small screen. And, during the 1983 general election, the staging of her set-piece speeches was organised by the same team that managed mass meetings for Billy Graham's evangelical crusades to Britain.

Much of this expert help, of course, had little or nothing to do with the specific problems faced by a female political leader. But some of the advice, such as that provided by Gordon Reece, was directly concerned with image-related matters like hair-styles, clothes, jewellery make-up and even which side of her face was supposed to be best for exposing to the camera.

This included advice that she should go for greater simplicity of appearance in television performances than when making major speeches. Reece and Millar were also concerned with the problems associated with pitch. To quote her biographers again:

"A full blast Commons speech can sound like raving hysteria in a broadcasting studio. The broadcasting of the Commons (which happened to coincide with Reece's arrival) caused him special problems. He was heard to remark that the selling of Margaret Thatcher had been put back two years by the mass broadcasting of Prime Minister's Question Time as she had to be at her shrillest to be heard over the din ... Millar had also taught her that lowering the voice brought the speed down to a steadier rate. He advised holding to a steady and equable tone at Question Time which would eventually drive through, not over or under, the noise.' (Wapshott and Brock, *Thatcher*, pp. 169-70)

Before the 1979 general election, the Conservative Party's advertising agents, Saatchi and Saatchi, were also worried about the prospects of convincing the electorate of the leadership potential not just of a woman, but of one who seemed to epitomise the typical suburban middle-class housewife.

Meanwhile, the various nicknames devised by her colleagues, such as "Mother", the "Leaderene", the "Bossette", "Attila the Hen", "the Immaculate Misconception", etc. can be seen as reflecting a sustained attempt on their part to come to terms with the fact that they were having to work under a woman leader.

Much the same could be said of the culturally available stereotypes of powerful women that cartoonists exploited in their caricatures of Mrs Thatcher, which included Bodicea, Britannia, a witch and the Queen. But the most astute attempt to come to terms with Mrs Thatcher's position as a political leader was supplied by the Soviet newspapers when, after a speech at Kensington Town Hall in 1976, they dubbed her the "Iron Lady". Of all the nicknames Mrs Thatcher attracted, it was as the "Iron Lady" that she became internationally best known. And this may well be because these two words aptly sum up one of the main secrets of her success in finding a solution to the problem of being a female in a position of power.

Given that successful women face the dilemma of being "damned if they behave like men, and damned if they don't", one solution is to behave in as efficient, tough and decisive a manner as possible, while at the same time making no concessions whatsoever when it comes to maintaining the external trappings of femininity. So Mrs Thatcher was committed to the importance of being smart in a conventionally feminine way, and consistently sought to make the most of her natural physical attractiveness. This included the preservation of her blonde hair by regular tinting as well as the elimination of gaps in her teeth by dental capping.

Nor was she afraid to be seen in the traditional female roles of wife and mother, even to the extent of being photographed at the kitchen sink just before competing as a candidate in the 1975 Conservative Party leadership election. Her uncompromisingly feminine appearance, and her repeated emphasis on the virtues of family life may not have endeared Mrs Thatcher to feminists. But, in the eyes and ears of a wider public, such factors had the effect of insulating her from being "damned" for lacking culturally acceptable feminine attributes, by leaving no one with any doubt that she was anything less than a 100 per cent female of the species.

At the same time, there was little or nothing in her conduct of government that could be singled out to expose her as "gentle", "weak" or not up to the job, and this enabled her to avoid being "damned" for possessing the sorts of stereotypical feminine attributes so often cited in attempts to demonstrate the unsuitability of women for positions of power and responsibility.

Her external image of unambiguously recognisable femininity effectively liberated her to pursue forceful policies without running any risk of being damned for behaving "like a man", because any such claim would have been so transparently at odds with all the other evidence that she was uncompromisingly female. And, with lines like "a general doesn't leave the field of battle just as it's reaching a climax", she showed no inhibitions at all about identifying herself closely with a powerful male role model, without having to worry about whether this would raise doubts about her essential femininity.

Nor was she averse to using a negative nickname to question the manliness of her male colleagues, as it was Mrs Thatcher herself who first used the word "wet", a colloquialism for describing men as feeble or lacking in masculinity, for referring to her more liberal Tory cabinet ministers.

As for the "Iron Lady", its aptness lay in the fact that it captured the two most visible and contrasting characteristics of her public image: toughness and femininity. And, when these two qualities are exhibited in the conduct and appearance of the same woman, she has found an effective way of deterring, resisting and neutralising any attacks based on male-chauvinist assumptions.

Mrs Thatcher was also quick to latch on to the advantages of this. Within weeks of the Russians dubbing her the "Iron Lady" (and still three years before she became prime minister) she was to be heard juxtaposing her feminine attributes with the toughness implied by the nickname in a speech she made in 1976.

Seven years later, when fighting for re-election in 1983, she was still confident enough about the nickname being an asset to woo her audiences with lines like these:

> Thatcher: "The Russians said that I was an Iron Lady."
> Audience: "Hear-hear."
> Thatcher: "They were right."
> Audience: "Heh-heh-heh"
> Thatcher: "Britain needs an Iron Lady."
> Audience: "Hear-hear" [applause]

Nor did she ever try to deny the appropriateness of another nickname that located her firmly within a long-standing and culturally familiar category of successful professional women in positions of power, namely head-teachers. In a report by John Cole, the BBC's political editor, during the 1983 general election, she showed no qualms about accepting the image he presented her with in a question formulated in blatantly male-chauvinist terms:

> Cole: "Other Prime Ministers after all have been bossy too, but Mrs
> Thatcher does undoubtedly keep a fussy watch on her ministers'
> performances with an occasional touch of motherliness. I asked her today
> what she said to suggestions that she had a headmistress image."

> Thatcher: "Well I've known some very good headmistresses who've
> launched their pupils on wonderful careers. I had one such and was very
> grateful. But I am what I am. Yes, my style is of vigorous leadership. Yes, I
> do believe certain things very strongly. Yes, I do believe in trying to
> persuade people that the things I believe in are the things they should
> follow. And Mr Cole I'm far too old to change now."

By saying that there is not only nothing wrong with being like a headmistress, but that it's a role model with positive virtues, Mrs Thatcher was able to identify herself with one of the relatively few widely respected positions of power and responsibility that have traditionally been available to women. Teaching is also one of the very few professions with job conditions that include a great deal of public speaking. For a female leader to be identified with the role of headmistress would therefore seem to be something worth cultivating if it's in your interests to promote the idea that women are perfectly capable of holding their own both on a public platform and in a position of power.

Indeed, one of Mrs Thatcher's major long term achievements may turn out to have been the undermining of age-old assumptions of the sort contained in Quintilian's observation that the perfect orator cannot exist "unless as a good man". And, by finding a workable solution to the problem of being damned for being like a man and damned for not being like a man, her combination of uncompromising femininity with equally uncompromising words and deeds may have laid the foundations for a new tradition within which women politicians of the future will be able to operate.

Postscript: After a year in which Hillary Clinton and Sarah Palin were at the forefront in the US presidential campaign, the question arises as to whether either of them showed any signs of taking on board any of these lessons from Margaret Thatcher – a theme to which I plan to return after posting this series of reflections on female charisma.

7th January 2009

Margaret Thatcher and the evolution of charismatic woman Part III The education of a female orator

Although Mrs Thatcher took the business of public speaking very seriously after becoming leader of the Conservative Party (see parts I & II), it's important to remember that she had already come a very long way in the years before she got there and must have found a way of surviving in the male-dominated world of politics long before Ronald Millar, Gordon Reece or Saatchi and Saatchi came on the scene. In this connection, her biography shows that, from a very early age, the former Margaret Roberts had far more opportunities than most English girls of her generation to become accustomed with being treated on equal terms with men.

Mrs Thatcher's father was very active both as a local town councillor in

Grantham, Lincolnshire, and as a Methodist lay preacher. According to her biographers, the young Margaret was not just exposed throughout her childhood to the political discussions that regularly took place in the Roberts household and across the counter of their grocery shop, but was also actively encouraged by her father to take part in them.

At the same time, she was listening to weekly Sunday sermons in the local Methodist church and, more occasionally, heard speeches by national politicians who were visiting the town. That she showed early promise in making the most of these experiences is shown by the fact that, at the age of nine, she won a poetry-reading competition at a local drama festival. It's also reported that such talents continued to blossom while she was a pupil at Kesteven and Grantham Girls' School:

> "She was a studious girl, but enjoyed the dramatic society, which made her at one time consider becoming an actress, and also question and answer sessions at the end of visitors' lectures, as long as the subject was current affairs. She is well remembered by a girl in the year above her, Margaret Goodrich, for cross-questioning Bernard Newman, the expert on spying, with a confidence not normally expected from such a young girl.'
> (Wapshott and Brock, *Thatcher*, pp. 34-5)

For her higher education, the future prime minister could hardly have gone to a university more dominated by men and male traditions than the Oxford of the 1940s. Nor could she have chosen a subject studied by fewer women or by fewer aspiring politicians than chemistry – Mrs Thatcher is not just the first woman, but also the first, and so far only, science graduate, to have become prime minister of the UK.

At the same time, part of the experience of living in an all women's college for three years involved taking it for granted that female academics were perfectly capable of performing on equal terms with men. Her chemistry tutor at Somerville was Dorothy Hodgkin, who subsequently went on to win a Nobel prize. During this period she also kept up an active interest in politics, and became president of the University Conservative Association, a post that brought her into direct contact with many of the then leading national politicians, as well as her own student contemporaries who were later to achieve cabinet rank, including Tony Benn, Anthony Crosland and Edward Boyle.

In her subsequent careers, first as an industrial research chemist and later as a tax barrister, Mrs Thatcher continued to live and work on equal terms with men in professions where women were still extremely under-represented. So, by the time she won a seat in parliament, she had already accumulated two decades of experience at succeeding in male-dominated environments. Even allowing for the inevitable tendency of biographers (and obituary-writers) to select facts from a life story which fit in with whatever the subject eventually became, it would seem that Mrs Thatcher underwent a lengthy and highly relevant apprenticeship, similar to that recommended by the classical Greek and Roman writers on the education of male orators.

As can be seen from her speeches, there is no doubt of her ability to deploy the full range of rhetorical techniques, and to do so in such a way that her essential femininity was never seriously called into question.

8th January 2009

Clinton, Palin and the legacy of Margaret Thatcher

In the last few blog entries on Margaret Thatcher, I've been suggesting that she had found a solution to the professional woman's problem of being damned if they behave like a man and damned if they behave like a woman – which involved being tough and decisive in her actions while being uncompromisingly female in her external appearance – and that this was summed up by the nickname the "Iron Lady". Although first used by the Soviet media, it was something that Mrs Thatcher was quick to take on board and use to her own advantage.

Whether or not Sarah Palin and her advisors were aware of this when she juxtaposed toughness and femininity by dubbing herself a "pit bull with lipstick", I do not know. But, judging from news reports of Republican campaign expenditure on her wardrobe, and widespread coverage of her enjoyment of rugged outdoor pursuits like hunting and shooting, it looks as though she or her advisors had taken on board Margaret Thatcher's lesson about combining unequivocal femininity with toughness.

However, leaks from Hillary Clinton's aides (and casual observation of her preference for trousers/pants over skirts/dresses) suggest that they hadn't quite got the point about Mrs Thatchers success in image management.

On 12th August 2008, the following headline appeared in the *Daily Telegraph*.

> "***Hillary Clinton's failed strategy inspired by Margaret Thatcher***
> "Hillary Clinton's flawed strategy for winning the White House was rooted in her chief strategist's admiration for Margaret Thatcher as the 'best role model' for her, according to a leaked campaign memorandum."

My immediate reaction on reading this was to wonder whether these "strategists" or Mrs Clinton herself had actually understood the key components of the "role model" so successfully established by Mrs Thatcher more than 30 years ago. What followed suggested that the author of the leaked document had not understood it at all, and that he'd made the mistake of concentrating exclusively on the mature Thatcher of later years (in her second and third terms in office) rather than on the younger Thatcher who had won her way to the top in the first place. The *Telegraph* article continued:

> "'We are more Thatcher than anyone else – top of the university, a high achiever throughout life, a lawyer who could absorb and analyse problems', Mark Penn wrote to the former First Lady in a 'launch strategy' document in December 2006."

The Democratic candidate, he argued, had to show the kind of decisiveness the former British prime minister had shown when she was first elected in 1979 – "her mantra was opportunity, renewal, strength and choice" – and avoid the temptation to try to be loved.

> "Margaret Thatcher was the longest serving Prime Minister in British history, serving far longer than Winston Churchill. She represents the most successful elected woman leader in this century – and the adjectives that were used about her (Iron Lady) were not of good humour or warmth, they were of smart, tough leadership."

The memo was part of a trove of internal Clinton campaign documents leaked to the *Atlantic Monthly* magazine that reveal a campaign that was fatally undermined by internal dissension, an incoherent strategy and – ironically, given the Thatcher comparison – Senator Clinton's hesitancy and failure to take decisions.

But what about the other half of the story?

The flaw in Penn's analysis was to concentrate only on those components of Thatcher's "role model" that had insulated her from being damned for behaving like a woman (e.g. "decisiveness", "strength" and "toughness") to the exclusion of those that had insulated her from being damned for being unfeminine (e.g. carefully coiffured hair, dental capping, make-up, dresses – yes, dresses, not trouser/pant-suits, à la Hillary Clinton).

How could Penn, Clinton or anyone else who bought into this "analysis" have missed such an obvious point as Thatcher's uncompromising femininity – even to the extent of making much of the "tough" implications of the first word in the "Iron Lady" nickname while completely ignoring the essentially female connotations of the second word?

The age factor?

At the risk of sounding "ageist", the most likely explanation of this extraordinary gaffe is that it did have to do with age, both of the advisor and of his client: in 2008, Mrs Clinton was ten years older than Mrs Thatcher was after she'd already spent six years as prime minister (and was only two years away from winning her third general election).

And unless Mr Penn, as a 21 year old, took far more interest in European politics than most Americans I know, it seems highly unlikely that he would even have noticed when a rather good-looking and well turned-out 50 year old English woman won the Conservative Party leadership campaign in 1975 (still four years away from making it to the top job). But by the time he became a strategist/consultant, all he could see was a much older woman who was, by then, more famous for her toughness than for her femininity.

Thatcher and Palin?

As for Mrs Palin, her record in Miss Alaska competitions, her willingness to wear skirts and dresses and to boast about being a "hockey Mom" suggest that, like Mrs Thatcher, she had no qualms about combining uncompromising femininity with the toughness associated with her outdoor sporting pursuits.

However, from a distance of 6,000+ miles away, and on the basis of cursory research into her education and career history, I have to say that her background seems to be a bit lacking in the impeccable credentials of Margaret Thatcher, who graduated from a top university (Oxford) and had worked as a research chemist and tax lawyer before winning a seat in the House of Commons and embarking on a career in politics.

20th January 2009

A line I don't want to hear in today's speech by President Obama

If there's one thing that irks me about speeches by American presidents, it's their tendency to overstate the case for their country being the first, finest or only example of freedom and democracy in the world.

The issue is summed up here in a thoughtful, and otherwise strongly recommended, piece by Clark Judge, a former Reagan speechwriter:

> "Inaugural addresses invariably remind us of America's historically unmatched commitment to popular sovereignty and individual liberty ..."

It was also there in a famous anecdote used by Ronald Reagan in his address at the 1964 Republican Convention that launched him on to the national political stage (*A time for choosing: Rendezvous with Destiny*):

> Reagan: Not too long ago two friends of mine were talking to a Cuban refugee, a businessman who had escaped from Castro, and in the midst of his story one of my friends turned to the other and said, "We don't know how lucky we are." And the Cuban stopped and said, "How lucky you are! I had someplace to escape to." In that sentence he told us the entire story. If we lose freedom here, there is no place to escape to. This is the last stand on Earth.

My point is not to criticise the particular form of democracy and freedom that's been developed in the USA. Nor is it to claim that we in the UK (or any other European country) have a come up with an even better version of democracy. But it is to register a complaint about this implicit criticism of other countries' democracy and freedom that's so regularly trotted out by American politicians.

Reagan was as wrong in saying that there was no place to escape to as he was wrong in claiming that the USA was "the last stand on earth". From the point of view of those of us lucky enough live in other countries where elections also determine who governs and also result in a peaceful transfer of power, such overstated claims are at best tactless, and at worst quite offensive.

That's why it's a line I would never recommend to any of my clients with a vested interest in staying friends with their closest allies.

21st January 2009

Rhetoric and applause in Obama's inaugural speech as a measure of what the audience liked best

When I first started studying bursts of applause in political speeches thirty years ago, some people couldn't see the point; others thought I was mad. But I did have a rational reason for doing it – because the absence of any instant positive response from jurors in the tape-recorded court hearings I was studying made it impossible to get empirical evidence about what might be having a positive impact on the twelve most important members of the audience in court.

In trying to solve this "methodological' problem, I was drawn to applause in speeches as a promising place to start, as it provides fairly concrete evidence that an audience is (a) awake and paying close attention and (b) approves of what's just been said strongly enough to join in a collective physical demonstration of their approval (by clapping hands, cheering, etc.).

The main finding – that most bursts of applause are triggered by a small number of simple rhetorical techniques – not only surprised me, but also launched me on a new career. More than a quarter of a century later, I still sometimes find it instructive to focus on the lines that were applauded in a particular speech to see which messages turned the audience on the most.

So the lines that prompted bursts of applause during President Obama's inaugural speech yesterday are reproduced below, along with some notes about the rhetorical techniques that were involved. Video clips of the first six examples can be seen on my blog.

For anyone unfamiliar with them, the main rhetorical techniques include: Contrasts: e.g. "I come to bury Caesar, not to praise him" (Mark Antony), three-part lists: e.g. "Education, education and education." (Tony Blair) and combinations of contrasts and lists: e.g by contrasting a third item with the first two: "We shall negotiate for it, sacrifice for it but never surrender for it." (Ronald Reagan). Add to these devices like alliteration, repetition, imagery and anecdotes, and you have the basic building blocks of the language of public speaking.

1. The first burst of applause came after the second of two three-part lists – in which the third item contrasts with the first two. Note also that the final item exploits the puzzle-solution format by getting the audience wondering what they're going to have to know before providing them with the solution to the puzzle.

> "Today I say to you that the challenges we face are real.
> They are serious
> and they are many.
>
> "They will not be met easily
> or in a short span of time.
> But know this, America – they will be met." [Applause]

So the audience liked being told that the country is up against some serious problems that will be hard to solve and his assurance that they will be overcome.

This was the first of four examples in the speech of his using the imperative form "know this", which is arguably a rather less high-sounding version of the repetitive "let" form of imperative favoured by Kennedy for directing his inaugural remarks to specific audiences in 1961:

> Kennedy: Let every nation know, whether it wishes us well or ill, that we
> shall pay any price, bear any burden, meet any hardship, support any
> friend, oppose any foe, in order to assure the survival and the success of
> liberty...

Let both sides explore what problems unite us instead of belabouring those problems which divide us.

Let both sides, for the first time, formulate serious and precise proposals for the inspection and control of arms – and bring the absolute power to destroy other nations under the absolute control of all nations.

Let both sides seek to invoke the wonders of science instead of its terrors. Together let us explore the stars, conquer the deserts, eradicate disease, tap the ocean depths, and encourage the arts and commerce.

Let both sides unite to heed in all corners of the earth the command of Isaiah – to "undo the heavy burdens ... and to let the oppressed go free."

2. The second burst of applause also came after two three-part lists, each of which had a third item that was longer than the first two:

"The time has come to reaffirm our enduring spirit;
to choose our better history;
to carry forward that precious gift, that noble idea, passed on from generation to generation:

"the God-given promise that all are equal,
all are free
and all deserve a chance to pursue their full measure of happiness."
[Applause]

So the audience liked hearing his reaffirmation of the American dream.

3. Another three-part list with longest item coming third:

"Starting today,
we must pick ourselves up,
dust ourselves off,
and begin again the work of remaking America." [Applause]

So the audience liked his recognition that there's work to be done in order to remake America (and, by implication, that America is in need of "remaking").

4. Another example of the "know" form of imperative, addressed this time to foreign audiences (identified by imagery contrasting "grandest capitals" with the

"small village" in Kenya where his father was born):

> "... to all other peoples and governments who are watching today, from the grandest capitals to the small village where my father was born: know that America is a friend of each nation and every man, woman, and child who seeks a future of peace and dignity, and that we are ready to lead once more." [Applause]

So the audience liked the idea of restoring America's reputation for positive leadership in the world (and, by implication, that it's in need of restoring).

5. Use of one three-part list to set up a puzzle ("what is it that he's going to say now?") that's solved by another three-part list that gets applauded.

> "We will not apologize for our way of life,
> nor will we waver in its defense,
> and for those who seek to advance their aims by inducing terror and
> slaughtering innocents, we say to you now that
> our spirit is stronger and cannot be broken;
> you cannot outlast us,
> and we will defeat you." [Applause]

So the audience liked hearing his commitment to defend the American way of life and defeat terrorism.

6. Contrast between negative status of a father being discriminated against 60 years ago and his son becoming president today:

> "This is the meaning of our liberty and our creed – why men and women and children of every race and every faith can join in celebration across this magnificent mall, and why a man whose father less than sixty years ago might not have been served at a local restaurant can now stand before you to take a most sacred oath." [Applause]

So the audience liked being invited to celebrate the election of an African-American as president as evidence that the central part of Martin Luther King's dream has come true.

Unexpected flutters of applause

There were a few other instances where a slight flutter of applause didn't build into a fully fledged burst, and where Obama didn't seem to have been expecting applause. In the following, it came in just after the second of two contrasts, the first of which contrasted the first item with the second two in the list. Evidence that he wasn't expecting it came from the fact that he can be seen abandoning an in-breath and a pointing gesture before waiting for the flutter of applause to subside.

> "The success of our economy has always depended
> not just on the size of our gross domestic product,
> but on the reach of our prosperity;
> on the ability to extend opportunity to every willing heart –
> not out of charity,
> but because it is the surest route to our common good." [Flutter of applause]

In this final example, the short burst of applause came in response to another "know this" imperative that ended with a contrast between "build" and "destroy". The start of the applause interrupted President Obama just after he'd embarked on another "to those ..." – which he cut short and then repeated as the applause was fading away.

> "To those leaders around the globe who seek to sow conflict, or blame their society's ills on the West – know that your people will judge you on what you can build, not what you destroy." [Flutter of applause]

22nd January 2009

Obama's inauguration rhetoric won approval for some uncomfortable messages

A point I made a couple of days ago was that bursts of applause can be used to identify which points in a speech an audience liked best.

If there are about 150 sentences, of which only six (4%) stood out enough to get a whole-hearted display of approval that lasted more than a few seconds – as happened on Tuesday – it's worth looking at them in a bit more detail to see what really turned the audience on.

On looking through them again, what I found interesting and surprising was that three of the six messages rated by the crowd as worthy of a decent round of applause were actually quite contentious or uncomfortable ones:

1. The USA is up against a lot of serious problems that can't be fixed easily or instantly, though the new administration will eventually fix them.

2. A lot of work needs to be done to remake America – where the use of the word "remake" implies that there's something so wrong with the country that it actually needs remaking.

3. The USA will be friends with any countries wanting to live in peace and dignity and is ready to provide leadership again – where "again" is presumably an admission that its foreign policy hasn't been making a very good job of it recently.

To foreign ears, the encouraging thing about all this is not just that the new president is willing to acknowledge that all is not well on a number of important fronts, but that the large numbers of Americans in the crowd were willing to applaud him for subscribing to such uncomfortable positions.

At the very least, these sentiments are a far cry from the over-stated claims about the unique greatness of the country that I was complaining about the other day – and which have put in another appearance in an article in the *Washington Post* by

Robert Ehrlich, Jr., former governor of Maryland, who writes of the need to "pray for the greatest democracy in the history of the world."

29th January 2009

Rhetoric and imagery in President Obama's inauguration speech

If the number of hits and emails are anything to go by, my earlier line-by-line analysis of rhetoric and imagery in Barack Obama's victory speech in Chicago (originally published in the British weekly newspaper, the *Independent on Sunday*) attracted a good deal of interest.

In response to those who have asked for something similar on his inaugural address, here's the text of the speech with comments just after the points to which they relate.

"My fellow citizens:
I stand here today humbled by the task before us,
grateful for the trust you have bestowed,
mindful of the sacrifices borne by our ancestors."

A three-part list.

"I thank President Bush for his service to our nation, as well as the generosity and cooperation he has shown throughout this transition.

Forty-four Americans have now taken the presidential oath. The words have been spoken during rising tides of prosperity and the still waters of peace."

A double contrast between rising tides and still waters and prosperity and peace, using sea imagery and alliteration.

"Yet, every so often the oath is taken amidst gathering clouds and raging storms."

Weather imagery is used to depict trouble ahead.

> "At these moments, America has carried on
> not simply because of the skill or vision of those in high office,
> but because We the People have remained faithful to the ideals of our
> forbearers, and true to our founding documents."

There is a contrast with indirect references to declaration of independence and the US constitution.

> "So it has been.
> So it must be with this generation of Americans."

A contrast between past and present.

> "That we are in the midst of crisis is now well understood.
>
> Our nation is at war, against a far-reaching network of violence and hatred.
> Our economy is badly weakened, a consequence of greed and
> irresponsibility on the part of some, but also our collective failure to make
> hard choices and prepare the nation for a new age.
>
> Homes have been lost;
> jobs shed;
> businesses shuttered. "

A three-part list.

> "Our health care is too costly;
> our schools fail too many;
> and each day brings further evidence that the ways we use energy
> strengthen our adversaries and threaten our planet."

Another three-part list.

> "These are the indicators of crisis, subject to data and statistics.
>
> Less measurable but no less profound is a sapping of confidence across our
> land – a nagging fear that America's decline is inevitable, and that the next
> generation must lower its sights."

A contrast between measurable and not so measurable.

"Today I say to you that the challenges we face are real.
They are serious
and they are many."

A three-part list.

"They will not be met easily
or in a short span of time.
But know this, America – they will be met."

The first burst of applause came after this second of two three-part lists in a row
– in which the third positive point also contrasts with the first two negative ones.
Note also that the final item exploits the puzzle-solution format by getting the
audience wondering what they're going to have to know before he provides them
with the solution to the puzzle.

"On this day, we gather because we have chosen hope over fear,
unity of purpose over conflict and discord."

Two contrasts are used.

"On this day, we come to proclaim an end to the petty grievances and false
promises, the recriminations and worn out dogmas, that for far too long
have strangled our politics."

A repetition of the first words of each line – "on this day" – known as "anaphora"
in classical rhetoric.

"We remain a young nation, but in the words of Scripture, the time has
come to set aside childish things.

"The time has come to reaffirm our enduring spirit;
to choose our better history;
to carry forward that precious gift, that noble idea, passed on from
generation to generation:
the God-given promise that all are equal,
all are free,
and all deserve a chance to pursue their full measure of happiness."

Two three-part lists, each of which with a third item longer than the first two.

"In reaffirming the greatness of our nation, we understand that greatness is
never a given.
It must be earned."

A contrast with alliteration (g-g) in the first part.

"Our journey has never been one of short-cuts or settling for less.
It has not been the path for the faint-hearted –
for those who prefer leisure over work,
or seek only the pleasures of riches and fame."

Imagery of a journey starts with a three-part list, which turns out to be the first
part of a contrast in which the second part is another three-part list.

"Rather, it has been the risk-takers,
the doers,
the makers of things –"

A three-part list

"some celebrated but more often men and women obscure in their labor,
who have carried us up the long, rugged path towards prosperity and
freedom."

A contrast between famous and obscure continues journey imagery with
alliteration – path/prosperity.

"For us, they packed up their few worldly possessions and traveled across
oceans in search of a new life."

The journey image is now extended to refer to the original immigrants to the USA,
with another alliterative "p-p" clause.

"For us, they toiled in sweatshops and settled the West;
endured the lash of the whip
and plowed the hard earth."

Repetition of the first words ("anaphora") and the "lash of the whip" image now
includes slaves among immigrants.

"For us, they fought and died, in places like Concord and Gettysburg;
Normandy and Khe Sahn."

The third "for us" now extends the list of heroes to more periods of struggle on our behalf, revolution, civil war, second world war and Vietnam, each identified with images of famous battles.

"Time and again these men and women struggled and sacrificed and worked till their hands were raw so that we might live a better life."

Imagery of painful hard work and struggle (for us).

"They saw America as bigger than the sum of our individual ambitions; greater than all the differences of birth or wealth or faction."

Two comparative contrasts, with a three-part list in the second one.

"This is the journey we continue today. We remain the most prosperous, powerful nation on Earth."

P-p alliteration as he turns to speak about the present.

"Our workers are no less productive than when this crisis began. Our minds are no less inventive, our goods and services no less needed than they were last week or last month or last year."

There are 3 comparative sentences starting with "our" (anaphora again), with the third one ending in a three-part list.

"Our capacity remains undiminished. But our time of standing pat, of protecting narrow interests and putting off unpleasant decisions – that time has surely passed."

A contrast in which the second part includes a three-part list (with more p-p alliteration).

"Starting today, we must pick ourselves up, dust ourselves off, and begin again the work of remaking America."

A three-part list with the third item longer than the first two.

"For everywhere we look, there is work to be done."

A puzzle to get people wondering what needs to be done

"The state of the economy calls for action, bold and swift, and we will act
– not only to create new jobs,
but to lay a new foundation for growth."

The first part of the solution to the puzzle ends with a "not only/but also" contrast
and starts with what turns out to be a sequence of repeated "we will…" lines (i.e.
more "anaphora").

"We will build the roads and bridges, the electric grids and digital lines that
feed our commerce and bind us together.

We will restore science to its rightful place, and wield technology's
wonders to raise health care's quality and lower its cost."

A contrast between raising quality/lowering cost.

"We will harness the sun and the winds and the soil to fuel our cars and run
our factories."

A 3 part list of things that will be harnessed.

"And we will transform our schools and colleges and universities to meet
the demands of a new age."

And 3 things that will be improved.

"All this we can do.
And all this we will do."

A contrast between what can be done and will be done.

"Now, there are some who question the scale of our ambitions – who
suggest that our system cannot tolerate too many big plans.
Their memories are short."

A puzzle is given.

"For they have forgotten what this country has already done;
what free men and women can achieve when imagination is joined to

common purpose, and necessity to courage."

A solution to the puzzle explains why their memories are short.

"What the cynics fail to understand is that the ground has shifted
beneath them"

Ground-shifting imagery is used to refer to changing ideas.

"that the stale political arguments that have consumed us for so long no
longer apply.

The question we ask today is not whether our government is too big or too
small, but whether it works –"

A question/puzzle formulated with a contrast between big and small that then
contrasts with the third item.

"whether it helps families find jobs at a decent wage,
care they can afford,
a retirement that is dignified."

A question/puzzle elaborated wit a three-part list.

"Where the answer is yes, we intend to move forward.
Where the answer is no, programs will end."

A contrast with anaphora.

"And those of us who manage the public's dollars will be held to account
to spend wisely,
reform bad habits,
and do our business in the light of day –"

The 3 things he'll be accountable for, with daylight imagery to refer to openness.

"because only then can we restore the vital trust between a people and their
government.
Nor is the question before us whether the market is a force for good or ill.
Its power to generate wealth and expand freedom is unmatched,"

A puzzle-solution.

"but this crisis has reminded us that without a watchful eye, the market can spin out of control – and that a nation cannot prosper long when it favors only the prosperous."

Spinning imagery and a contrast between national and individual prosperity.

"The success of our economy has always depended not just on the size of our Gross Domestic Product, but on the reach of our prosperity;"

A contrast.

"on our ability to extend opportunity to every willing heart –
not out of charity, but because it is the surest route to our common good."

Another contrast.

"As for our common defense, we reject as false the choice between our safety and our ideals.
Our Founding Fathers, faced with perils we can scarcely imagine, drafted a charter to assure the rule of law and the rights of man, a charter expanded by the blood of generations."

A writing image to refer to the US constitution; and a blood image to refer to changes since the Civil War.

"Those ideals still light the world, and we will not give them up for expedience's sake."

A lighting up the world imagery to say that US ideals are widely admired.

"And so to all other peoples and governments who are watching today, from the grandest capitals to the small village where my father was born:"

Contrasting images of the "grandest capitals" and a "small village".

"know that America is a friend of each nation and every man, woman, and child who seeks a future of peace and dignity, and that we are ready to lead once more.

"Recall that earlier generations faced down fascism and communism not just with missiles and tanks, but with sturdy alliances and enduring convictions."

A contrast between the first item and the second two in a three-part sequence.

"They understood that our power alone cannot protect us, nor does it entitle
us to do as we please.
Instead, they knew that our power grows through its prudent use;
our security emanates from the justness of our cause,
the force of our example,
the tempering qualities of humility and restraint."

The second part of a contrast ends with a three-part list.

"We are the keepers of this legacy."

Guardians/inheritance imagery.

"Guided by these principles once more, we can meet those new threats that
demand even greater effort – even greater cooperation and understanding
between nations.
We will begin to responsibly leave Iraq to its people, and forge a hard-
earned peace in Afghanistan.
With old friends and former foes, we will work tirelessly to lessen the
nuclear threat, and roll back the specter of a warming planet.
We will not apologize for our way of life, nor will we waver in its defense,
and for those who seek to advance their aims by inducing terror and
slaughtering innocents, we say to you now"

The 3 "we will" (anaphora) starts followed by a puzzle (what is he going to say
now?).

"that our spirit is stronger and cannot be broken;
you cannot outlast us,
and we will defeat you."

Followed by a 3 part solution.

"For we know that our patchwork heritage is a strength, not a weakness."

A contrast.

"We are a nation of Christians and Muslims, Jews and Hindus – and non-
believers."

A contrast between religious believers and non-believers.

"We are shaped by every language and culture, drawn from every end of this Earth;
and because we have tasted the bitter swill of civil war and segregation, and emerged from that dark chapter stronger and more united, we cannot help but believe that the old hatreds shall someday pass; that the lines of tribe shall soon dissolve; that as the world grows smaller, our common humanity shall reveal itself; and that America must play its role in ushering in a new era of peace.
To the Muslim world, we seek a new way forward, based on mutual interest and mutual respect."

First in a sequence with repetitive starts (anaphora).

"To those leaders around the globe who seek to sow conflict, or blame their society's ills on the West – know that your people will judge you on what you can build, not what you destroy."

A contrast.

"To those who cling to power through corruption and deceit and the silencing of dissent,"

We are given three unacceptable ways of holding power.

"know that you are on the wrong side of history;
but that we will extend a hand if you are willing to unclench your fist."

A contrast with imagery of shaking hands and an unclenching fist.

"To the people of poor nations, we pledge to work alongside you to make your farms flourish"

Then there is p-p and f-f alliteration.

"and let clean waters flow; to nourish starved bodies and feed hungry minds."

There are 3 water and feeding images.

"And to those nations like ours that enjoy relative plenty, we say we can no

longer afford indifference to suffering outside our borders; nor can we
consume the world's resources without regard to effect.
For the world has changed, and we must change with it.
As we consider the road that unfolds before us,"

A return to the journey imagery from earlier in the speech implies he's moving
towards the end, or at least changing the subject.

"we remember with humble gratitude those brave Americans who, at this
very hour, patrol far-off deserts and distant mountains."

"Desert" and "mountain" imagery is used to refer to difficulties troops face in
Iraq and Afghanistan.

"They have something to tell us today, just as the fallen heroes who lie in
Arlington whisper through the ages."

He compares a message from current troops with that from dead ones – referred
to with an image of whispers from the national cemetery.

"We honor them not only because they are guardians of our liberty, but
because they embody the spirit of service;"

A contrast.

"a willingness to find meaning in something greater than themselves.
And yet, at this moment – a moment that will define a generation – it is
precisely this spirit that must inhabit us all.
For as much as government can do and must do, it is ultimately the faith
and determination of the American people upon which this nation relies."

The American people contrasted favourably with the American government.

"It is the kindness to take in a stranger when the levees break, the
selflessness of workers who would rather cut their hours than see a friend
lose their job which sees us through our darkest hours.
It is the firefighter's courage to storm a stairway filled with smoke, but also
a parent's willingness to nurture a child, that finally decides our fate."

Imagery is used to provide examples of American people's virtues.

"Our challenges may be new.

The instruments with which we meet them may be new.
But those values upon which our success depends – hard work and honesty,
courage and fair play, tolerance and curiosity, loyalty and patriotism –
these things are old."

A contrast between two new things and a third old thing.

"These things are true.
They have been the quiet force of progress throughout our history.
What is demanded then is a return to these truths.
What is required of us now is a new era of responsibility – a recognition, on
the part of every American, that we have duties to ourselves, our nation, and
the world, duties that we do not grudgingly accept but rather seize gladly,
firm in the knowledge that there is nothing so satisfying to the spirit, so
defining of our character, than giving our all to a difficult task."

Another comparative contrast.

"This is the price and the promise of citizenship.
This is the source of our confidence – the knowledge that God calls on us
to shape an uncertain destiny.
This is the meaning of our liberty and our creed – why men and women
and children of every race and every faith can join in celebration across
this magnificent mall, and why a man whose father less than sixty years
ago might not have been served at a local restaurant can now stand before
you to take a most sacred oath."

Three repetitive starts (anaphora) ending with a contrast between the negative
status of a father being discriminated against 60 years ago and his son becoming
president today.

"So let us mark this day with remembrance, of who we are and how far we
have traveled."

A return to earlier journey imagery implies he's close to the end.

"In the year of America's birth, in the coldest of months, a small band of
patriots huddled by dying campfires on the shores of an icy river."

Historical imagery that echoes water and weather images from start of speech
confirms that he is indeed moving into the peroration.

"The capital was abandoned.

The enemy was advancing.

The snow was stained with blood."

A three-part list of images depicting threats and struggle during the war of independence.

"At a moment when the outcome of our revolution was most in doubt, the father of our nation ordered these words be read to the people: "Let it be told to the future world...that in the depth of winter, when nothing but hope and virtue could survive...that the city and the country, alarmed at one common danger, came forth to meet [it]."

A quotation from George Washington as the first part of a contrast between then and now.

"America. In the face of our common dangers, in this winter of our hardship, let us remember these timeless words."

A continuation of weather imagery.

"With hope and virtue, let us brave once more the icy currents, and endure what storms may come."

A continuation of water and weather images.

"Let it be said by our children's children that when we were tested we refused to let this journey end, that we did not turn back nor did we falter;"

A three-part list of what we did and didn't do when tested.

"and with eyes fixed on the horizon and God's grace upon us, we carried forth that great gift of freedom and delivered it safely to future generations."

He concludes with three-part journey images ("horizon", "carried forth", "delivered") of the destination.

4th March 2009

Unexpected poetry in Gordon Brown's speech to the US Congress

Readers of my books will know that they emphasise the importance of simple poetic elements, such as alliteration and imagery, in the tool-kit of effective public speakers. But such poetics have never been very evident in past speeches by Gordon Brown.

That's why the most surprising thing about his speech to the US Congress earlier today was his use of at least 37 examples of alliteration and/or imagery (see below for more detail) – though his alliteration score was somewhat boosted by his repetitive use of the phrase in the first half of the alliterative title of the speech: With faith in the future, we can build tomorrow today.

For someone who has spent most of his life on the political platform, his sudden conversion to poetics raises the interesting question of whether there are new speechwriters at work in Downing Street – and, if so, who are they?

(P.S. Answer: Eight months later, I was fascinated to discover that there were indeed new speechwriters at work, but not in Downing Street. The PM apparently paid West Wing Writers, a Washington company run by former Democrat speechwriters, $7,000 to work on the speech – bringing the total paid to them since he became Chancellor of the Exchequer to more than $40,000).

Meanwhile, here are the examples spotted so far (alliteration in bold, imagery in italics):

F-f and b-b alliteration + imagery (building):

"The very creation of America was a bold affirmation of faith in the future: a future you have not just believed in but built with your own hands."

Imagery (writing a book):

"And on January 20th, you the American people began to *write the latest chapter in the American story...*"

B-b and s-s alliteration + topographical imagery (plains, streets, sands, beaches, bridges to denote battle fields in different wars):

> "And let me pay tribute to the soldiers, yours and ours, who again fight side by side in the *plains of Afghanistan* and the *streets of Iraq*, just as their forefathers fought side by side in the *sands of Tunisia*, on the **beaches of Normandy** and then on the **bridges over the Rhine**."

F-f alliteration:

> "And let it be said of our **f**riendship – **f**ormed and **f**orged over two tumultuous centuries, a **f**riendship tested in war and strengthened in peace"

F-f alliteration (echoing Churchill's use of same f-words):

> "And when banks have **f**ailed and markets have **f**altered…"

P-p alliteration (+ contrast):

> "Not an alliance of convenience, but a **p**artnership of **p**urpose."

W-w, f-f and r-r alliteration (+contrast):

> "…**w**ealth must help more than the **w**ealthy, good **f**ortune must serve more than the **f**ortunate and **r**iches must en**r**ich not just some of us but all."

W-w and d-d alliteration + imagery (contagion):

> "And **w**e need to understand **w**hat **w**ent wrong in this crisis, that the very financial instruments that were **d**esigned to **d**iversify risk across the banking system instead *spread contagion across the globe*."

C-c and f-f alliteration:

> "And this is not blind optimism or synthetic **c**onfidence to **c**onsole people; it is the practical af**f**irmation for our times of our **f**aith in a better **f**uture."

F-f alliteration:

> "Every time we rebuild a school we demonstrate our **f**aith in the **f**uture."

S-s and f-f alliteration:

> "… every time we increase **s**upport to our **s**cientists, we demonstrate our

faith in the future."

F-f alliteration:

"... we conquer our fear of the future through our faith in the future."

M-m and p-p alliteration:

"And I believe that you, the nation that had the vision to put a **man** on the **moon**, are also the nation with the vision to **p**rotect and **p**reserve our **p**lanet earth."

Weather imagery + c-c-c-c alliteration:

"An economic *hurricane has swept the world*, **c**reating a **c**risis of **c**redit and of **c**onfidence."

T-t alliteration:

"We are summoned not just **t**o manage our **t**imes but to **t**ransform them."

W-w and d-d alliteration + imagery (contagion, again):

"And we need to understand **w**hat **w**ent wrong in this crisis, that the very financial instruments that were **d**esigned to **d**iversify risk across the banking system instead *spread contagion across the globe*."

T-t and s-s alliteration:

|And America and Britain will succeed and lead if we **t**ap into the **t**alents of our people, unleash the geniu**s** of our **s**cientists and **s**et free the drive of our entrepreneurs.|

C-c and f-f- alliteration:

"And this is not blind optimism or synthetic **c**onfidence to **c**onsole people; it is the practical affirmation for our times of our **f**aith in a better **f**uture."

S-s and f-f alliteration:

"... every time we increa**s**e **s**upport to our **s**cientists, we demonstrate our **f**aith in the **f**uture."

C-c and f-f alliteration:

"And so I say to this Congress and this country, something that runs deep in your character and is woven in your history, we conquer our fear of the future through our faith in the future."

F-f and p-p alliteration:

"And it is this faith in the future that means we must commit to protecting the planet for generations that will come long after us."

Imagery (sowing seeds):

"As the Greek proverb says, why does anybody *plant the seeds of a tree whose shade* they will never see?"

M-m and p-p alliteration:

"And I believe that you, the nation that had the vision to put a man on the moon, are also the nation with the vision to protect and preserve our planet earth."

Imagery (water and rippling):

"No matter where it starts, an economic crisis *does not stop at the water's edge. It ripples across the world.*"

P-p, f-f and t-t alliteration and "building' image:

"Let us restore prosperity and protect this planet and, with faith in the future, let us together *build* tomorrow today."

6th March 2009

Brown's "poetry" heads up news of his speech to Congress

The previous post highlighted the frequency with which Gordon Brown used "poetic" devices, like alliteration and imagery, in his speech to the US Congress earlier this week.

When it comes to getting key messages across, the advantage of using these and other rhetorical techniques is that they are they much more likely to be noticed (and perhaps even remembered) by the audience than if the same point had been made in a more bland or mundane way.

I first discussed how the way a message is packaged in a speech can affect its chances of reaching a wider audience in my book *Our Masters' Voices* (1984), using examples from speeches by Ronald Reagan, Margaret Thatcher and other leading politicians of the day.

Luckily for politicians, then and now, their audiences also include the media, whose reporters and editors react in much the same way as any other member of an audience, and are therefore likely to turn similar lines into prime-time soundbites.

A nice example of this came from the top of Sky News reports of Mr Brown's speech to Congress, which opened by quoting his most-repeated alliterative phrase and one of his more powerful metaphors:

> "Gordon Brown has told America to have 'faith in the future' that 'the economic hurricane that has ravaged the world's financial system can be overcome'".

8th March 2009

How to improve impact by sequence, repetition and a rhetorical technique

In Vince Cable's speech at the spring conference of the Liberal Democrats in Harrogate a couple of days ago, there was a sequence that would have been more effective had he (or his speechwriter) reversed the order in which he mentioned the two points, used repetition and packaged it as a contrast.

The line went as follows:

> "Public companies should publish full pay package of all their highly paid employees [applause starts] as well as the directors."

You can see the sequence by looking 1 minute, 25 seconds into the video on my blog, and will notice that the audience started applauding immediately after he said "employees" and before he got to the key phrase "as well as the directors."

As the current situation is that pay packages of directors already have to be published and Cable's new/controversial point was that this should also apply to all highly paid employees, this would have worked better if the "news" had come second rather than first.

It was also crying out to be turned into a more explicit contrast between directors and other highly paid employees, with key words repeated, along the lines of the following:

> "Public companies should not just publish the full pay package of their directors. They should publish the full pay package of all their highly paid employees."

Rhythmically and for adding emphasis, it would arguably have been improved further by making the second part of the contrast slightly longer, as in:

"They should publish the full pay package of each and every single one of their highly paid employees."

Either way, the applause would still have come immediately after the word "employees", but it would have sounded more emphatic and there would have been no risk of the key point being drowned out by the applause.

"From Stalin to Mr Bean": putting two parts of a contrast in the most effective order

In case anyone thinks that the last posting was intended as a criticism of Vince Cable's rhetorical skill, I haven't forgotten that his most famous line came when, as acting leader of the Liberal Democrats, he produced a devastating contrast at Question Time in the House of Commons.

If he had said that Mr Brown "had become more like Mr Bean than Stalin", the contrast between a bumbling fool and an autocratic dictator would still have been there and would no doubt have raised a laugh or two.

But on that occasion, he got the order of the two parts of the contrast the right way round, and not only had a tremendous impact there and then, but also did his own longer term reputation no harm at all.

18th March 2009

Check the fixtures and fittings before you speak

Prince William recently gave a speech that, not surprisingly, received national media coverage. After all, here was a very famous person who had lost his mother at a young age and in tragic circumstances becoming patron of the Child Bereavement Charity, which helps children and families who have lost a parent.

It must have been difficult for him not to accept their invitation – and even more difficult to have to make a speech in which he could hardly not mention his mother, the late Princess Diana.

If that wasn't going to be tough enough, he then had to speak without a lectern and without a stand for the microphone, even though the organisers must surely have known that it was going to be broadcast to a mass television audience.

The result was that the viewers saw a nervous young man standing at the bottom of a staircase with sheets of paper in one hand and a microphone in the other.

Not surprisingly, it could hardly be said to be a model example of how to deliver a speech. However difficult Prince William was going to find it speaking about something so close to his heart, it would have been a little bit easier if he (or the organisers) had made sure that clutching paper and a microphone would not be necessary parts of the performance.

The very obvious general point is that, whenever speakers can, they should always check out – in advance – the room, layout, fixtures, fittings and equipment. Otherwise you risk falling foul of the inadequate arrangements made by your hosts.

25th March 2009

It's time Gordon Brown stopped recycling other people's lines

I've warned Gordon Brown and his speechwriters before that it's not a good idea to lift lines from other people's speeches. This was prompted by one of the lines from a speech he made in July last year:

> "There's nothing bad about Britain that cannot be corrected by what's good about Britain ..."

This bore an uncanny resemblance to something Bill Clinton had said in his inaugural address in January 1993:

> "There is nothing wrong with America that cannot be cured by what is right with America."

Then, when Brown spoke to the US Congress three weeks ago, he came up with:

> "There is no old Europe, no new Europe, there is only your friend Europe."

Not surprisingly, this got some commentators wondering if his scriptwriters had now started borrowing from the collected works of Barack Obama, whose address at the 2004 Democratic Convention had included the following:

> "There is not a liberal America and a conservative America – there is the United States of America. There is not a Black America and a White America and Latino America and Asian America – there's the United States of America."

Obama subsequently recycled a similar version in other speeches, including the one in Chicago after he had won the election:

> "We have never been just a collection of individuals or a collection of red states and blue states. We are and always will be the United States of America"

Recycling your own material may be acceptable, but there is nothing whatsoever to be gained from recycling material that sounds as though it's been lifted from someone else – other than the kind electoral disaster Joe Biden experienced when his unattributed use of lines from a Neil Kinnock speech brought his otherwise promising 1987 campaign for the Democratic nomination to an abrupt end.

But Brown and his speechwriters still don't seem to get it. So, here we are, hardly three weeks since he told the US Congress:

"There is no old Europe, no new Europe, there is only your friend Europe"

we hear him telling the European Parliament:

"There is no old Europe, no new Europe, no east or west Europe. There is only one Europe – our home Europe."

Pass the sick bag please ...

26th March 2009

Does Daniel Hannan's attack on Brown tell us what makes a speech memorable?

When I first started doing research into political speeches in the early 1980s, I concentrated on sequences that prompted applause – as it seemed a fairly obvious and unequivocal barometer for measuring audience approval. What attracted most attention about the results was the observation that most bursts of applause are triggered by a small number of simple rhetorical techniques (*Our Masters' Voices*: the Language and Body Language of Politics, 1984).

But the book also included some observations about the content of the messages that get applauded in political speeches, the main finding being that 84% of the bursts of applause occurred after a boastful statement about the speaker's own party or an insult/attack on an opposing party – or some combination of the two (OMV, p. 45).

When I was actively involved with the Liberal Democrats during the Ashdown years, we had some interesting arguments, thanks to their rather pious tradition of trying to stand aside from "Yah-boo" politics – which would make it sound inconsistent if they were to use too much in the way of knocking copy.

But my point was (and still is) that to abstain from the insult/attack option means signing up to a self-denying ordinance that deprives you of one of the main techniques for generating audience approval – and the success of Vince Cable's suggestion that Gordon Brown had changed from Stalin to Mr Bean suggests that there is at least one member of the current leadership team willing to deploy an insult now and then.

So the first thing that struck me about Daniel Hannan's speech was that almost every sentence conveyed an insult or attack – not just directed at Labour in general, but highly personalised ones aimed at the leader of the Labour Party in particular. Add to this the fact that it was in front of MEPs in Strasbourg and in the presence of Mr Brown, a distinguished guest who had just made a speech, and the context becomes comparable with that of a cheeky schoolboy standing up at speech day and telling the headmaster exactly what he and others thought of him in full view of all the other pupils, teachers and parents.

If Mr Hannan's repetitive use of the insult/attack option, packaged with some neat rhetoric and appropriate imagery, may have set the speech up to attract more attention than usual, it's obviously not the only reason for its success.

Since writing *Our Masters' Voices,* I've been asked many times: what makes a truly memorable speech? However intellectually and financially rewarding it would be to have a definitive answer, I can't claim to have got there yet. But I do have the beginnings of a theory.

Effective use of rhetoric and imagery to package the key messages is important, but it doesn't really provide anything like a complete answer, not least because the same techniques are to be found in all famous speeches.

So I started trying to get together samples of speeches that qualified as such to see if they had anything in common. After asking scores of people which speeches they considered "memorable", what surprised me was the frequency with which they mentioned the same four speeches (remember that I was doing this 25 years ago):

Harold Macmillan's "Wind of change" in the South African parliament in 1960

John F Kennedy's "Ich bin ein Berliner" in front of the Berlin wall in 1963

Martin Luther King's "I have a dream" in front of the Lincoln Memorial in 1963

Enoch Powell's "Rivers of blood" in Birmingham, 1968

So what, if anything, did these particular speeches have in common that made them stand out as more memorable than most?

The best I've been able to come up with is that, in each case, the speaker managed to hit the jackpot by saying something that struck just the right chord with just the right audience in just the right place at just the right moment in history – which means that it's more or less impossible to predict "memorability" with any certainty in advance of any particular speech – though I did wonder whether this was what Barack Obama had in mind when he tried unsuccessfully to speak at the Brandenburg Gate when visiting Berlin last year – given the previous Berlin successes of Kennedy in 1961 and Ronald Reagan's "Tear down this wall" in 1987.

Much the same can be said of three more recent specimens of the commonest answers to the same question about memorable speeches:

Ronald Reagan's "Challenger" speech after the shuttle disaster in 1986

Tony Blair's "People's Princess" speech on the death of Princess Diana in 1997

Lord Spencer's eulogy at the funeral of Princess Diana (his sister) in 1997

At this point, I should make it clear that I am not suggesting that Daniel Hannan's speech in Strasbourg the other day will ever get anywhere close to the long-term "memorability" of the above examples. But I do think that, when it comes to explaining its sudden success, the same factors – right chord/right audience/right place/right time – may help to answer the question appearing on blogs and in the media, namely why has it taken off in the way that it has?

Right chord: challenging one of the favoured solutions to the current economic crisis.

Right audience: including a prime minister and people around the world who are also unconvinced by such solutions.

Right place: in the European Parliament where there is disagreement between countries about the alternative solutions.

Right Time: Just before the G20 meeting about agreeing a global solution to the economic crisis.

What brought me back to this question after so many years was reading through some of the 5,573 comments (at the time of writing) about the speech on YouTube.

You don't have to read many of them to see that the right chord, the right audience, the right place and/or the right time are recurring themes from those who liked the speech well enough to want to put their own comments on the record.

27th March 2009

Rhetorical techniques and imagery in Hannan's attack on Brown – edited highlights

As promised the other day, here are some notes on the rhetorical highlights of Daniel Hannan's attack on Gordon Brown.

At its simplest, the more use a speaker makes of the main rhetorical techniques and imagery to get key messages across, the more likely it is that a speech will achieve high audience ratings.

Given the impact of this particular speech, it's therefore hardly surprising to see just how frequently he uses them – at a rate that comes close to the frequency to be found in some of Barack Obama's speeches.

Edited footage of the following five highlights can be seen on my blog.

1. The opening:

Attention grabbing opening with a puzzle (that sounds as it though it could be a compliment) followed by a solution packaged as a contrast (that turns out to be an insult/attack):

Puzzle: Prime Minister, I see you've already mastered the essential craft of the European politician,

Solution: (A) namely the ability to say one thing in this chamber
(B) and a very different thing to your home electorate.

2. Attack packaged as a "you/our " contrast:

The truth, Prime Minister, is that you have run out of our money.

3. Extended metaphor introduced by two contrasts:

(A) It is true that we are all sailing together into the squalls.

(B) But not every vessel in the convoy is in the same dilapidated condition.

(A) Other ships used the good years to caulk their hulls and clear their rigging; in other words – to pay off debt.

(B) But you used the good years to raise borrowing yet further.

As a consequence, under your captaincy, our hull is pressed deep into the water line under the accumulated weight of your debt.

4. Insult/attack packaged as a"not (A) but (B)" contrast with alliteration:

(A) Now, it's not that you're not apologising; like everyone else I have long accepted that you're pathologically incapable of accepting responsibility for these things.

(B) It's that you're carrying on, wilfully worsening our situation, wantonly spending what little we have left.

5. Contrasts followed by simile, four 3 part lists (with repetition) and a concluding puzzle-solution:

(A) Prime Minister you cannot go on forever squeezing the productive bit of the economy

(B) in order to fund an unprecedented engorging of the unproductive bit.
[applause]

(A) You cannot spend your way out of recession
(B) or borrow your way out of debt.

And when you repeat, in that wooden and perfunctory way, that our situation is better than others, that we're well placed to weather the storm, I have to tell you, you sound like a Brezhnev-era Apparatchik giving the party line.

(1) You know,

(2) and we know,

(3) and you know that we know that it's nonsense.

Everyone knows that Britain is worse off than any other country to go into these hard times.

(1) The IMF has said so.

(2) The European Commission has said so.

(3) The markets have said so, which is why our currency has devalued by 30% – and soon the voters, too, will get their chance to say so.

Puzzle: They can see what the markets have already seen:

Solution: that you are the devalued Prime Minister of a devalued government.

29th March 2009

Another Tory speech that marked the beginning of the end for a prime minister

There was an interesting comment the other day on one of my postings about Daniel Hannan's speech by Charles Crawford, a former speechwriter to Sir Geoffrey Howe. It reminded me of another Tory speech that marked the beginning of the end of a prime minister – and also met the right chord/right audience/right place/right time test for "memorability".

Sir Geoffrey Howe's resignation speech to the House of Commons included a fine example of sporting imagery (a cricketing simile) to describe what it had been like working for Mrs Thatcher.

> "It's rather like sending your opening batsmen to the crease, only for them to find, the moment the first balls are bowled, that their bats have been broken before the game by the team captain."

The speech ended with a fairly explicit invitation to other discontented colleagues to stand against her for the leadership, and it wasn't long before she was gone:

> "The time has come for others to consider their own response to the tragic conflict of loyalties with which I have myself wrestled for perhaps too long."

Mr Crawford says he didn't write the speech, but I wonder if he or anyone else could shed any light on a rumour that was circulating at the time, namely that Sir Geoffrey's wife had had a major hand in writing it.

30th March 2009

"The Lost Art of Oratory" by a BBC executive who helped to lose it in the first place

Well, well, well – after decades of showing fewer and fewer speeches (and shorter and shorter extracts from the few that ever do get shown) on television, the BBC is now trailing a programme entitled "Yes We Can: The Lost Art of Oratory" next Sunday night, presented by none other than Alan Yentob – who, in his former roles as controller of BBC 1 and Director of Programmes, was one of the few people who could actually have done something to prevent the "Art of Oratory" from being more or less lost from our television screens in the first place

Having posted a piece entitled "Obama's rhetoric renews UK media interest in the 'lost art' of oratory" back in December, I suppose I should be gratified to see my point being endorsed by the BBC.

But it does seem rather ironic that the programme is being put out on the same channel (BBC 2) that broadcast a half an hour programme of speeches every night during the 1979 election, but where you'll never see any now – unless they feel it's time for a bit of speculation about the declining importance of oratory in British politics, helped along the way by authoritative experts like Bob Geldof and Germaine Greer.

Or maybe it's just their way of trying to justify part of the huge amount of licence payers' money spent on sending Mr Yentob and the swarms of other BBC employees to Washington for inauguration day.

Having just heard him plugging the programme on BBC Radio 4's Start the Week, I'm not expecting much in the way of news or insight into the subject. But it should be worth recording in case they play any clips that I don't already have in my collection.

31st March 2009

Gordon Brown is finding the Jacqui Smith expenses story more "delicate" than he says

Long ago, I heard one of the founders of conversation analysis (and I can't remember whether it was Emanuel Schegloff or Gail Jefferson) talking about "pre-delicate hitches" – a rather cumbersome piece of jargon for referring to a fairly common occurrence in conversation.

"Hitches" are things like "uh-" and "um-", restarts of a word, or slight pauses, and the observation was that these are regularly found at those points in a conversation where the speaker is leading towards a word or a topic that they know is rather "delicate" (e.g. a swear word, obscenity or potentially controversial news, gossip, etc.).

The general argument was that such hitches are used to give advance notice that we're about to say something that we know is rather delicate – and know that others might find delicate too.

I was therefore fascinated to notice that there were at least ten pre-delicate hitches in the first four sentences of Gordon Brown's comments about the scandal of the Home Secretary's expenses claim for a blue movie watched by her husband – which you can check out by following the transcript below (hitches in bold).

> Brown: **This is- this is** very much **a-a** personal matter **(pause) uh- for- for** Jacqui. She's made her **uh-** apology. Her husband has made it **uh-** clear that **he is- he is** apologised (sic). **Uh I-I think** that the best thing is that Jacqui Smith **gets- gets on** with her work **as-** which is what she wants to do.

What these hitches suggest is that Mr Brown is finding the whole episode much more delicate than he's letting on in the words that he actually uses.

2nd April 2009

Gordon Brown's G20 address ignores an important tip from Winston Churchill

Whenever I'm asked about the biggest single problem I've come across since migrating from academia into training and coaching, my answer is always the same, namely the sight and sound of speakers trying to get far too much information across – aided and abetted by programs like PowerPoint that implicitly encourage presenters to load up the screen with far too much detail.

It's something that was very well understood by Winston Churchill, who said:

> "If you have an important point to make, don't try to be subtle or clever. Use a pile driver. Hit the point once. Then come back and hit it again. Then hit it a third time with a tremendous whack."

But it's never been very well understood by Gordon Brown, as was evidenced yet again in his address at yesterday's pre-G20 press conference.

Announcing that there are *five* tests for the G20 summit may not have been quite as daunting to the audience as showing a slide listing *seventeen* items to be covered, as was once tried by someone I was trying to cure. But it hardly makes you sit up eagerly waiting to hear what's coming up.

20th April 2009

Obama's rhetoric identifies with Martin Luther King but appeals to a wider audience

The oratory of Martin Luther King was clearly derived from the style of preaching he had grown up with in the Southern Baptist Church. That same tradition was also reflected in the way crowds responded to his speeches like congregations, punctuating them at regular intervals with chants like "Holy, holy, holy", "Amen", etc.

This was very evident in the last speech he ever made on the night before he was assassinated (see transcript and video on the blog):

MLK: I just want to do God's will.
Crowd: Yeah-
MLK: And he's allowed me to go up to the mountain.
Crowd: Go ahead
MLK: And I've looked over,
Crowd: Yeah
MLK: and I've seen the promised land.
Crowd: Holy, Holy, Holy.
Crowd: Amen.
MLK: I may not get there with you.
Crowd: Yeah – holy.
MLK: but I want you to know tonight
Crowd: Yeah -
MLK: that we as a people
Crowd: Yeah -

MLK: will get to the promised land.

Crowd: Yeah [Applause] Holy, holy.

MLK: So I'm happy tonight, I'm not worried about anything, I'm not fearing any man. Mine eyes have seen the glory of the coming of the Lord (Cheers and Applause).

Moving though his use of biblical imagery and references to 'God' and 'the Lord' may have been, a question that never occurred to me when I first wrote about Martin Luther King's oratory twenty five years ago (*Our Masters' Voices* pp. 105-111) was how such language must have sounded to American Muslims, Jews, Hindus and non-believers, all of whom who were explicitly included in the nation's "patchwork heritage" referred to in President Obama's inaugural address.

Nor was his inaugural speech the first time that Obama's rhetoric had broadened and extended his appeal to a much wider constituency than King's fellow Southern Baptists and/or committed Christians. The following sequence from his victory speech in Chicago last November included clearly recognisable echoes with its mountain-climbing imagery and the claim that "we as a people will get there":

Obama: The road ahead will be long. Our climb will be steep. We may not get there in one year or even in one term, but America – I have never been more hopeful than I am tonight that we will get there. I promise you – we as a people will get there.

"We as a people will get there" may have sounded a good deal less dramatic than "We as a people will get to the promised land", but it has the great benefit of being much more inclusive than was implied by the religious connotations of "the promised land" – while at the same time clearly identifying Mr Obama with the well-known words of the person whose dream he was implicitly claiming to have fulfilled by winning the election.

The crowd also responded with a secularised version of the kind of chanting that brought such life to Martin Luther King's speeches, replacing words like "holy" and "amen" with repetitive refrain of the non-religious "Yes we can", but still echoing or harking back to the close speaker-audience interaction of the Southern-Baptist tradition of worship.

As an outside observer of Barack Obama's oratory and rhetoric, I have been fascinated by the way he managed, by stripping out religion from well-known words of Martin Luther King, to broaden his appeal to a much wider audience, while leaving the identification with his distinguished African-American predecessor clearly in view.

The questions I'd be fascinated to hear answered by him and his team of insiders is whether this was a deliberately contrived strategy and, if so, whose idea was it and when it was first conceived?

22nd April 2009

Inspiring banking imagery for Budget day from Martin Luther King

I'm currently preparing for a trip to the University of Michigan next month, where I'll be running a course for Genome scientists and giving a lecture in the Political Science Department.

So, quite by chance, I've spent most of Budget day rummaging through video clips to take with me and came across one of my all time favorites, namely Martin Luther King's extraordinary use of what, on the face of it, might seem like a rather unpromising source of imagery during the early part of his "I have a dream" speech.

When working with clients in the banking and finance sector, I sometimes find it quite difficult to convince them that they too could be making effective use of imagery to get their business points across.

Yet here we have someone developing an image drawn from banking to get a powerful political message across extremely effectively.

So, if you weren't too inspired by Mr Darling's speech earlier today, here's something completely different: read and enjoy. `

Martin Luther King:

  "In a sense we have come to our nation's capital to cash a check.

When the architects of our republic wrote the magnificent words of the Constitution and the Declaration of Independence, they were signing a promissory note to which every American was to fall heir.

This note was a promise that all men, yes, black men as well as white men, would be guaranteed the unalienable rights of life, liberty, and the pursuit of happiness.

It is obvious today that America has defaulted on this promissory note insofar as her citizens of color are concerned.

Instead of honoring this sacred obligation, America has given the Negro people a bad check, a check which has come back marked "insufficient funds."

But we refuse to believe that the bank of justice is bankrupt.

We refuse to believe that there are insufficient funds in the great vaults of opportunity of this nation.

So we have come to cash this check — a check that will give us upon demand the riches of freedom and the security of justice."

25th April 2009

David Cameron's attack on the Budget used some well-crafted rhetoric

Having used the neat alliterative phrase "decade of debt" early in his reply to Mr Darling's Budget speech on Wednesday, David Cameron returned to it in the second part of a contrast as he began to wind up his reply.

He then followed it up with another contrast between the last Labour government and this one, a repetitively constructed three-part list and a question – technically pretty faultless, and hardly surprising that he was rewarded with a good deal of positive media coverage.

Cameron:

[A] The last Labour government gave us the Winter of Discontent.

[B] This Labour Government has given us the Decade of Debt.

[A] The last Labour Government left the dead unburied.

[B] This one leaves the debts unpaid.

[1] They sit there, running out of money,

[2] running out of moral authority,

[3] running out of time.

[Q] And you have to ask yourself what on earth is the point of another fourteen months of this Government of the living dead?

30th April 2009

Joanna Lumley's rhetoric outshines Clegg and Cameron

In a previous posting, I suggested that actors, with the notable exception of Ronald Reagan, aren't always very effective speech-makers.

But yesterday, we saw actress and Gurkha justice campaigner Joanna Lumley showing two party leaders the virtues of brevity and enthusiasm when it comes to delivering a highly useable sound bite (rounded off with a nice simple three-part list):

Lumley: When it came through – we saw it on the screen in the corner – I can't tell you the sense of elation, the sense of pride: pride in our country, pride in the democratic system, pride in our parliament …

By comparison, the reactions of Messrs Clegg and Cameron came across as rather long-winded and their impact was arguably weakened by their eagerness to use the victory to get other political points across:

Clegg: It's a victory for the rights of Gurkhas who have been waiting for so long for justice. It's a victory for Parliament over a government that just wasn't prepared to listen. But actually the biggest victory of all ... it's a victory of decency. It's the kind of thing that I think people want this country to do – that we pay back our obligations, our debt of gratitude towards generations of Gurkhas who have laid their lives on the line for our safety. I'm immensely pleased that David Cameron and I have been able to work on this together, that Labour backbenchers have also been brave enough to vote with their consciences. It was a cross-party effort. It was a great, great day for everybody who believes in fairness and decency in this country.

Cameron: Today is an historic day where Parliament took the right decision, that the basic presumption that people who fight for our country should have a right to come and live in our country has been set out very clearly. And the government now have got to come back with immediate proposals, so that those Gurkhas that have been waiting so long now for an answer can have that answer. It can be done. We've set out a way for it to be done that doesn't ruin our immigration system and it should be done. And I think everyone should say congratulations to Joanna Lumley for the incredible campaign that she's fought, with all these brave Gurkhas, some of them very old and very infirm, coming to Parliament again and again. The government attempted a shoddy deal today to try and buy off some of their backbenchers. And I'm proud of the fact that it didn't work and I'm proud of all those Labour MPs who joined us in the lobby – and actually got the right result for Britain and the Gurkhas.

9th May 2009

Eye contact, public speaking and the case of President Zuma's dark glasses

Having just watched Jacob Zuma being sworn in as South Africa's new president, I was reminded of the importance of eye contact in holding the attention of an audience.

It wasn't so much that he hardly looked up from the text, which was excusable given the importance of getting the words right when reading out an oath, as the fact that he was wearing dark glasses.

Readers of my books will know that I regard some of the widely circulating claims about body language and non-verbal communication as being at best over-stated, and at worst false (e.g. see *Lend Me Your Ears*, Chapter 11). But eye-contact is definitely not one of these.

In fact, here's what I wrote about the subject twenty-five years ago that bears on the case of President Zuma'a dark glasses:

".. humans are the only primate species in which the irises are framed by visible areas of whiteness, and it is generally considered that the evolutionary significance of this has to do with the communicative importance of our eyes: the whites of the eyes make it relatively easy for people to track even slight movements over quite large distances. An illustration of the importance of eye visibility for holding the attention of an audience is provided by an anecdote in the autobiography of the Oxford philosopher, A.J. Ayer (Part of My Life, 1977). He reports that, after sustaining a black eye as a result of bumping into a lamp post during a wartime blackout, he took to wearing dark glasses. He goes on to say that he subsequently found when lecturing in them that it was quite impossible to hold the attention of an audience. Given his reputation as an effective speaker, this suggests that the invisibility of a person's eyes can seriously interfere with his ability to communicate with an audience. It may therefore be no coincidence that there have been very few great orators who have worn spectacles, even with plain glass in them, when making speeches." (*Our Masters' Voices*, 1984, pp.89-90).

There's much more on why eye-contact is so important for effective public speaking in *Lend Me Your Ears* (pp.36-43), but an additional point about President Zuma's choice of dark glasses is that it tends to make him look more like a South American dictator than a democratically elected president, an implicit association that he would presumably be quite keen to avoid.

All of which is to say that, if I were advising him, I'd definitely tell him to get some new glasses.

I'd also suggest that his aides should pay a bit more attention to camera angles and back-drops, because there's someone just behind him wearing a black bowler hat, the brim of which at times pokes out from the sides of the president's head – a seemingly trivial point perhaps, but I bet I'm not the only viewer who found it distracting.

11th May 2009

Gordon Brown's interview technique: the tip of a tedious iceberg

Yesterday, Iain Dale posted a plug for a new book about handling media interviews and included the following observation (by Dale) about Gordon Brown (or "Boredom Frown', as my granddaughters prefer to call him):

> "Gordon Brown has catchphrases he uses over and over again. Whatever the question he's asked he'll come out with the same five catchphrases. Someone should tell him people are getting bored. They know what the answers are going to be. He doesn't seem to have the ability to think on his feet in the way that Blair did. He doesn't come across well in interviews like Blair."

I think Brown's problem is even more serious than this. More than 20 years ago, I heard the late great Robin Day complaining that the TV interview had been hijacked by politicians. In the good old days, he said, interviewers could have a really good argument with the likes of Harold Macmillan, who would perk up at the prospect of engaging in serious debate – whereas now (i.e. more than 20 years ago), they just treat questions as prompts to say anything they like about whatever they like.

14th May 2009

Why it's so easy for politicians not to answer interviewers' questions – and what should be done about it

I mentioned in an earlier post that I'd once heard the late Robin Day complaining that the news interview had been "hijacked" by politicians who had discovered that they could get away with ignoring questions and talk about whatever they felt like.

David Dimbleby made much the same point in a clip I found the other day. If interviewers as experienced as Day and Dimbleby can be so easily thwarted, there must be some quite deep-seated reason why it's so easy for politicians to get away with it. And I think Dimbleby is on to it when he says that he doesn't have a gun to point at them if they don't answer a question.

The thing about pointing a gun at someone is that it is about as hostile and aggressive an action as you can think of. And the trouble is that the only conversational techniques available to us for trying to get someone to answer questions also come across as hostile and aggressive.

Hostility & Neutrality

Consider, for example, the kind of thing that happens when a witness in court fails to answer a question during cross-examination.

Barristers can ruthlessly intervene and demand an answer:

Counsel: Did you make any attempt to persuade the crowd to go back before you baton-charged them?

Witness: I don't see how you could persuade them to go back.

Counsel: Never mind that – just answer the question first and then give your reason. Did you make any effort to persuade the crowd to go back before you baton-charged them?

Witness: No.

Or they may refer the matter to the judge for a ruling, as in this sequence where the alleged victim in an American rape trial is being cross-examined:

Counsel: Didn't you tell the police that the defendant had been drinking?

Witness: I told them there was a cooler in the car and I never opened it.

Counsel: May the balance of the answer be stricken, your honour, and the answer is "no".

Judge: Yes – the answer is "No".

If the lawyers sound hostile or aggressive towards the witnesses, this is of course perfectly acceptable in an adversarial legal system in which barristers are paid to take sides.

But the insurmountable obstacle that our news interviewers are up against is that they are paid to be neutral, which means that appearing to take sides can get them into serious trouble – so that they are, in effect, barred from using the kinds of hostile conversational techniques used in other settings to force people to answer a question without also coming across as aggressive and, by implication, politically biased (unless, of course, they're willing to court controversy and take the risk of losing their job).

A solution?

So here's my formula for sparing us from having to watch the repetitive evasiveness of politicians in interviews: they would be conducted in front of an audience equipped with handsets that would enable them to press a "yes" or "no" button, according to whether or not they felt a question had been adequately answered. These would be instantly added up and displayed on a scoreboard behind the interviewer and interviewee.

Whenever more than 50% of the audience felt that the politician had not answered the question, the interviewer would have the right and duty to press further on the same question – and to continue doing so until more than half the audience had rated the answer as adequate.

Such an approach would have three advantages over the present situation:

1. It would liberate interviewers from the risk of being accused of hostility or political bias, because they would merely be acting as representatives on behalf of a dissatisfied audience.

2. By making it more difficult for politicians to be so evasive, it would give viewers and listeners a clearer idea about where the interviewees really stand on a particular issue.

3. It would be much more entertaining television than the tedium currently inflicted on us (and might even have the added bonus of getting people more interested in politics than they are at present).

26th May 2009

Two tips for David Cameron after today's speech on political change

I suppose it's of the nature of the Open University that they're a bit short on decent lecture theatres for speeches like the one David Cameron gave there earlier today. But I did think they could have done a bit better than to position his lectern in front of a distracting and rather unattractive bookshelf – distracting, because anoraks like me start trying to see which books are waiting there to be picked up and read.

The need to check on furniture and fittings before you make a speech is something I've commented on before after Prince William had to hover at the bottom of some stairs trying to hold his script in one hand and a microphone in the other.

The OU did a bit better than that, but if I'd been Mr Cameron or one of his aides, I'd have done my best to arrange for a rather more suitable backdrop than a few bookshelves.

One other thing he should be doing something about is that he's still spending far too much time looking towards one side of the audience before looking in the other direction. On this occasion, it wasn't quite as marked as it has been in the past, but his gaze was quite often fixed in one direction for 11-19 seconds (i.e. too long) before being redirected towards the other half of the audience.

Given that his delivery is much better than the average currently prevailing among British politicians, it's a pity he doesn't do something about such a simple error that's so easy to correct.

27th May 2009

Obama's nomination of Judge Sotomayor received five times more applause than "normal"

Soon after I started studying applause in political speeches, it emerged that there is a "normal" burst of applause that lasts for about eight (plus or minus one) seconds (see *Our Masters' Voices*, 1984).

Less than this and it sounds half-hearted; more than this and it sounds more enthusiastic than usual – with the result that the media are more likely to select lines that get longer bursts for headlines in newspapers or sound bites on news programmes.

Nor is this norm only to be found in political speeches, but is also to be heard in award ceremonies, at conferences when speakers are introduced or when the identity of guests on television talk shows is revealed.

A few years ago, I went to a concert by Donovan, a pop star contemporary of the Beatles. In the first half, all his performances of familiar hits from the 1960s attracted 15-20 seconds of applause (i.e. considerably more than usual), whereas none of the applause for his numbers from his latest album in the second half fell outside the standard 7-9 second range – polite enough, but nowhere near as enthusiastic as the responses to songs that the audience had known for years.

If you want to check out what the difference sounds like for yourself, compare the two clips on my blog from President Obama's introduction to his nominee for the vacancy on the Supreme Court. In the first one, Judge Sotomayor gets a "standard" eight-second burst of applause after saying that she loves her family; in the second one, the applause for the President's introduction to her goes on for five times longer than that.

As such, it suggests that the audience was very well pleased with the announcement. But to find out if it was a more enthusiastic response than usual, we'd have to compare it with some clips of presidents introducing previous nominations for the post of Supreme Court judge.

28th May 2009

Clinton on North Korea: "There are consequences to such actions"

When I first saw this this statement on the news, it fascinated me enough to want to hear it again. So I looked it up on YouTube, dug out the verbatim transcript from the US State Department's website and am still working on it.

What baffled me the first time round was that "sounded" as though she was saying something very important, but I was left wondering what it all meant. This is why I'm going to have a look at it in more detail to see if I can put a more precise finger on what made it seem so vague and uncertain the first time I heard it (and the first time is, of course, the last and only time that most normal members of the viewing public get to see of it).

Mrs Clinton:

"North Korea has made a choice.

It has chosen to violate the specific language of the UN Security Council Resolution 1718.

It has ignored the international community.

It has abrogated the obligations it entered into through the Six-Party Talks.

And it continues to act in a provocative and belligerent manner toward its neighbors.

There are consequences to such actions.

In the United Nations, as we speak, discussions are going on to add to the consequences that North Korea will face coming out of the latest behavior, with the intent to try to rein in the North Koreans and get them back into a framework where they are once again fulfilling their obligations and moving toward denuclearization of the Korean Peninsula.

But they have chosen the path they're on, and I'm very pleased that we have a unified international community, including China and Russia, in setting forth a very specific condemnation of North Korea and then working with us for a firm resolution going forward.

I want to underscore the commitments that the United States has and intends always to honor for the defense of South Korea and Japan.

That is part of our alliance obligation, which we take very seriously.

So we hope that there will be an opportunity for North Korea to come back into a framework of discussion within the Six-party process, and that we can begin once again to see results from working with the North Koreans toward denuclearization that will benefit, we believe, the people` of North Korea, the region, and the world.

29th May 2009

The "delicacy" of Mrs Clinton's "consequences" for North Korea

First of all, thanks to those of you who took the trouble to make comments about Mrs Clinton's "Consequences" statement (posted yesterday) – not only because I found them interesting and agree with much of what you said, but also because it was a relief to discover that I wasn't alone in thinking that there was something rather odd about it.

Some of you may have seen something I posted about the concept of "pre-delicate hitches" a while back, where the general argument is that such hitches (e.g. ums, ers, pauses, etc.) occur when a speaker is about to say something that he or she knows is likely to come across as delicate to their listeners.

On watching this sequence again, I realised that it was the first two paragraphs (reproduced and re-transcribed below) that were what had really caught my attention in the first place. In the course of 120 words, there are more than 40 such hitches (i.e. one every three words), not to mention the abstract vagueness of some of the language ("violate the specific language", "abrogated the obligations it entered into", "consequences", "behaviour", "framework", etc.).

The "uhs" and frequency and duration of pauses bring down the speed of her delivery to about 92 words per minute (i.e. words other than "uh" or "um"), which is extremely slow compared with the ideal speed for public speakers of somewhere between 120-140 words per minute (which is also much slower than normal conversational speeds of around 180 words per minute).

Interestingly, the number of hitches diminishes once she moves on to the second part of the statement, which was delivered at the much more satisfactory rate of 130 words per minute.

Two factors may have influenced this. One was that the hitches came at their thickest and fastest when the key audience most likely to find what she was saying particularly delicate was the North Koreans themselves.

The other was that, to be fair to Mrs Clinton, this was not a pre-prepared speech but came in answer to a question at a press conference taking place in Egypt, very soon after the news from North Korea had come through. So it's possible that there hadn't been enough time for her to get a full briefing from State Department specialists, which meant that she had no choice but to make it up as she went along (i.e. "busk" it).

(N.B. This revised transcript uses a convention that's also useful for marking up scripts of speeches before delivery that's described in *Lend Me Your Ears*, pp. 299-301, where a single slash indicates a slight pause of a fifth to half a second and a double slash indicates a longer pause of half a second to a second).

Mrs Clinton:

"North Korea has made // uhh //a choice. // It has chosen to // violate the // u-specific language / of the / uh // UN Security Council Resolution 1718. // It has ignored the international community. // It has abrogated the obligations it entered into / through the Six-Party Talks. // And it uh continues to act in a provocative and belligerent manner / uh toward its neighbors.// There are consequences to such actions.//

"In the United Nations uh as we speak / discussions are going on to // uh // add to the / uh / consequences that North Korea / will face // u-coming out of the latest uh // u-behavior / u-with the // uh / intent to // u-try to rein in / uh the North Koreans // uh and get them back into a framework where they are once again // uh fulfilling their obligations and moving toward denuclearization of the Korean Peninsula."

29th May 2009

Planning to say "um" and "uh"

For non-native speakers of English, learning how to use our definite article must be an absolute doddle compared with the problems I've always had in handling "le", "la" and "les" in French and the even more complicated "der", "die", "das", "die", etc. in German (for which I achieved my worst failure ever with a pitiful 7% at O level).

English nouns don't have genders so "the" works fine for all of them – except, of course, when we're speaking. Nouns beginning with a consonant are indeed preceded by "the", but, if the noun starts with a vowel, "the" is pronounced "thee" – so we say "the pub" but "thee egg".

Interestingly, the definite article often comes before "uhs" and "ums" when we're speaking. Even more interesting is the fact that, when it does, speakers invariably use the "thee" form: "thee-uh". The fact that the "the" is fitted to an upcoming vowel sound presumably means that we know that an "uh" or an "um" is on its way before we select "thee" rather than "the".

On the evidence of Mrs Clinton's recent "consequences" statement, she does it quite a lot as you can see from the video clips on the blog:

1. "It has chosen to violate thee u-specific language of thee uh UN Security Council Resolution 1718."

2. "... discussions are going on to uh add to thee uh consequences"

3. "I want to underscore thee uh commitments that the United States has"

The interesting question for people who know more than I do about languages other than English is whether they too involve planned "ums" and "uhs" – and, if so, what form does it take?

For example, do German speakers project an upcoming masculine, feminine or neutral noun with "der uh", "die uh" or "das uh"? And what happens in languages that don't have definite articles at all?

15th June 2009

Combining rhetoric and imagery to get your point across in a speech

I've just been going through some video clips in preparation for a presentation I have to give next week and came across an old favourite, in which a 90 year old speaker shows how effectively imagery and the main rhetorical techniques can be combined to get a point across in a mere 75 words.

As audiences are getting younger and fewer still remember former prime minister Harold Macmillan (who later became Lord Stockton), I tend not to use this example much these days, but it's such a fine specimen of rhetorical techniques in action that it deserves a wider audience.

In lines 1-8, he uses a metaphorical puzzle about a sinking ship that juxtaposes a contrast between two alternatives, [A] "sinking" or [B] making a new cross-party effort.

The first part of this contrast ends with a third item ("go slowly down") that contrasts with the first two ("drastically" and "tragically"), and the second part includes a three-part list ("new, determined, united").

The solution to the puzzle (lines 9-12) then comes in the form of another contrast, this time between [A] "decline and fall" and [B] "a new and glorious renaissance".

Add to this his delivery, with pauses (marked by / in the transcript) coming at an average rate of one pause per 3.75 words, and it's hardly surprising that the commentator refers to it as "another masterly speech".

I used to say that, if I had to illustrate as many of the key points about rhetoric and imagery as possible with reference to a single example, this would be it – a view I'm not so sure about having looked in detail at some of Barack Obama's speeches.

Lord Stockton:

1. Do we just / slowly / majestically / sink /

2. not perhaps drastically

3. or tragically /

4. but go slowly down like a great ship? /

5. Or shall we make / a

6. new /

7. determined /

8. united effort, / putting as far as we can / party aside. /

9. Let us / do the latter,

10. and then / historians of the future /will not describe the end of this century /

11. as the beginning / of the decline and fall of Britain /

12. but as the beginning / of a new / and glorious renaissance.

15th June 2009

Politician answers a question: an exception that proves the rule

Given previous posts about politicians not answering interviewers' questions I was delighted last week to see former Home Secretary Charles Clarke giving as straight an answer to a question as anyone could ever hope for:

Q: Will you tell us what you think about Gordon Brown?

A: No.

19th June 2009

Imagery worthy of Obama in speech by the Governor of the Bank of England

I've thought for some time that Mervyn King, Governor of the Bank of England, has some pretty good speechwriters, and this isn't the first time I've thought it worth posting an example from one of his speeches.

The night before last at the Mansion House, he used and developed a neat simile, that was singled out and used as a headline in the print and broadcast media.

King:

> "To achieve financial stability the powers of the Bank are limited to those of voice and the new resolution powers.

> "The Bank finds itself in a position rather like that of a church whose congregation attends weddings and burials but ignores the sermons in between.

> "Like the church, we cannot promise that bad things won't happen to our flock – the prevention of all financial crises is in neither our nor anyone else's power, as a study of history or human nature would reveal.

> "And experience suggests that attempts to encourage a better life through the power of voice alone is not enough.

> "Warnings are unlikely to be effective when people are being asked to change behaviour which seems to them highly profitable.

> "So it is not entirely clear how the Bank will be able to discharge its new statutory responsibility if we can do no more than issue sermons or organise burials."

You can watch this part of the speech on Youtube - and was there a slight smirk on his face as he finished the punch line about "sermons" and "burials"?

22nd June 2009

Body language, nonverbal communication and the myth about folded arms and defensiveness

A recent posting on Olivia Mitchell's Speaking about Presenting blog led to a lively exchange about the absurdly overstated claims that 93% of communication is non-verbal.

The chapter on "Physical Facts and Fiction" in my book *Lend Me Your Ears* was aimed at debunking some of these modern myths, and I'd like to know what others think about the claim that folding your arms means that you're being defensive.

It's one that prompted me years ago to start asking people sitting in lectures with their arms folded whether they were feeling defensive.

The immediate and invariable reaction is that they quickly unfold their arms – because they too know exactly what I'm referring to and they too know that it's alleged to be a sign of defensiveness.

The commonest response is that they're feeling quite comfortable, thank you very much.

Sometimes they point out that there are no armrests on the chairs; occasionally they complain that the room is a bit cold.

But never once has anyone among the hundreds of people I've now put he question to ever said that they felt on the defensive.

The body language "experts" would no doubt tell me that I'm a naïve idiot for being taken in by them, that I'm failing to read what their non-verbal behaviour is really telling me, that they're covering up what their real feelings are in order not to offend me, etc, etc.

My problem is that I see no reason not believing them. Nor, until someone provides a convincing demonstration to the contrary, do I believe that these self-appointed "experts" have any evidence to support their position, or to prove that people like me have got it so wrong.

But, and this is perhaps the most depressing thing of all, I do nonetheless advise people not to fold their arms when speaking, whether in a conversation, presentation, job interview or anywhere else where they're hoping to make a good impression – not because I believe that folded arms signals defensiveness, but because I know that there's almost certain to be someone in the audience who's been misled into believing that it does.

24th June 2009

"Check against delivery"

Charles Crawford has a very interesting post today about David Miliband's speech in Poland that's prompted me to try something I've never done before.

I've seen plenty of speeches (and have even penned a few) that started with the instruction "Check against delivery" in the first line, but had never bothered to do so in any detail. Thanks to the wonders of the internet and YouTube, it's now become something that's easier to do than ever before.

What's more, you can go beyond checking against the speaker's delivery and check against what anyone else might be saying about a particular speech.

So, whilst checking the press release of Miliband's speech against his delivery, I was able to see exactly what Charles Crawford meant about the opening passages being "clunky". An attempt by a speech-writer who knows little of Poland to rummage around and find a few historical examples by way of "filler". The examples used cast no light of insight on what follows, and might as well have been omitted.

Mr Miliband too seems to have found them a bit clunky, or presumably wouldn't have felt himself prompted to ad-lib so many changes as he went along.

It's as if, having declared himself "deeply conscious of the history between our two countries", he realised that he hadn't until that moment been in the least bit conscious of King Canute's Polish ancestry (and one has to wonder if the Poles in the audience were any more conscious than him about King Canute's genealogy).

Then, with his quip about the speech becoming a "pronunciation test", he openly confesses that he's just reading out stuff that's news to him (supplied by the local ambassador and/or his staff).

The parts of the speech in italics below were what was actually delivered and did not appear in the official press release.

Mr Miliband:

"*I think for obvious reasons* any *visiting* British Foreign Secretary *coming* to Poland is deeply conscious of the history between our two countries.

"It goes back a long way. *I didn't know that* Canute *er – was* the half Polish King of Denmark who, in 1015, *actually* invaded England, bringing with him Polish soldiers and his mother, Princess Swietoslawa, who *er – is buried* – is buried – Winchester castle.

"*When I asked for a historical lesson from our ambassador, I didn't realise it would be a pronunciation test, but it has become such.*"

14th July 2009

Puzzle-Solution formats

One important rhetorical technique that wasn't mentioned in Denise Waterman's recent piece on the BBC website, is what I refer to in my books and courses as the puzzle-solution format. It's based on the very simple principle that, if you say something that gets the audience wondering what's coming next, they'll listen more attentively and, if it's a good "solution", they'll applaud it.

An example I often use when teaching is from a speech that Ronald Reagan made when declaring his candidacy for the Republican presidential nomination in 1980. What's puzzling is why this should be a moment of "mixed emotions" for him:

Puzzle: This is a moment for quite some mixed emotions for me.

Solution: I haven't been on prime-time television for quite a while.

Another of my favorite examples comes from a speech by William Hague when he was leader of the Conservative Party.

This one poses as big a puzzle as anyone who knows anything about the recent history of British politics could ever pose, namely the suggestion that former Tory prime ministers Margaret Thatcher and Edward Heath could actually agree on something in a debate about Europe.

To appreciate the solution, it also helps to know that, on the previous day, the conference stage had been furnished with some chairs supplied by the Swedish furniture company IKEA:

Puzzle: Ted and Margaret came on to the platform for the debate on Europe yesterday and they were both in instant agreement.

Solution: They both hated those chairs.

Combining rhetorical techniques

Something else not mentioned in the post on the BBC website is the way in which you can combine rhetorical techniques to achieve greater impact.

In this clip, from the 1987 UK general election, Mrs Thatcher poses a metaphorical puzzle (why is the Labour Party's manifesto going to be like an iceberg), the solution to which comes in the form of a simple contrast:

Puzzle: From the Labour Party expect the iceberg manifesto.

Solution: (A) One tenth of its socialism visible.
(B) Nine tenths beneath the surface.

17th July 2009

How to stay awake during a repetitive ceremony

Graduation ceremonies are important landmarks for graduates, families and universities.

But seeing 125 youngsters trooping across a stage to shake hands and receive their degrees can hardly be said to be the most gripping of theatrical events, especially when there's only one of the 125 that you actually know and care about.

I've just been to such an event, at which it quickly became apparent that we were in for a long wait (over half an hour, as it turned out) before our candidate got anywhere near the stage. Nor were we alone, because there were about 250 other people in the audience in exactly the same position as us.

All of which raises the interesting question of how you stay awake, as one unfamiliar name after another is read out, and as one unfamiliar smiling face after another appears on stage. For me, the answer is easy, because occasionally there's an advantage in having a technical interest in how such ceremonies work.

And I have to say that this particular one worked like clockwork, and did so in two intriguing respects that probably weren't even noticed by anyone else in the audience.

The first was the supreme efficiency with which the "clap on the name" technique ensured that every candidate was applauded as they walked into the limelight, with the applause coming in on cue a fraction of a second after each name was read out.

The second piece of clockwork was that the ovation in every single case lasted for exactly 7 seconds. No one told the audience to time their clapping to fit within the standard 7-9 second span found in the vast majority of bursts of applause, but the fact is that they did – with mechanical precision.

And the fact that they did so meant that, in every case, it sounded about right –

less than 7 seconds wouldn't have sounded complimentary enough; more than 9 seconds would have sounded more enthusiastic than necessary.

The only reason I'm able to report this extraordinary 100% regularity is that I sat there timing them all, which not only kept me wide awake, but also enabled me to test a hypothesis or two.

At the start, for example, I wondered whether there might be a difference between the amount of applause awarded to men and women, younger and older graduates, members of different ethnic groups, etc. But there was no hint of any such difference, as all of them got exactly the same 7 second ration.

Such negative results can sometimes be disappointing, but not if the process of coming up with them keeps you awake and attentive from the beginning to the end of what might otherwise have been a rather tedious experience (apart from our 30 second reason for being there).

There were, however, two exceptions that did get an outstanding 15 seconds of applause (outstanding because it's twice as long as normal). One was for the collected assembly of graduates themselves, and the other was for their teachers – which is also exactly as it should be.

20th July 2009

Moon rhetoric from Neil Armstrong, JFK & Werner von Braun

About twelve years after the moon landing in 1969, I started writing about the power of rhetorical techniques like the contrast, and remember being vaguely amused and delighted when I realised that, of all the possible things that Neil Armstrong could have said 40 years ago, it was a simple contrast that was beamed back to earth.

[A] That's one small step for man;
[B] one giant leap for mankind.

But this historic achievement was also the fulfillment of earlier memorable rhetorical flourishes from President Kennedy, who'd committed the USA to land a man on the moon within a decade. And here he is cranking out a contrast and rounding off his message off with a three-part list:

> We choose to go to the moon in this decade and do the other things,
>
> [A] not because they are easy,
> [B] but because they are hard,
>
> because that goal will serve to organize and measure the best of our energies and skills, because that challenge is
>
> [1] one that we are willing to accept,
> [2] one we are unwilling to postpone
> [3] and one we intend to win.

(The full text of the speech is www.space-video.info/speech/19620912-jfk-rice-text.html).

Rocket scientist though he may have been, Werner von Braun, without whose brains NASA might never have met Kennedy's deadline, was no slouch when it came to coining memorable quotations.

When the first of the V2 rockets he'd designed for Hitler hit London, it's been claimed that his mind was already on space – as he was quoted as saying: "The rocket worked perfectly except for landing on the wrong planet."

Other famous lines from von Braun include the following:

> "Man is the best computer we can put aboard a spacecraft, and the only one that can be mass produced with unskilled labor."

> "Our sun is one of 100 billion stars in our galaxy. Our galaxy is one of billions of galaxies populating the universe. It would be the height of presumption to think that we are the only living things in that enormous immensity."

> "Research is what I'm doing when I don't know what I'm doing."

> "Don't tell me that man doesn't belong out there. Man belongs wherever he wants to go – and he'll do plenty well when he gets there."

"We can lick gravity, but sometimes the paperwork is overwhelming."

"There is just one thing I can promise you about the outer-space program – your tax-dollar will go further."

"Crash programs fail because they are based on theory that, with nine women pregnant, you can get a baby a month."

"It will free man from the remaining chains, the chains of gravity which still tie him to this planet."

"For my confirmation, I didn't get a watch and my first pair of long pants, like most Lutheran boys. I got a telescope. My mother thought it would make the best gift."

For someone who helped the Nazis to develop the V2 rockets that launched so much terror and destruction on London, US citizenship wasn't such a bad gift either.

27th July 2009

How many numbers can you get into a minute?

A few months ago, I made the point that Gordon Brown tends to pack far too much information into his speeches and still has to take notice of a crucial tip from Winston Churchill about simplicity. In his final press conference before the Summer recess, he was at it again. At one stage, as you can see below, he managed to mention nine numbers in less than a minute.

The trouble is that a lot of people glaze over when numbers come at them so thick and fast – a problem that's even worse if, as in this case, they're delivered in a flat monotonous tone of voice.

And the importance of speakers conveying enthusiasm for their subjects cannot be overestimated – for the very obvious reason that, if a speaker sounds bored by his or her subject matter, why should the audience feel any less bored, let alone be inspired by it? Add to this Mr Brown's earnest facial expression and it's hardly surprising that he's so often referred to "dour".

29th July 2009

Thatcher had more teleprompter troubles than Obama

Bert Decker has just posted a very interesting piece arguing that President Obama's use of the teleprompter isn't doing any favours for his reputation as a great communicator.

This doesn't surprise me, because I've always thought it a rather mixed blessing since seeing Margaret Thatcher's performance deteriorate after she moved from using a script on a lectern to reading from teleprompter screens.

Before 1982, she never used a teleprompter. But, on seeing Ronald Reagan using it in a masterly speech to both houses of parliament that year, she was apparently so impressed that she told her aides that she wanted one too – and, a few months later she tried it out at the annual conference of the Conservative Party.

The immediate result was a dramatic fall in the amount of applause she received. In her 1981 Conference speech, she'd achieved the astonishing average of one burst of applause for every three sentences she uttered. A year later, aided, or rather abetted, by the teleprompter, her applause rate fell by about 35%.

One reason for this was that it interfered with an extremely regular part her delivery. When using a script on a lectern, she would routinely lower her eyes and head towards the text during the last two or three syllables as she approached a completion point (e.g. the end of the second part of a contrast or the third item in a list).

If anyone in the audience still wasn't sure that she'd finished and it was time to respond (i.e, applaud), any such doubt was eliminated by two more non-verbal signals: she would close her mouth tightly and audibly clear her throat.

In some of her speeches from a lectern, this didn't just happen now and then, but on every single occasion she was applauded. You can see examples of the routine as she delivers two consecutive contrasts at the start of her third successful general election campaign in 1987 (see my blog for video clips).

Whereas this all worked pretty smoothly to trigger instantaneous applause, it was a very different story when Mrs Thatcher's eyes were fixed on teleprompter screens instead of a lectern. She no longer looked down towards the script as she came to a completion point, but gazed beyond the screens into thin air.

The removal of these decisive and unambiguous signals that she'd definitely finished and it was time to applaud meant that it didn't happen as often as it did when could return her eyes to the lectern.

The line in this first example should have been guaranteed to get applause from any Tory Party audience in 1982:

> Thatcher: ... this is why we need nuclear weapons, because having them makes peace more secure.

But nothing happens, other than some rapid eye-blinking and a long pause from Mrs Thatcher before continuing, perhaps indicating that she'd both noticed and was surprised by the lack of applause:

In another example, the audience does applaud after the second part of a contrast, but only after a delay of about half a second and then for noticeably less than the "standard" 8 seconds.

> Thatcher: We all want peace, but not peace at any price; peace with justice and freedom.

Once the slight delay is over and the applause is underway, you can see that Mrs Thatcher half closes her mouth and then, looks down towards the lectern – after the applause had started rather than before it, as would have happened had she been reading from the lectern:

Although these may seem to be small details, there were so many of them in her 1982 conference speech that it's easy to pick out enough similar examples to be unsurprised that she got so much less applause than in the previous year.

For Mrs Thatcher, it brought with it other new, and rather odd-looking, changes to the way her eyes and body had previously moved. Sometimes, her eyes would remain fixed on one screen as her shoulders started moving towards the other one. Then, once the shoulders were in position, her head and eyes would dart very quickly and suddenly from one screen to the other, as if she wasn't going to take any chances about losing her place.

So this is why I started by saying that teleprompters are a mixed blessing for speakers. Few, including, it appears, President Obama can match Ronald Reagan's mastery of the technology. And some, like Margaret Thatcher, were considerably more effective reading from a script on sheets of paper resting on a lectern than when reading from transparent screens in front of them.

I first came across teleprompters when writing *Our Masters' Voices* 25 years ago. In those days, they used to be called "sincerity machines" – and that, perhaps, is precisely the problem with them.

31st July 2009

Impersonators as masterful analysts of non-verbal communication

The recent debate on various blogs about some of the myths about body language and non-verbal communication has reminded me of a minor frustration from my days as a full-time academic. When I worked in Oxford during the 1970s-80s, there were quite a few social psychologists doing research into body language and non-verbal communication.

Although they were always good company and interesting to talk to over lunch, they knew and I knew that there were some quite important methodological differences between their approach and that of conversation analysts like me. Put briefly, and from my point of view, they didn't seem to let empirical data constrain their claims to the same extent as we did.

Invite an impersonator to give a seminar?

Some of the people I knew used to arrange for visiting academics to speak at their regular seminars, and I was continually trying to persuade them to invite Mike Yarwood. He wasn't an academic, but was the top showbiz impersonator at the time (and, if I were still there today, I'd no doubt be trying to get them to invite Rory Bremner, for the same reason).

As for why I thought Yarwood would have some interesting things to say, it was because, for his impersonations to convince the mass television audience so successfully, he must have developed some very effective techniques for observing the way celebrities speak and behave – and for analyzing at such fine levels of detail that he was then able to reproduce instantly recognisable versions of them in his own performances.

In fact, as far as I could see, he must have been better at it than those of us who were supposed to be "experts", and should therefore be able to teach us a thing or two that would help us to improve our own observational skills.

What's the point?

My conversations with the psychologists about this always ended in failure, so we never did get to hear Mr Yarwood revealing any of his secrets.

In retrospect, I suspect my argument may have too threatening, or perhaps too undiplomatic, for them to agree to invite him to a seminar.

When they asked "Why?", "What would the point of that be?", etc., my reply went along the following lines:

> "Because his observations and analyses have to be accurate enough not just to describe their behaviour in detail, but to be able to reproduce it so effectively that anyone can recognize who it is. If Yarwood gets it wrong, his shows will fail and he'll be out of a job, whereas academics can be wrong for the next 30+ years and still get paid."

Such were the luxuries of the academic life.

18th August 2009

PowerPoint and the demise of Chalk & Talk: 1. The beginning of the end

We may have reached the 25th anniversary of PowerPoint, but how many of us will be celebrating?

This is the first in a series of three posts on one particularly destructive part of its legacy of collateral damage to our ability to communicate with each other.

When new universities were being built during the 1960s, there were arguments at some of them about whether to install blackboards or whiteboards in the lecture theatres. The pro-blackboard lobby opposed change because, they claimed, it would spell the end of tax relief for damage to clothes from chalk dust. Advocates of white boards thought them trendy, modern and more in keeping with the architecture of the new universities.

But one thing that was never questioned by either side was that writing or drawing on boards, whether black or white, was an indispensable part of the presentational process.

Today, the debate would be about what kind of computer and projection systems should be installed, and what would never be questioned would be the effectiveness of PowerPoint presentations – even though there remain serious questions about whether this dramatic technological shift in the way visual aids are used was a change for the better.

Like a 20th century Pandora's box, the computer, aided and abetted by Microsoft, has unleashed new and previously unheard of maladies on millions of unwary victims. Chronic slide-dependency has reached pandemic proportions, its main symptoms being a compulsive urge by speakers to put up one boring slide after another, and an inability to say anything without reading from prompts on the screen. It has inhibited the ability of presenters to convey enthusiasm for their subjects and infects those on the receiving end with confusion and self-doubt as they slip quietly into a coma, blaming themselves for their inability to absorb so much information in so short a space of time.

Ask people how they like listening to the modern slide-driven style of delivery, and you'll soon discover a deep groundswell of dissatisfaction. Go a step further and ask how they rate the slide-dependent majority as compared with the eccentric and tiny minority who still use chalk and talk, and the verdict invariably comes down against the new orthodoxy.

As for how a style of speaking that audiences don't much like became the norm I've discussed in more detail elsewhere (along with the relative merits of other types of visual aid). Part of the story is that it probably all came about because of a terrible accident.

An unexpected result of technical innovation

Slide-dependency can be seen as the legacy of a change in the way the overhead projector – PowerPoint's immediate ancestor – was originally intended to be used. The invention of the OHP, if anyone can remember that far back, was designed to overcome a problem with using chalk and talk when speaking to large audiences, namely that people couldn't see what was being put on the board from a long distance away. So the original natural habitat of the OHP was the large auditorium, where speakers used them in much the same way as they'd used blackboards, writing on a roll of acetate and winding it forward whenever they ran out of space.

Then came what must surely be the darkest day in the history of the modern presentation: the arrival of a new breed of photocopiers in the 1970s that was no longer limited to copying on to paper, but could print directly on to sheets of acetate. What seemed rather a small technological step turned out to be a giant leap into a completely new way of presenting. More and more speakers stopped writing and drawing as they went along and started using pre-prepared slides made up of lists that were, in effect, their notes.

This new style of delivery not only survived the replacement of OHPs by computerised graphics, but was also implicitly encouraged by assumptions built into programs like PowerPoint.

Most of the initial templates it offers to users are for producing lists of bullet points. What's more, a fairly recent version came equipped with the added bonus of a set of 23 "model" presentations to make your life easier. They were made up of 214 slides, 94% of which – yes, more than nine out of ten of them – consisted entirely of written words and sentences.

In the light of this, there's something very strange to hear a Microsoft executive announcing that one of the best PowerPoint presentations he ever heard had no slides with bullet points on them, or when Bill Gates himself didn't use them in his TED presentation.

Perhaps the most extraordinary thing of all about the PowerPoint revolution was that no one seemed to notice what was happening, let alone stop and ask whether anything important was being lost by the sudden death of chalk and talk.

But, having continued to advocate the effectiveness of using blackboards, whiteboards and flip-charts, I can report that none of my pupils who has tried it out has ever regretted it, and most say that they achieved better rapport with their audiences than they had ever experienced when using slides. This, together with other evidence accumulated over the past twenty years, has convinced me that a wider discussion of its forgotten benefits is long overdue.

19th August 2009

PowerPoint and the demise of Chalk & Talk: 2. The lost art

A more "natural" form of communication

One of the great advantages of chalk and talk is that there is something very natural about it: unlike speaking from slides, it has a close parallel in everyday life. We're very used to showing others where a place is by drawing a map on a scrap of paper; sometimes, we'll sketch out a diagram to explain what something looks like or how it works. Chalk and talk simply extends the practice of writing on the back of an envelope to the bigger canvas of a large vertical surface that everyone can see. But the lack of an everyday equivalent of speaking from slides makes it a more contrived and less natural form of communication.

Less interference with eye-contact

Slides also have negative side effects that make it more difficult for presenters to hold the attention of audiences, central among which is the serious disruption of eye-contact. This is partly because speakers spend so much time looking at the screen, and partly because audiences have to keep glancing from speaker to screen and back again for however long the presentation lasts.

With chalk and talk, these repeated breaches in eye-contact are less of a problem – for the very obvious reason that you are never more than an arm's length away from whatever it is you are showing to your audience.

Better coordination between the talk and the visual aid

Speaking about what you're putting on the board while you're doing it more or less guarantees that there'll be a very close connection between what you're saying and what everyone is looking at – which makes it much easier for listeners to stay on track than when they have to read up and down lists, trying to find a connection between what they're hearing and what they're reading.

Protection from information overload

Of all the innovations that came with the arrival of slide-dependency the most disastrous was the ease with which you can project large amounts of detailed written and numerical information on to the screen, a practice based on the dubious assumption that people can readily absorb complex detail at a glance.

By contrast, chalk and talk protects audiences from being overwhelmed by such massive and painful information overload, because it forces speakers to develop their arguments step-by-step and at a comfortable pace that's easy for listeners to follow and take in.

Spontaneity and authoritativeness

Writing things up as you go along also involves a degree of spontaneity, authoritativeness and liveliness that's hardly ever achieved with slides. I've now asked hundreds of people how many really enthusiastic and inspiring slide-driven presentations they have seen, and most of them have trouble in coming up with a single example.

But with chalk and talk, whatever's being written or drawn on the board is being done here and now for the sole benefit of everyone in the room, rather than being a pre-packaged list that's been cooked up in advance and perhaps even been circulated beforehand. Unlike speakers who have to look at their slides before they know what to say next, someone using a board or flip-chart has to be in full control of their material and can convey an air of confidence, authority and command over the subject matter that's much more difficult to achieve when using slides as prompts.

20th August 2009

PowerPoint and the demise of Chalk & Talk: 3 Glimmers of hope

As it's probably too late for a cultural counter-revolution that would take us back to the good old days when chalk and talk ruled supreme, the best we can hope for is that salvation may be at hand in three glimmers of hope built into presentational software like PowerPoint.

Dynamic and animated functions

The first is that the dynamic and animated functions make it fairly easy to simulate some of the benefits of chalk and talk by enabling you to put things up as you talk about them – whether by building points up step-by-step, or by creating diagrams that appear to draw themselves on the screen.

Pictorial and graphical functions

Another glimmer of hope is that PowerPoint has tremendous pictorial and graphical capabilities that make it easy for speakers to make the most of the fact that audiences find genuinely visual slides, such as pictures, simple graphs, etc., much more helpful than ones made up of nothing but words and numbers.

Blank slides

Finally, you can bring considerable relief to your audiences by switching everything off for a while – either by pressing the relevant button on the keyboard or by inserting slides consisting of nothing but a black background, both of which make it look as though there's nothing on the screen at all.

This is, in effect, the electronic equivalent of turning over to a blank page on a flip chart or rubbing chalk off a blackboard, and forces listeners to focus on nothing else but you and what you are saying – at least until the appearance of the next slide.

Unfortunately, only a tiny minority of presenters are making any use of any of these options. The vast majority of slides I see still consist of seemingly endless lists of bullet points, and the full potential of PowerPoint is still a long way from being realised.

The 1960s argument about blackboards versus whiteboards may be a thing of the past, but it is surely time for an urgent debate about the relative merits of using slides, chalk and talk and other types of visual aid.

Otherwise, the danger is that the real cost of the new orthodoxy will not be the millions spent on computers, software and projectors, nor the enormous waste of time and money resulting from people attending presentations from which they get little or no benefit – which, for the UK, I've estimated at more than £7.8 billion a year.

The real price and the real tragedy will be the incalculable long-term damage that will come from continuing to believe that PowerPoint is a foolproof panacea for presenters, when it's no more than a tool. And, like any tool, its effectiveness depends on its users understanding its limitations, as well as its strengths.

26th August 2009

On the death of Edward Kennedy: "the dream shall never die"

Speeches by all three of the Kennedy brothers are to be found in the top 100 American speeches listed on the website *American Rhetoric*.

For me, one of the most memorable ones by Edward Kennedy was delivered shortly after I had started studying political speeches in 1980: his address to the Democratic National Convention, now ranked at 76th in the top 100.

To mark his death, here are the final few sentences, which, somewhat unusually, end with a 4 part list that has been much quoted since:

"And someday, long after this convention, long after the signs come down and the crowds stop cheering, and the bands stop playing, may it be said of our campaign that we kept the faith.

"May it be said of our Party in 1980 that we found our faith again.

"And may it be said of us, both in dark passages and in bright days, in the words of Tennyson that my brothers quoted and loved, and that have special meaning for me now:

"I am a part of all that I have met
To [Tho] much is taken, much abides
That which we are, we are -
One equal temper of heroic hearts
Strong in will
To strive, to seek, to find, and not to yield.
For me, a few hours ago, this campaign came to an end.
For all those whose cares have been our concern, the work goes on, the cause endures, the hope still lives, and the dream shall never die."

28th August 2009

Joe Biden's moving tribute to Edward Kennedy

Of the all the tributes to Edward Kennedy I've heard over the past couple of days, the one that stood out for me came from Vice-president Joe Biden.

A bit long, maybe, but there were moments of genuine sincerity that could perhaps only have been said by someone who'd lost a wife and child in a road accident and knew from his own experience the importance of support from friends and relations when you're struggling to come to terms with such trauma.

Interestingly, two of the most quoted passages from Biden's speech came from the following short sequence – one was a simple piece of imagery – "he was kind of like an anchor" – and the other a reasserted contrast "it was never about him. It was always about you. It was never about him."

There were other neat rhetorical flourishes as well, such as the opening three-part list in which the third item contrasted with the first two, another neat contrast and the anecdotes about Kennedy phoning him every day and arranging for doctors from Massachusetts to turn up out of the blue and about what Kennedy's wife had said to him near the end (another contrast).

But, as I've so often said and written in the past, seeing a speaker exhibiting such technical skill in no way diminishes either the sincerity or the positive impact conveyed by his message.

Biden:

I literally would not be standing here were it not for Teddy Kennedy,

(1) not figuratively,
(2) this is not hyperbole
(3) but literally.

He was there – he stood with me when my wife and daughter were killed in an accident. He was on the phone with me literally every day in the hospital, my two children were attempting, and, God willing, God thankfully survived very serious injuries.

I'd turn around and there would be some specialist from Massachusetts, a doc I never even asked for, literally sitting in the room with me.

(A) You know, it's not just me that he affected like that.
(B) It's hundreds upon hundreds of people.

I was talking to Vicki this morning and she said – she said,

(A) "He was ready to go, Joe,
(B) "but we were not ready to let him go."

He's left a great void in our public life and a hole in the hearts of millions of Americans and hundreds of us who were affected by his personal touch throughout our lives.

People like me, who came to rely on him.

He was kind of like an anchor.

And unlike many important people in my 38 years I've had the privilege of knowing, the unique thing about Teddy was

(A) it was never about him.
(B) It was always about you.
(A) It was never about him.

31st August 2009

Obama on Kennedy got more applause than "normal"

I mentioned in an earlier post an observation, first reported in my book *Our Masters' Voices*, about there being a standard or "normal" burst of applause that, in many different settings and across several different cultures, lasts for about 8 seconds. Less than 7 seconds and it sounds feeble; more than 9 seconds and it sounds more enthusiastic than usual.

The most powerful piece of cross-cultural evidence came from a group of Iranian students who had collected some tapes of speeches by Ayatollah Khomeini after the Shah had been deposed. Applause had been banned as a "decadent Western practice" and replaced by chanting ("Death to the Americans..." "Down with imperialists..." etc.).

The students reported that the chanting occurred immediately after Khomeini had used exactly the same rhetorical techniques as the ones that trigger applause in the West and, even more interestingly, regularly faded out after 8 plus or minus 1 second.

The last time I remember the congregation applauding a eulogy was after Lord Spencer finished speaking at the funeral of his sister, Princess Diana.

But it happened again on Saturday after President Obama's eulogy at the funeral of Edward Kennedy, where the clapping went on for 35 seconds or just over four times longer than a standard burst of applause.

3rd September 2009

Claptrap 1: The movie

This is the first in a series of posts to mark this month's 25th anniversary of a television documentary that completely changed my life.

Before that, I'd spent nearly twenty years working in universities and doing research that was widely regarded at the time as being thoroughly "useless" (i.e. lacking in any theoretical or practical implications whatsoever).

But a series of lucky breaks led to my getting the chance to take part in a World in Action documentary based on my book *Our Masters' Voices: the Language and Body Language of Politics World in Action* series frequently attracted audiences of 15 million or more viewers – though "attracted" is probably the wrong word, because it came on immediately after the nation's most popular soap (*Coronation Street*): it was also before everyone had remote controls, which meant that viewers still had had to make the effort of getting out of their chairs if they wanted to switch channels.

Such was the impact of the programme that, on the following morning, my phone hardly stopped ringing, with everyone asking the same question: "can you do the same for me?" Without realising it at the time, I had embarked on an irreversible journey from the peaceful seclusion of an Oxford college to the more hectic world of freelance consultancy.

Over the next few weeks, I'll be blogging about some of the background leading up the publication of *Our Masters' Voices* and the making of the film *Claptrap*.

It was called *Claptrap* because one of the definitions of the word in the *Oxford English Dictionary* is a "trick, device or language designed to catch applause". I'd originally thought of using it as the title of the book, but decided against it because it would be too much of a hostage to fortune for reviewers.

Gus Macdonald, the film's producer who'd dreamt up the idea in the first place, had no such qualms about using it as the title for the programme – but by then, of course he did have the advantage of knowing that the experiment had been a success.

You can watch the film in four consecutive episode on the blog (and I hope you're impressed by my new Apricot computer!).

4th September 2009

Claptrap 2: Eureka!

Such is the nature of the social sciences that "eureka" moments are very few and far between. That's why I count myself lucky to have had one, and there was only one of them, in the last 40 years.

Why study clapping?

After starting to collect tape-recordings of political speeches during the 1979 UK general election, I started looking at bursts of applause about a year after that. It was prompted by a "methodological" problem in the research I was doing into courtroom language.

We had plenty of tapes of court hearings, but the absence of any audible responses from jurors during the proceedings meant there was no way of knowing which parts of what was being said were having a positive impact on the audience that really matters.

The reason why applause in political speeches seemed a promising place to start was because it provides instant and unambiguous evidence that listeners are (a) awake and paying close attention and (b) approve strongly enough of what's just been said to show their approval of it (by clapping hands, cheering, etc.).

Collecting the data was also extremely cheap and easy, requiring no more effort than recording speeches from radio and television in the comfort of your own home.

Orderliness beneath the surface?

If I had even the slightest hunch that it might be worth the effort, it was largely thanks to Gail Jefferson, one of the founders of conversation analysis, who'd already come up with some remarkable observations about the organisation of laughter in everyday conversation.

After all, if something that seems, on the face of, it to be as disorganised as laughing can exhibit such unexpected regularities, there was at least a possibility that there might be something regular about clapping too.

Apart from being willing to look for orderliness in the least obvious places, another crucial lesson I learnt from Gail Jefferson was that by far the best way of observing the details of talk is to transcribe the tapes yourself (as she always did).

So the time-consuming part of the research consisted of finding a burst of applause, winding the tape back a minute or two and then transcribing it, then going on to the next burst of applause, winding the tape back and transcribing it, etc., etc., etc.

Eureka!

The eureka moment came fairly quickly. I can't remember exactly how many transcripts I'd done before noticing that the applause wasn't just happening at random, but was occurring immediately after a small number of very simple verbal formats (e.g. contrasts, three-part lists, etc.). But I do know that the main regularities had started to fall into place well before I'd got to the fiftieth example.

At about the same time, I got a phone call from the organisers of a sociology of language conference in Cambridge: one of the scheduled speakers had dropped out, and could I stand in for him? I agreed to do so on condition that they advertised my paper as "title to be announced". Yes, I did have another courtroom language paper in the pipeline that would have fitted the bill, but I'd already started wondering whether it was time to try out the clapping data on a wider audience.

Time to go public?

When the conference flyers went out, the phone rang again. This time, it was John Heritage, my most regular partner in crime when he was still at Warwick University and I was still in Oxford.

Coming straight to the point, he demanded to know: "What's all this nonsense about 'title to be announced'?"

"I'm thinking of doing something on – er – clapping."

"What?" he demanded, "Everyone thinks we're mad enough already without you going around doing something as off the wall as that."

There was no point in trying to tell the full story on the phone, but I was pretty keen to get an opinion from someone else before deciding whether or not to take the plunge. So we arranged to meet the next day when I'd be able to play him the tapes and show him the transcripts.

Which device I began with I can't remember. But I do remember the gasps and startled expressions on his face as I kept saying "here's another" and pressing the "play" button, over and over again.

By the time I asked him if he thought it would be too much of a risk to air such stuff at the conference, he was more than a little encouraging: "That's not just a paper you've got there; it could be the first of quite a few."

It turned out he was right. Within a couple of years, I'd started writing a book and he was running a much larger scale follow-up study funded by the Social Science Research Council – and you can hear him talking to Ann Brennan about some of his findings in part 2 of the *Claptrap* film.

Long before that, however, news of this first conference presentation, for which "Title to be announced" had become "Some Techniques for Inviting Applause", spread much wider than expected – as will be seen from the next post in this series.

7th September 2009

Claptrap 3: News leaks out of the lecture theatre

The first time I spoke in public about the clapping research was at a conference in Cambridge, where there must have been someone from (or with a hotline to) *New Scientist* magazine in the audience.

Hardly a mass-market publication, but, as I learnt when the BBC phoned a few days later, it's one that the rest of the media regularly scour through for stories that might be of wider interest. What they'd picked up that Thursday was a short report on the findings I'd just presented in my talk on "Some Techniques for Inviting Applause". Could I come to London to appear on *Nationwide*, their (then) early evening news programme, to be interviewed about it by Sue Lawley?

Well, yes I could, except that I had two children to pick up from school that day – a problem quickly solved by allocating some BBC licence payers' money to pay for a taxi.

When I got to the studio, I was surprised to discover that they'd abandoned their normal coverage of the final day of the Labour Party conference in favour of interviewing me about political speeches.

But, as has so often happened in similar brushes with the media since then, they'd already picked out some clips from the week's speeches without any consultation with me. And this was live TV, so the "expert" would just have to hope for the best and busk it.

Luckily, the findings about what triggers applause were so robust that there was a very good chance of there being some nice examples before any of the bursts of applause they'd chosen. And so there were, which made busking rather easier than I'd feared.

A book?

Talking to other guests who were waiting in the hospitality room to be interviewed that evening, I learnt something else that surprised me: everyone else there had just published a book that they were there to be given a few minutes to plug in front of an audience of millions, whereas all I'd done was to have given a lecture to a few dozen academics at a fairly obscure conference.

That was the moment when the idea of writing a book first entered my head, as too did a quiet vow to myself not to go on television again until I'd finished it.

And, as there seemed to be so much interest from a wider public, maybe I should try to write a book aimed at a much more general readership than had been the case with my previous academic ones.

Science?

Back in Oxford, there were plenty of regular *New Scientist* readers, one of whom invited me for dinner at his college a week or two later.

Seen & Heard

He was a zoologist interested in human-animal interaction and was thinking of doing some work on how people talk to their cats and dogs. The problem was that, if they were going to be able to make any sensible observations or comparisons, they'd first have to know something about how humans talk to each other. Before reading the piece in the *New Scientist* he hadn't been aware that there was a field of research called "conversation analysis", so he'd invited me to dinner to learn more.

While drinking the regulation glasses of pre-dinner sherry, my host introduced me to one of his colleagues, a physicist who also read the *New Scientist*.

"Ah," he said "I hope you don't mind me saying this, but, until I read about what you're doing, I'd never realised that sociologists ever did anything as scientific as that."

I didn't mind him saying that at all.

He probably didn't have much idea at all about what most sociologists actually do. But after nearly 20 years of doing pretty much nothing else, I did. I also knew that many, and probably most, professional sociologists would have been grossly offended by what he said.

But I found his reaction thoroughly agreeable and very comforting. After all, what had drawn me into conversation analysis in the first place was that it's approach to observing human interaction was so much more rigorous than all the other methodologies on offer.

So to hear a natural scientist recognising anything at all from the social sciences as "scientific" was recognition indeed – and I decided to conveniently ignore the fact that a proper scientist ought really to have observed more than one example before coming to such a momentous conclusion!

9th September 2009

Claptrap 4: How to get a book published

For academics in the 1970s, getting your work into print was never much of a problem. Publisher's reps used to tour the universities with two simple missions. One was to try to persuade you to put some of their books on your reading lists and get the university bookshop to order a few copies. The other was to ask if you had any books in the pipeline – and, if you had, they'd more or less sign you up there and then.

As the first lecture I'd given on the clapping research had revealed wider interest in the subject than I'd expected, I assumed that it would be just as easy to get it published as had been the case with my previous "academic" books.

I could not have got much further from the truth: by the time I finally signed a contract for the publication of *Our Masters' Voices*, I'd collected a grand total of twenty- two (yes, 22) rejection slips.

It was probably a mistake to write the whole manuscript before sending it to any publishers. After all, my other academic books had been accepted on the basis of a few notes, an occasional paper or two and a good deal of waffle on my part.

So, unlike these unfortunate publishers on whose desks there dropped a complete draft of *Our Masters' Voice*, the previous ones never had to wade through hundreds of pages of tedious prose before reaching a decision.

Twenty years later, when I was writing *Lend Me Your Ears*, I learnt from my agent that it was much more effective (and much less time-consuming) to send a proposal out to likely publishers – and, though he'd be too modest to say it, having a reputable agent is half the battle.

A promising start falters

Initially, things looked quite promising. Desmond Morris, zoologist and best-selling author of *The Naked Ape* and *Manwatching* was a fellow of the same Oxford college as me. He loved the book enough to fix me up with an introduction to his own publisher, the legendary Tom Maschler (and eventually wrote some nice glowing words on the back cover of the book).

Mr Maschler was friendly enough, but said that he thought the book would be much better if he recruited what he called a "co-author", which I took to be a polite word for ghost-writer.

"I'm a bit surprised by that," I said, " because one of the few kind things reviewers have said about my other books is that they found them very readable."

"But" he came back decisively "that merely reflects the abysmally low standard of writing in the academic world."

I've no doubt in retrospect that I should have taken his advice. I was trying something that was completely new to me – to write in a way that would be accessible to any average reader of a serious Sunday newspaper, a book with plenty of pictures, no extensive bibliography and no footnotes citing every last chapter and verse.

The road to rejection

Looking at *Our Masters' Voices* now, I realise that I never got anywhere near the style I was aiming for until the third chapter – which also happened to be the most important one in the book. If the publishers I'd inflicted it on had never got as far as that, it was hardly surprising that they rejected it.

Many of them also had backing for their decision from learned assessors, from whom they'd sought an expert opinion.

Quite a lot of these reflected the vested interests of hostile camps within sociology, psychology, and linguistics, the main disciplines in which the (then) new field of conversation analysis was already having a significant, if controversial impact after little more than ten years in business.

Others were more straightforward in their dislike of the book, and I'll never forget the one that said "people are already cynical enough about politicians without publishing this kind of stuff."

A key crops up on a Croatian beach

By the time the twenty-second rejection came in, we were on family holiday on the Makarska riviera, where I met a British school teacher who was grappling with the problem of how to get another new subject (media studies) across to her pupils.

She was complaining about something I knew all too well from my background in sociology, namely that most of the available literature was relentlessly Marxist in approach, and she was having trouble finding anything that took a took a different line.

When I told her about the clapping research and *Our Masters' Voices*, she was extremely encouraging and said that it sounded just the kind of thing they needed.

She also had a practical suggestion. Methuen were just starting a new series of books on communication studies, had I tried them and, if not, why not send them a copy of the manuscript when I got back to Oxford?

Without either of us realising it at the time, she had handed me the key to the door that had so far refused to open.

Fate comes to the rescue

I thought no more about it until about a week later. I was back in college having lunch for the first time since getting home. In the common room afterwards, I sat down for coffee with a colleague from the Psychology Department who had a guest with him.

She was an editor with a firm of publishers, and not just any old publishers, but one that was very fresh in my mind: Methuen!

"Don't disappear until I get back" I blurted out as I sprinted back to my office. Five minutes later, the manuscript was in her brief case.

No, she wasn't in charge of the new series on communication studies, but knew who was and would make sure it landed on the right desk as soon as she got back to London.

A few weeks later, I signed the contract with Methuen – 23rd time lucky.

My only regret is that I didn't exchange names and addresses with the teacher on the beach in Croatia, so I've never been able to thank her for mentioning Methuen and their interest in communication studies.

If she hadn't, it might never have occurred to me to thrust the manuscript into the hands of my colleague's lunch-time visitor.

Seen & Heard

21st September 2009

Not the Lib Dem conference in Bournemouth

Before last week, I'd only ever been to Bournemouth to attend Lib Dem annual conferences – and I haven't done that for at least 10 years.

But I did go to another conference in Bournemouth on Friday, the first Annual Conference of the UK Speechwriters' Guild, whose founder, Brian Jenner, is to be congratulated for making it possible for about fifty people with this apparently esoteric interest to spend a day together.

One of the most fascinating talks was by Phil Collins, former speechwriter to Tony Blair, who had an interesting and plausible line on the main theme of the conference, "Why is there no British Obama?" – which he developed further by explaining why he thinks it unlikely that there will ever be a British Obama.

But for speechwriters, one of his more interesting revelations was about the difference between Tony Blair and Gordon Brown in their approaches to speechwriting.

Blair was not only a good writer (as we've all known since long before he became leader of the Labour Party) who wrote quickly and effectively with a fountain pen, but he also understood the importance of using other people's material as well.

The more computer-literate Brown apparently prefers DIY and makes little or no use of material from other writers. Instead, he's continually composing, reworking and storing his own lines about different subjects on his hard disk, and then cuts and pastes different sections according to whatever his next speech is going to be.

For me, this shed interesting light on some of the comments I've posted over the last year, and especially those bemoaning his tendency to pack far too much information and far too many numbers into his speeches.

If he had a better understanding of the importance of keeping things simple, or listened to and/or used speechwriters who do, this might be less of a problem for him.

And, in the unlikely event of his still having to give so many speeches at this time next year, he might pick up a few helpful tips if he came along to the second annual conference of the UK Speechwriters' Guild.

Claptrap 5: In the right places at the right times

If a chance meeting on a Croatian beach had broken the deadlock of 22 rejections slips, another similar encounter resulted in *Our Masters' Voices* being promoted to a much wider audience than expected.

How it happened and where it happened made it difficult not to believe that fate was working in mysterious ways – as it's unlikely that any of it would ever have happened if I hadn't been a research fellow at Essex University more than fifteen years earlier.

Another chance meeting

I mentioned in Claptrap 4 how easy it had been to get academic books published during the 1970s – so easy, in fact, that my PhD thesis had been published, more or less verbatim, by the Macmillan Press (*Discovering Suicide*, 1978).

Although I knew that sociology students, from A level to universities, were all required to know about Emile Durkheim's classic *Le Suicide* (1898), it hadn't occurred to me there was therefore a market for secondary reading on the subject, especially if it was cheeky enough to question the methodology of such a famous founding father of the discipline.

One result of this was that some of my earliest publications had penetrated as far as the A level syllabus. A spin-off from that was that I found myself being invited to speak at sixth form conferences, where bus-loads of reluctant school children were treated to the dubious pleasure of listening to some of the authors whose work they were supposed to know about.

At one such conference, I bumped into someone I'd known from when I was working at Essex University. By then, Ivor Crewe had become a professor in the department of government, and his work on elections meant that he too was getting invited to speak at sixth form conferences.

When I told him about the clapping research, he became interested enough to ask me to send him some samples of what I'd written so far – which I did.

An invitation to meet the media

A few months later, he invited me to speak at one of the most fascinating conferences I'd ever been to. In those days, Ivor Crewe and Tony King used to organise a weekend at Essex University on "Political Communications" during the most recent general election campaign.

They were planning the one on the 1983 election, which was scheduled for the early spring of 1984. A paper from me comparing the performances of Margaret Thatcher and Michael Foot during the campaign, they thought, might give a novel angle on their usual proceedings.

What made their conferences so different from all the other academic conferences I'd ever been to was that it wasn't just attended by academics, but also attracted people from politics, the media, opinion polling, etc. So speakers at that first one I attended included Cecil Parkinson, fresh from presiding over Margaret Thatcher's second election victory, Austin Mitchell, M.P., Robin Day and Peter Snow from the BBC, Gus Macdonald from Granada Television, Bob Worcester from MORI, representatives from the advertising agents used by the main political parties – as well as leading academics from politics and government departments around the country.

The mood of these conferences was best summed by the delegate who told me that what newcomers had to understand about them was that all the academics there wanted to be on the media and all the media people there really wanted to be academics.

"Opening Pandora's box"

As no one there knew who I was, let alone anything about this still unpublished research into clapping, the comparison between Thatcher and Foot depended on my starting off with a selection of introductory video clips illustrating the main rhetorical devices that trigger applause in speeches.

Before the session was over, two notes had been passed up to me at the front. One was from someone asking for a copy of (the yet to be published) *Our Masters' Voices* to review in his column in *The Times*. Another was from someone asking me to go on his TV show.

By the end of the weekend, people were saying that what I'd shown them had been like watching someone opening Pandora's box, and I'd been approached by five different producers and/or presenters about my work being featured on five different television news and current affairs programmes.

It was as if the media interest in that first lecture I'd given a few years earlier had suddenly started to explode. It also reminded me of the secret vow I'd made not to go on television again until I'd published a book on the subject.

A kindred spirit?

Of all the media people I met at the conference, the one who intrigued me most was Gus Macdonald, who was then still with Granada. It wasn't just his unusual background – a former ship builder from the Upper Clyde with little in the way of a formal education – but he was the only person there who'd spotted that there might be a connection between what I was doing and the work of one of my heroes, Erving Goffman. Gus, it turned out, was a Goffman fan too and one of our meal-time conversations must have made those nearby wonder what on earth we were talking about.

I was also intrigued by his parting words as we were all leaving. He shook me firmly by the hand and said "Don't sign up with any of these other bastards until you've spoken to me."

There'd been no promises and no hints about what he might have in mind. But he sounded so emphatic and decisive that I couldn't get his words out of my mind when some of the "other bastards" did start phoning a few days later.

23rd September 2009

25 years on, and all I remember about the day is baldness and chewing gum

Twenty five years ago today, Methuen published *Our Masters' Voices* and Granada Television began a new season of their *World in Action* series with the film *Claptrap*.

The story of how the book came to be written, published and eventually used as the basis for a televised experiment is continuing in the *Claptrap* posts on this blog, and I'd been vaguely aiming at getting to the end of it by today. But it's turned out to be a rather longer story than I'd expected and there are at least two or three more episodes that will be posted during the next week or so.

The curious thing about today is that the main things I can remember were two details in the way Ann Brennan and I reacted when we saw the film for the first time at the London offices of Granada for the press preview before the film went on air later that day.

Ann was upset by a close-up shot of her chewing gum just before going up to make her speech. She never chewed gum, didn't like the sight of people chewing gum and certainly didn't want people to think that chewing it was a normal part of her everyday behaviour.

The only reason she was chewing it was that Cicely Berry, then head of voice at the Royal Shakespeare Company, had given it to her to help relax her jaw and moisten her mouth before making the speech. But that wasn't mentioned in the commentary and it was far too late to change anything before the film went out.

I experienced a similar shock about my appearance that was beyond repair. When congratulating her at the end of the speech, the camera brought the top of my head into view, revealing the beginnings of a bald patch – that has progressed a great deal further during the 25 years since then.

Apart from these two trivial details, I remember hardly anything else about what happened that day.

Given some of my posts criticising over-stated claims about the importance of body language and non-verbal communication, I find it rather depressing that, 25 years later, the only things I remember clearly about that day had to do with what we looked like, rather than anything either of us actually said in the film!

24th September 2009

Clegg's conference speech: "definitely OK, absolutely fine, without any doubt not bad"

The last thing party leaders want when making their annual conference speeches is for something in the news to knock coverage of them down in the list of the day's headlines.

So it was bad luck for Nick Clegg that he was wrapping up the Lib Dem conference at the same time as President Obama was speaking to the United Nations in New York, one result of which was that *Sky News* opted for live coverage from across the Atlantic rather than from Bournemouth. Another was that, if you look at the online versions of today's newspapers, it's actually quite difficult to find any references to his speech at all on their home pages.

But the fact that much of the reaction was as feint in its praise as the quote from former Blair speechwriter Phil Collins in today's title can't just be put down to "bad luck".

Noticeable absences

Something else that Party leaders should be aware of is that "noticeable absences" from their speeches don't make good headlines.

The concept of a noticeable absence is a simple but important one in conversation analysis. It refers to instances where conversationalists notice that something that had been expected to be (or should have been) said is missing – e.g. if you don't say "hello" in response to someone who's just said "hello" to you.

Speeches are obviously different from conversation, but you really don't want the media giving higher priority to what you didn't say than to what you did say, as happened in the following headline and opening few lines in *The Times* (which wasn't the only paper that highlighted the absences):

> Nick Clegg ignores Lib Dems' week of woe with pitch for Downing St
>
> Nick Clegg urged voters yesterday to elect him Prime Minister in a brazen attempt to put a difficult and divisive pre-election conference behind him.
>
> Speaking in Bournemouth Mr Clegg failed to discuss his promise of "savage cuts", he ignored the dispute over tuition fees and made only a fleeting mention of the "mansion tax" proposal for properties worth more than £1 million, which was intended to be the flagship policy for the week.

Walkabout woe?

Given Mr Clegg's obsession with not being regarded as a clone of Tory leader David Cameron, repeated in yesterday's speech with jokes about Brad Pitt, I remain baffled as to why he insists on aping the management guru – apparently unscripted – walkabout style of delivery that made Cameron stand out at the Tory leadership beauty parade in 2005 – and set him on course to win the top job.

If you want to assert how different you are from someone else, why on earth would you copy that person's distinctive (for a British politician) style of delivery? Why would you do it if you aren't as good at it as him? And why would you do it when even Cameron has increasingly given it up in favour of looking more "statesmanlike" at a lectern?

I've asked a number of Lib Dem insiders why he does it, whose idea it was and what the advantage is supposed to be, but they either don't know or won't tell me.

Time to abandon Autocue?

One comment submitted to *The Times* "Live chat" feature on Clegg's speech raised an important question:

"Does he have an Autocue problem or does he just talk that way?"

This could well be at the heart of what's holding him back – because without giant teleprompters, he wouldn't be able to pretend that he's speaking off the cuff.

One problem of wandering about, with or without Autocue assistance, is that you have to find something to do with your hands. Another is the question of what to do when the audience applauds – an issue touched on previously .

The trouble is that how you handle such apparently trivial details is likely to be noticed by reporters, and you really don't want valuable column inches being wasted by such distractions, as in the following accurate observations (in italics) from Ann Treneman in *The Times*:

> "I want to be prime minister," said Nick Clegg, *hands clasped* as he stood in a spotlight. Nick, basking in their love, *stepped back for a moment*, preparing himself to deliver his next bombshell announcement.

Similar details also got a mention in *The Daily Mail*:

> "Captain Clegg looked neat and tidy and *waved his hands about* ... He spoke fluently, *strode around the stage* and *clasped his palms together at appropriate moments* ... Once or twice *he waggled a forefinger* in a way that reminded me of John Major'.

I'm not sure how far his insistence on walking about and reading from teleprompter screens at the same time is diminishing his performance. But his delivery does seem to attract a good deal of feint praise like that from Phil Collins in today's title and other similar reactions to yesterday's speech, like:

> "he gave a workmanlike version of what a modern Opposition Party leader's speech tends to be these days. But that is as far as it went", "a decent performance', "fluent but strangely unpersuasive", "there is no change in timbre in his voice, no rise and fall", "I don't get the sense he really believes this", "it makes you nostalgic for the rabble-rousing charisma of, er, Menzies Campbell".

However, one thing I am sure of is that, if I were advising him, I'd get him to have a go at speaking from a lectern to see if it helped him to lift his performance beyond "OK" and "not bad".

25th September 2009

What's wrong with saying "Hi"?

One of the (many) things about Twitter that irritates me is that messages from would-be "followers" start with "Hi" – and presumably anyone I decide to "follow" gets an identical "Hi" from me – even though it's a word I do my best to use as rarely as I can.

This isn't just because I don't much like imports from American English into British English, but is because "Hi" is so much less efficient as a greeting than alternatives like "Hello" or "Good morning" – especially if you're making a phone call and can't see the person who's answered it.

Some of the early work in conversation analysis took a detailed look at greeting sequences, and came up with the idea that the first thing we do when we hear a voice on the other end of a phone is a "voice recognition test".

The rule is: if you can recognise the voice, you should immediately let the other person know that you've recognised who it is.

So, if someone answers the phone by saying "Neasden 456789", you have quite an extended voice sample (9 syllables) on which to do the voice recognition test before the answerer reaches the end of the number. By then, if you have recognised it, you should promptly acknowledge the fact by saying something along the lines of "Hello Ron" or "Hello Mr Knee."

The advantage of this for Mr Knee is that he doesn't have to go to the trouble of introducing himself or explaining who he is or where he's from, because you've already established that you know perfectly well who he is.

Like quite a lot of rules in conversation, the rule has an "if you can" clause to it. In other words, there's a preference for showing instant recognition over failing to show recognition – so the first option is to show that you've recognised the answerer – if you can.

This is why the word "Hi" is such an inefficient or inadequate form of greeting when you can't see the person who's speaking – for the obvious reason that a single syllable on its own may not be enough for you to be sure who it is within the split second before they've finished. As a result, you'll have to admit to them that you didn't recognise their voice, which can sometimes have quite embarrassing consequences.

This might seem a rather trivial reason for suggesting that multi-syllable words and phrases like "Hello" and "Good morning" are more efficient than "Hi". But it's not at all trivial when you're on the phone, or if you happen to be blind or visually impaired.

I know this because the person I've heard objecting most strongly about people greeting him with "Hi" is someone who's been blind from birth. What's more, the reason he gives for detesting it so much is precisely because it doesn't give him enough time to know who it is that's speaking to him – and makes him feel impolite for having to confess that he'd failed to recognise them.

28th September 2009

Why doesn't anyone warn politicians about becoming Autocue automatons?

When we were being taught about road safety at primary school, we had to learn a slogan that's still firmly entrenched in my mind:

"Look right, look left and right again and quick march across the road you go."

What brought it back into my head this morning was the sight of Alistair Darling speaking to the Labour Party conference, where he seemed to be following a revised version of the slogan:

"Look right for 10 seconds, look left for 10 seconds, look right for 10 seconds and turn your head when you get to the end of the sentence."

In other words, like David Cameron, Gordon Brown and Margaret Thatcher, he has a problem with reading from teleprompter screens.

The commonest one, involves spending too much time looking in one direction rather than the other. Sometimes, it creates the impression that you're so tied to your script that you daren't look at the other screen until you get to the next full stop (even though you're supposed to be pretending you don't have a script). Sometimes it creates such regular movements of the head from side to side that the regularity becomes noticeable. And sometimes it excludes half the audience for very extended periods of time (e.g. Cameron and Brown).

Given the high stakes involved in some of these speeches, I never cease to be amazed that no one alerts the speakers to such an obvious problem, let alone spends a few minutes coaching them to make a better job of it.

28th September 2009

If Mandelson has to struggle to win applause, what are the Labour Party faithful saying?

In discussing Nick Clegg's leader's speech at the Liberal Democrat conference a few days ago, I touched on the concept of a "noticeable absence":

> "a simple but important concept in conversation analysis. It refers to instances where conversationalists notice that something that had been expected to be (or should have been) said is missing – e.g. if you don't say 'hello' in response to someone who's just said 'hello' to you."

Although speeches obviously differ in various interesting ways from conversation, "absences" can be "noticeable" there, as, for example, when audiences don't applaud when they might have been expected to have done (e.g. after the speaker has just used one of the main rhetorical techniques that trigger applause).

Quite often, speakers not only notice when this happens, but implicitly acknowledge the absence of a response by using a "last resort" technique, that's been referred to as "pursuing" or going "in "pursuit" of applause.

A neat example of this happened in the 1987 election, when Neil Kinnock used a three-part list to describe the Labour Party's manifesto as "cool, tough and unsinkable". In the absence of instant applause, he went in pursuit with "That's our manifesto that we launched today", whereupon the audience started clapping.

Observation

There were several more examples of "noticeable absences" and "pursuits" in the excerpt from Peter Mandelson's speech to the Labour Party conference that was shown on the BBC website earlier today.

The first absence came after he'd just used an alliterative three-part list and a contrast between Labour and the Conservatives – to which he responded with a pursuit – "That's what we've got to do" – that eventually got the applause under way.

After that, there were four more contrasts in succession, none of which (surprisingly) managed to prompt any applause at all – which only came after Mandelson had used another "pursuit" as a last resort: "That's the choice for the British people at the next general election."

Interpretation

Although it may be of technical interest to note that the Labour Party audience were withholding applause at places were it should have happened, it's arguably of greater political interest to inspect the content (rather than the rhetorical structure) of the messages that came before each of these noticeable absences. These were:

1. the leadership of Gordon Brown
2. the party is in the progressive centre of British politics
3. the party knows it will have to meet global changes
4. the shallowness of David Cameron

Taken together, it's difficult not to conclude that the Labour Party loyalists at the conference are less than enthusiastic when it comes to "showing their approval in the usual manner" for Gordon Brown (1 and 4), being positioned in the centre of British politics (2) or being willing to change to meet global events (3).

If I'd been one of the original architects of new Labour or a strategist aiming for electoral success next year (like Brown and Mandelson), I'd find these particular noticeable absences, coupled with the need to use "pursuits" to get any applause at all, more than a little worrying.

You can see what you think by reading the transcript below.

Lord Mandelson:

"We need to fight back. Of course we do.

But to do so successfully it is up to us to explain – with confidence, and with clarity and conviction – what the choice is between us and the Conservatives."

No applause.

Pursuit: "That's what we've got to do."

Applause

(A) "The choice between a Conservative Party – the choice between a Conservative Party whose judgements on the credit crunch were wrong,

(B) or a party providing leadership (points at Gordon Brown) in the toughest of times."

No applause (for Gordon Brown?).

(A) "A choice between a party A choice between a party that lurches to the right the second it sees a chance of doing so,

(B) or our party that is resolutely anchored in the progressive centre of British politics."

No applause (for being in the centre?).

(A) "A choice between a party that does not understand the new world we live in or even what has happened in the last year,

(B) or a Labour Party that knows the world has changed and we that we have to change with it."

No applause (for the Labour Party?).

"That's the choice, conference, and I tell you too

(A) experience and change with Gordon's leadership

(B) or the shallowness of David Cameron."

No applause (for criticism of Cameron?).

Pursuit: "That's the choice for the British people at the next general election."

Applause.

29th September 2009

Was it Mandelson's self-deprecating humour that won the day for him?

Having suggested yesterday that the Labour Party faithful had withheld applause from some rather important points in Peter Mandelson's conference speech and that he'd had to use the "last resort" technique for winning applause (the "pursuit") a few times, I was surprised that no one in the media seemed to notice.

I was even more surprised at just how positive most of the media coverage has been – so much so that I've taken a closer both at it and at the speech itself.

What was widely featured both by TV news programmes and newspaper reports were Mandelson's jokes. Given that his departures from Tony Blair's cabinet had been clouded with controversy and that his recall by Brown as an unelected Peer, his use of self-deprecating humour may well have been the smartest thing he did to win over doubters in the audience (and in the media).

But I've had one email that summed the whole thing up as "pantomime performance" – and these three examples almost make you wonder whether Rory Bremner has has joined the Mandelson speech writing team:

1. "And I know that Tony said that our project would only be complete when the Labour Party learned to love Peter Mandelson, well I think perhaps he set the bar a little too high, though I am trying my best"

2. "But conference let me say this, if I can come back, we can come back"

3. "Yes they've made changes to their presentation, the image making department has done its job, it's done it well. Who am I to criticise?"

29th September 2009

Brown surfs applause (briefly) before reverting to type

I've never seen Gordon Brown surfing applause before, but it got his speech off to such a lively start that he got a premature standing ovation. But once that was over, it was back to Brown-style speaking business as usual. As a result, instant media comments a few minutes after he'd finished were already saying that the opening had got them expecting something better and that they were disappointed by what followed.

I obviously don't know whose idea it was that he should have a go at surfing, but the irony for me was that this is exactly what I had recommended David Cameron to do in order to up his game for last year's Conservative Party conference.

Gordon Brown surfs applause through a very long list

The video clip of Brown surfing applause can be seen on my blog. There are a number of points worth noting on viewing it:

First, it's the most extreme case I've ever seen since I first noticed it about 30 years ago – where what I mean by "extreme" is that it goes on for longer and more persistently than I've ever seen before. As such it comes over as contrived and bears little resemblance to the more natural sounding way in which more skilled exponents like Benn and Obama do it. That's why I think this was carefully planned to provide a rabble-rousing opening to what turned out to be a rather typical Brown speech.

Second, this list is not included in the full tex of the speech on any of the websites I've looked at so far, which suggests that the ploy was either a last minute decision, or was designed to spring a surprise on the media (or both).

Third, I was fascinated to see that the applause got under way immediately after the 3rd item in a 24-part list.

Fourth, in the first cut-away to cabinet ministers clapping on the front row, all of them look more despondent than delighted, none of them are clapping particularly vigorously and Alistair Darling comes in so late that Stalin would certainly have had him dispatched to Siberia on the first available transport.

15th October 2009

Claptrap 7: On location

The two most common questions I've been asked since the *Claptrap* programme was first shown are (with answers in brief):

1. How long did it actually take to coach Ann Brennan to make her speech?

Answer: A few hours on five separate days.

2. Which parts of the process played the biggest part in her success?

Answer: They were never filmed or shown.

Five days on location

1. Voice coaching at the Royal Shakespeare Company's London rehearsal rooms.

2. Oxford & Stratford upon Avon: John Heritage and I showing Ann the main rhetorical techniques; Cicely Berry coaching her on stage at the Royal Shakespeare Theatre (by far the busiest single day).

3. Ann & I watching Arthur Scargill in action at the TUC in Brighton

4. Ann's encounter with Joe Haynes, Harold Wilson's former speechwriter.

5. Filming the speech in Buxton (plus Scargill speech analysis that had had to be deferred).

The most important parts of the process that were never shown were the actual writing of the speech (as opposed to the sequence in which Joe Haynes, former speechwriter for Harold Wilson, came up with some brilliant lines) and Cicely Berry's work with Ann rehearsing the speech the night before she gave it.

The scene that nearly wasn't

Before the meeting with Joe Haynes, he'd been sent a copy of *Our Masters' Voices* and asked to write a speech using the main rhetorical techniques described in it.

As the camera was being set up, Ann was asked to read through the draft. Her initial reaction was that Haynes was trying to put Labour words into her mouth – to which he retaliated by accusing her of being a "closet Tory", and it began to look as though there might not be anything to film that day.

So we asked her to go through it again and mark anything that she liked or might feel comfortable saying.

If only the camera had been ready by then! Because if it had been, it could have have shown a close up her hand marking particular lines with comments like "I like this bit" and "Yes, that's exactly the kind of thing I want to say". Viewers would have been able to see the same fascinating sight that we saw – it was as if the contrasts, puzzles and three-part lists that were later to have such an impact on the audience in Buxton were already jumping off the page and having an impact on her.

And that's how the lines recommended by Joe Haynes on the film were selected for when the camera started to roll.

The two missing links

The final text of the speech took a whole day to write at a meeting attended by Gus Macdonald, Ann and me at the Macdonald's home in Islington with no cameras present. We were careful to weave in some of the lines from Joe Haynes, and very careful to make sure that Ann felt comfortable with every word we wrote.

In other words, contrary to what some critics later tried to make out, we merely translated the messages she wanted to get across into rhetorically effective words, and were determined throughout not to put any of our own views into her mouth.

Apart from the script, the other most crucial part of the exercise took place in a hotel room in Buxton on the night before Ann gave the speech. Present were Cicely Berry, then head of Voice at the Royal Shakespeare Company, Gus Macdonald and I – and it was in that hour or two that I learnt almost everything I know (and still teach) about the importance of rehearsing speeches.

Not present, unfortunately, were any cameramen. Otherwise that particular part of Cicely's genius could have been made available to an audience of millions. And that's why I think that the omission of the rehearsal was the film's biggest weakness.

Claptrap 8: Sparks in the background

In the summer of 1984, the miners' strike was still dragging on as a daily reminder of the woeful state of industrial relations in Britain at the time.

Of the many ways in which those of us who worked in universities were privileged, one was that we had little or no first hand experience of the irritating frustrations that so many industries were up against – especially, I soon learnt, in the world of the media.

When the Granada Television crew came to film in my study at home, I remember being amazed at just how many of them there were – and quite shocked by how little there was for some of them to do.

How many electricians does it take to check a plug?

There was an electrician, for example, who spent about a minute poking a gadget into one of the electrical sockets on my study wall before giving the crew the "all clear" to set up the camera and lighting. It was a warm sunny day, so he went to the village shop, bought a newspaper and spent the rest of the time reading in the garden.

How many electricians does it take to light a theatre?

I'd also got wind of rumblings between Granada and the Royal Shakespeare Theatre in Stratford upon Avon, where more filming was scheduled for later that day. Granada needed to know exactly how many RSC electricians would be doing the stage lighting. If there were three, there would have to be three from Granada, if four then four from Granada, and so on. It wasn't that there would be anything for them to do, or even that they would have been allowed to do anything by the local electricians, but the rule was that same number would have to be there (and paid) for the same number of hours as the theatre's own electricians.

How many production assistants does it take to carry a film to Manchester?

Meanwhile, Granada was also constrained by some fairly bizarre demarcation issues among its own staff. After filming at the TUC in Brighton, Don Jordan, the researcher in daily charge of the production, had arranged a business meeting in London the next day. *World in Action* was filmed on 16mm film that had to be developed before editing could begin, so he asked a production assistant to do him a favour that would let him get straight on to London: could she take today's film back to Manchester and drop it off at the labs for him.

"No", she replied, "that's not part of my job."

Don knew the union rules well enough to know that he had no choice but to cancel his meeting in London and go back to Manchester – sitting next to the same woman on the same flight from Gatwick – for the sole purpose of carrying the film from the airport to the laboratories (which she had to go past on her way home).

How many films were never made? Ann Brennan's standing ovation may have been a major victory for Granada. But so too was the fact that they ever managed to make any television programmes at all.

20th October 2009

Churchill's perfect timing of his "iron curtain" gesture

Watching Churchill's "iron curtain" clip again yesterday got me thinking about posting a note on the timing of his gesture – at which point, there suddenly appeared a Twitter link to a book by a body language expert that included "iconic" gestures as one of three types of gesture:

"**Different types of gesture**

"Iconic-gestures whose form displays a close relationship to the meaning of the accompanying speech.

"Metaphoric-gestures that are essentially pictorial but the content depicted here is an abstract idea rather than a concrete object or event.

"The Beat-movements that look as though they are beating out musical time."

Although I always advise that three-part typologies, whether from Marx, Freud or countless other theorists, need to be treated with caution (because the theorist probably stopped looking for more after the third one made the story seem complete enough to get it published), I don't have a problem with the idea that "iconic gestures" are a distinct and frequently used type of gesture that do indeed relate to words that are coming out of a speaker's mouth.

I'm less certain, however, about the above distinction between "iconic" and "metaphoric" gestures – as it's not clear to me whether Churchill's downward hand movement relates to the words "has descended" or the metaphor of an "iron curtain" falling across Europe. Nor do I think there's any way of determining which of these it is, any more than I think it matters very much.

The timing of iconic gestures

As far as I'm concerned, the most interesting thing about it is that it's a splendid illustration of perfect timing of an iconic gesture.

Seen & Heard

The first time I ever heard the term used was in a lecture by Emanuel Schegloff, one of the founders of conversation analysis, back in 1979, in which he observed that iconic gestures anticipate a word that's coming up any second now – i.e. they get under way just before the speaker actually says the word to which the gesture relates (E.A. Schegloff, "On some gestures' relation to talk", in Atkinson & Heritage, Eds. *Structures of Social Action: Studies in Conversation Analysis*, Cambridge University Press, 1984, pp. 266-298.

This can be clearly seen in the Churchill clip, where his hand begins to move just as he starts to say "an iron curtain" and has fully descended by the time he gets to the word "descended".

If you watch the video (on my blog), an interesting question to ask yourself is what it would have looked like had he started the gesture after saying the word "descended". Or think of an angler telling you that the fish he'd just caught was "huge" and then moving his hands apart to show just how huge it was.

In both cases, your answer is likely to be something like "odd", "mistimed", "later than it should have been" or even "vaguely amusing".

This is because one of the intriguing things about the way we use these iconic gestures is that timing them "correctly" (i.e. start before saying the word) is something we learn in early childhood. Something to look out for if you have young children. Sometimes, very young children will describe something before doing a gesture that relates to it – e.g. "It was really round", followed by drawing a circle in the air with their hands – the timing of which, is likely to be regarded by adults as "cute" – but, as they grow older, they discover how to get the timing right.

No one ever tells them they'd been doing it "wrong" or coaches them to get it "right" – just as I have never found it necessary to coach adult speakers how to use iconic gestures (or would ever dream of doing so).

21st October 2009

Steve Jobs shows how to use an object as a visual aid (and how to speak about it)

When teaching and writing about the effectiveness of different types of visual aid, one that I always recommend for getting a positive response from audiences is the use of an object or prop to get your point across.

If you've seen Ann Brennan's speech (4th video clip in Claptrap 1 on my blog), you might have noticed that the audience laughed and applauded when she held up a copy of the paper on equality that she was speaking about.

Earlier posts on the same theme include a clip showing the Archbishop of York taking off his dog collar and cutting it into pieces during a TV interview, another in which Bill Gates appears to release some mosquitos from a box in a TED talk about malaria and one in which a Nobel prize winner commends a lecturer for using a mock-up of turbine blades.

And so to the case of the announcement in 2008 of the MacBook Air notebook by Apple's Steve Jobs that was recently brought to my notice by Twitterers (to whom thanks) – and on which there may well be a few more posts in the near future.

Steve Jobs takes the rabbit out of an envelope

One of the high spots, widely hailed as such in reviews of the event, was the way Jobs introduced the new notebook by pulling it out of a very ordinary looking office envelope – which occurred after an extended build-up in which he'd been contrasting the thinness and other virtues of the yet to be revealed MacBook Air with the thickness and other (inferior) features of its competitors.

Details worth noting in the video clip on my blog include:

1. A well-timed open armed "iconic" gesture that gets under way just before he says "... floating around the office."

2. The leisurely four seconds he takes to move across to where he can pick up the envelope.

3. The instant positive audience response as he picks up the envelope.

4. The way this response grows into hoots, cheers and applause when he holds it up in the air.

5. The fact that he lets the applause continue for 8 seconds before his first attempt to continue speaking.

6. His slow and unhurried removal of the MacBook Air from the envelope.

7. After saying "there it is", waits until 9 seconds of applause has elapsed (i.e. within the 8 ± 1 second standard burst again) before saying anything else.

8. Shows the keyboard and display before saying "full size keyboard full size display" (iconic gesture precedes the words again).

9. On average, he pauses every 5.5 words – i.e. at a very similar rate to that found in speeches by accomplished orators like Churchill, Thatcher, Reagan, Clinton, Blair and Cameron.

10. He walks (unhurriedly) large distances from one side of the stage to the other.

11. And smiling for some of the time (but not all of the time) is no bad thing either.

The devil is in the detail

Were any of these details actually noticed by any of those who were there at the time and/or who wrote about it as a masterful performance?

Probably not – other than, perhaps, that it was like a magician pulling a rabbit out of a hat whilst talking about it in a natural, confident and enthusiastic way.

The fact that it's almost certain that few, if any of these details were consciously identified by the audience is one of reasons why I think it's such an excellent example of effective speaking in action (as it was widely recognised as having been) – for the obvious reason that it confirms pretty much everything I've learnt, taught and written about in nearly 30 years of research, namely that the more details you can get right, the more impressed will your audience be.

Below is a transcript. The line-breaks indicate where pauses occur:

So
it's so thin
it even fits inside
one of these envelopes we've all seen
This is it.
Let me take it out here.
This is the new
MacBook Air
And you can get a feel for how thin it is.Yeah – there it is.
Right.
Amazing product here – full-size keyboard
Full size display.

23rd October 2009

How rhetorical techniques work: an example from last night's Question Time

I'm quite often asked how rhetorical techniques actually work to trigger a positive response from members of an audience.

Part of the answer is because their structure provides listeners with implicit instructions that enable them to anticipate exactly when the speaker will finish – so that they can be ready to respond as soon as he/she gets to the end (in much the same way as we're able to know when to respond in a conversation without interrupting or leaving a potentially embarrassing silence before we start to speak).

So, once someone in an audience notices that a speaker has launched into a contrast, it's pretty easy for them to recognise when the second part of it comes to an end. Or, if you hear a rhetorical question, you'll know that you'll be able to respond as soon as the answer is completed.

In this sense, audience responses like booing, cheering and clapping are collective versions of the individual turns we take when talking to someone in a conversation.

It's not often that television editors let us see members of an audience visibly anticipating one of these completion points, though I've already posted a very clear example of a woman anticipating the answer to a question being posed by David Cameron.

On BBC Question Time last night, there was a similar example of a listener anticipating the third item in a three-part list as the person in front of her was putting a question to the leader of the BNP.

As he launches into his list, watch the woman behind him on the left, and you'll see her nodding in approval just as he starts the third item in his list – which is also exactly the point at which the applause begins:

> Where do you want me to go?
> This is my country
> I love this country
> I'm part of this country

27th October 2009

Claptrap 9: Broadcasters' bile and SDP sulks

An earlier posting of an excerpt from Ann Brennan's speech prompted the following comment from Chris Rodgers, a former member of the SDP:

> "I was a member of the audience that day in the autumn of 1984, in Buxton's Pavilion Gardens, as the SDP debated a typically learned (but dry) paper on equality.

"Then Ann Brennan rose to speak. I can confirm that her well crafted and superbly delivered speech was a breath of fresh air. It was accompanied throughout by applause, cheering and the stamping of feet. When Shirley Williams tried to 'call time', at the end of the allotted four minutes, she was shouted down by party members. Ann Brennan left to a deserved standing ovation."

BBC approves and disapproves

As the standing ovation got under way, Sir Robin Day, the commentator on BBC Television's live coverage of the conference, described it as "the most refreshing speech we've heard all week and the audience would have liked her to go on ..."

Meanwhile, his colleague Peter Snow, who had wanted me to appear on *Newsnight* after the Chesterfield by-election a few months earlier (see Claptrap 6), had seen us being filmed by the Granada crew as we left the hall – and lost no time in telling Robin Day what was going on.

A few minutes later, Day was almost spluttering with rage as he interrupted a later speech to tell viewers:

"An extraordinary story is beginning to emerge. It seems that Ann Brennan who's just got a standing ovation was coached by a Dr Max Atkinson, an Oxford don who's an expert in – er – an expert – er -in how people wave their hands about when making speeches – for a television programme being made by Granada Television – and there'll be a tremendous row between the SDP and Granada for interfering with the proceedings of their conference."

Meanwhile, Peter Snow was hot on the trail outside the hall and had rounded up three delegates to interview live on air.

When he tried to get them to denounce us for what we'd done, the first two seemed quite relaxed about it, saying that they were applauding the sentiment of what Ann Brennan had been saying.

The third interviewee, to Snow's obvious disappointment, rounded off his comment by saying: "In any case, if you can be coached to get a standing ovation, I'd like to have a course of their coaching."

Seen & Heard

Broadcasters' bile

Until then, it had never really occurred to me just how fierce the competition between the BBC and commercial broadcasters was – a fact that was amplified further by an invitation to Ann Brennan and me to appear on BBC Radio 4's Woman's Hour – that was withdrawn as soon as they realised that Granada would be broadcasting a documentary on it about ten days later.

SDP sulks

After posting Claptrap 1, an exchange between David Cox and me discussed the way the SDP had reacted at the time:

Cox: I think the SDP used the speech on their party political broadcast. I think I'm right in saying more people joined the SDP after her speech as well.

Atkinson: As far as I remember, the SDP never used anything from Ann's speech for a PPB. They did however use Rosie Barnes (in one of the worst PPB's I've ever seen) and a lot of people used to confuse the two of them.

It wouldn't surprise me if new members came in after the speech. What did surprise me was that the SDP leadership, Owen included, were fuming about it. They thought it a disgraceful "stunt", and I remember trying to convince them that it was excellent PR for them that they should make the most of. If nothing else, it meant that the 1984 conference got far more media coverage than it otherwise would have done.

Cox: "Disgraceful stunt"! What is false or distasteful about giving somebody the skills to communicate and articulate their ideas; after all, Ann was given the training, but the message was Ann's, and it was Ann who delivered it.

"Here today, gone tomorrow" politician walks out of interview with Robin Day

John Nott was the Secretary of State for Defence in Margaret Thatcher's government during the Falkland's war in 1982.

The following year, he announced that he would not be standing for re-election at the next general election – after which he moved on to become chairman and chief executive of a merchant bank.

His imminent departure prompted Robin Day to refer to him during an interview as a "transient here today, if I may say so, gone tomorrow politician".

This prompted Nott to get to his feet, announcing that that that he was "fed up" with the interview – whereupon he took off his microphone and threw it down on the table in front of him.

If that wasn't enough of a high spot, Day's calm response – "Thank you Mr Nott" – was arguably the crowning glory of this remarkable sequence.

Two other points are also worth noting:

1. Nott didn't forget what Day had said, *Here Today, Gone Tomorrow* resurfaced nearly ten years later as the title of Nott's autobiography.

2. It's another nice example of a gesture coming just before the word(s) to which it relates. Nott looks away with an irritated expression on his face and starts to stand up before he gets to saying "I'm fed up with this interview" – illustrating again that iconic gestures start before the speaker says the actual words to which they relate.

14th November 2009

Claptrap 10: Academic acclaim?

Before trying to get *Our Masters' Voices* published (Claptrap 4), I'd been warned by Desmond Morris, who was a fellow of the same Oxford college as me, that I would have to be prepared for a sniffy reaction from other academics if I went ahead with my plan to write a book with no footnotes and lots of pictures.

If anyone should know about such things, it was him. Distinguished ethologist though he certainly was, he'd committed the cardinal sin of "popularisation" by writing *The Naked Ape* – world sales of which had, by then, reached a mere 15 million copies.

So I should have been ready for the deathly silence that greeted me at lunch on the day after the *Claptrap* film was shown on television – and should not, I suppose, have been surprised that several days went by before anyone said anything at all.

After all, I knew that the programme had been seen by 12 million people and, however much Oxford dons might pretend that they never watched television, it was statistically improbable that none of them had seen it.

Then, about three days after my phone had hardly stopped ringing – from people asking if I could do the same for them and help them to speak as well as Ann Brennan had done – the silence finally broke.

Standing next to a famous psychologist in the queue for our free lunch (yes, there really was, and probably still is, such a thing as a free lunch in Oxford colleges), I discovered that at least one other member of the college had seen the programme.

"Ahh" he said "now about that programme you made a few days ago."

For a split second, this sounded promising, until he went on:

"I think I would need to see the results of more than one experiment to be convinced by your findings."

I was tempted to reply by asking him which funding agency he thought would be willing to finance such a project, and how anyone other than a television company would have the contacts and resources to make all the complicated arrangements that would be needed to replicate it.

It also crossed my mind to launch into a full frontal attack on what I considered to be the rather dubious methodology and facile nature of some of the "findings" from his own research. But, by then, I'd been in Oxford for ten years, and had become far too polite to do either.

And however "unconvinced' my lunchtime colleague may have been by the *Claptrap* project, within a year or two, I'd been invited to apply for jobs by two well-known American universities, head-hunted by a British business school and seen several follow-up studies published by other researchers.

Within the first ten years, *Our Masters' Voices* was reprinted five times and, 25 years on, still appears to be in print.

All of which would I think, even if I'd stayed in the ivory tower, have been quite pleasing.

As it was, all the phone calls that came in after the *Claptrap* experiment led me in much more interesting directions and, somewhat ironically, gave me the chance to replicate the results thousands of times over.

17th November 2009

An example of rhetorical virtuosity from rhetoric denier Tony Benn

Readers from outside the UK have probably never heard of Tony Benn, and quite a few here will be too young to remember just how effective an orator he was. So, having looked at his rhetorical denial in a post about Obama from last year, I thought it might be useful to look at his rhetorical virtuosity in action.

This particular extract comes from a Labour Party conference in the early 1980s, when he was at the height of his powers and a prime mover in his party's electorally disastrous lurch to the left after Margaret Thatcher came to power in 1979.

Seen & Heard

It shows how he was so in tune with the way the audience was reacting that a slight response to his news about that day's record stock market fall was enough to prompt him to break off from what he was going to say and launch into an impressively constructed contrast, each part of which ends with the phrase "the wealth of the nation":

> Benn: For a moment between debates the stock market had its biggest fall was it within living memory 30 points – and uhh that is an indication that indeed it was rather appropriate that ITN was swinging

> [A] from the stock market where they're gambling with the wealth of the nation

> [B] to Brighton where we represent the people who create the wealth of the nation.

Iconic gestures

The sequence also provides more examples of the way iconic gestures come before the word(s) to which they relate, as discussed in earlier posts. Benn's swinging hand movements get under way quite a while before the word "swinging" comes out of his mouth – whereupon his hands start moving to his left just before the words "stock market" and to his right just before he say's the word "Brighton".

Then the slightest pause after "create" followed by the coordinated downward movements of his head and hands are reminiscent of the precision with which an orchestral conductor brings in the whole of the chorus on time – and the audience starts applauding just before he's finished repeating "the wealth of the nation".

Surfing applause

But, as was typical of Benn, he didn't stop there but carried on trying to surf the applause – not that he says anything more important than "and that is also-" and "now uhh-" while the applause is still preventing his words from being heard.

Historical context

One point of interest is that, as the applause gets under way, the camera switches away the from the audience to focus on Benn's former Labour cabinet colleague and arch-enemy of the day, Denis Healey, who had just narrowly defeated Mr

Benn in an election for the party's deputy-leadership – but who seems to be thoroughly enjoying this particular line.

Another is the fact that a stock market fall as pitifully small as 30 points was treated as such dramatic news in those days!

18th November 2009

The enormity of my debt to Tony Benn – without whom ...

Writing the last two posts on Tony Benn has reminded me of the enormity of my debt to him, and I think it's time I went public on recording my thanks to him.

I'm not just talking about the rich source of videotaped data his speeches supplied for the research on which my first book on public speaking (*Our Masters' Voices*) was based, grateful though I am to him for that.

But he played a much more direct part, albeit unwittingly, in changing my life for good – many years before I ever got interested in public speaking.

My first proper academic job

First of all, he was responsible for providing me with two whole years of gainful employment at a crucial and formative stage in my career.

Harold Wilson had appointed Anthony Wedgewood-Benn, as he was still known in the mid 1960s, to be Postmaster General, a job that included responsibility for the country's publicly owned telephone system.

The Labour government was under pressure to supply free and/or subsidised telephones to the elderly – but then as now, research is always cheaper than action because it provides a "respectable" way of postponing hugely expensive demands on the public purse. So Postmaster General Benn decided set up a two year project to look into the problem.

Conveniently for him, one of his friends and neighbours at the time was a leading expert on old age and poverty, Professor Peter Townsend, who'd recently been appointed to the first chair in sociology at the new University of Essex – where, conveniently for me, I'd just started research for a PhD on the sociology of suicide.

So a two-year Post Office research fellowship was set up at Essex to investigate "communication and isolation in old age" and, if I hadn't been lucky enough to get the job, it's unlikely I'd have ever have got anywhere near to completing the doctorate, let alone embarking on an academic career.

My first encounter with conversation analysis

But it wasn't just the two years of salary that came my way thanks to Mr Benn, but the initial work on the project led to a discovery that would have a much more profound impact on my life's work. Dorothy Smith had just moved to Essex from Berkeley, where she'd come across a young graduate student called Harvey Sacks, who'd recently finished a PhD based on tape-recorded telephone conversations on a helpline at a suicide prevention agency in California.

This held out the prospect of being able to kill both my research birds (into telephones and suicide) with a single stone. The only trouble was that, insofar as anyone in British sociology had heard of Sacks in 1968, his work was already being written off as far too methodologically innovative, daring, eccentric and controversial to be acceptable by the mainstream of the discipline.

Fascinated though I was by it, I didn't have the guts to try to sell the idea of doing something similar to my Post Office sponsors or to my senior colleagues at Essex – so I ended up playing safe and did a thoroughly boring, though worthy enough, survey of a national random sample over 65 year-olds.

Meanwhile, Harvey Sacks, along with Emanuel Schegloff and Gail Jefferson were beginning to attract wider recognition as founders of the new field of conversation analysis. So, by the time I eventually finished my PhD thesis, the gist of the final chapter concluded with the modest proposal that all hitherto existing sociology, from Durkheim's Le Suicide onwards, was methodologically flawed and that the future lay with ethnomethodology and conversation analysis.

At the time, I didn't have much of a clue as to how you would actually get to such a promised land, let alone what the results would look like if ever you got there. But it eventually took me into research aimed at applying the methodology of conversation analysis to more formal settings like court rooms and, eventually political speeches and public speaking more generally.

And all because of Tony Benn. If Tony Benn had never been Postmaster General and if he hadn't known Peter Townsend, none of this would ever have happened – which is why I'm so thankful to him for his hidden, but nonetheless profound and far-reaching, impact on my life and work.

2nd December 2009

Steve Jobs shows how to time the changing of slides in a presentation (and how not to)

A few weeks ago, I posted a video showing how effectively Steve Jobs used an object as a visual aid when introducing the MacBook Air, and hinted that there might be some more comments to come about his performance in the same presentation

In addition to showing how to make the most of pulling a rabbit out of a hat, Jobs also demonstrated how (and how not) to time the changing of slides with what you're saying.

1. Sooner rather than later

One very common habit in this slide-dependent age is that speakers can't wait to press the button to bring up a new slide or a new bullet point. This creates the impression that they don't know what to say until the prompt has appeared on screen to remind them. It also gives the game away to the audience before you've had chance to deliver the news to the audience from the horse's mouth (i.e. yours).

The advantage of saying something before it appears on screen is that it makes it look as though you're in charge, you know what's coming next and you're in control of slides that are merely supporting you (rather than being controlled or prompted by them). This is why my books and courses recommend that later rather than sooner is the safest guide to when you should press the button to bring on a new slide.

Seen & Heard

During the presentation I originally commented on Steve Jobs was going through the characteristics of note book computers before the super-thin MacBook Air that he was about to announce. But each of the bullet points appeared before he had made the various points about them. Then, when he started to allocate ticks and crosses to the list, the tick and crosses again came up on the screen before he pronounced verdicts on each one of them.

Would his performance have been improved if he'd waited to press the button later rather than sooner?

2. Later rather than sooner

Shortly after the sequence noted above, Jobs started using the power of contrast to show how thin the MacBook Air was compared with the Sony TZ series notebook computers – and this time his timing was much better.

The the green pictorial image of the MacBook Air appeared just after he said "This is the MacBook Air" – prompting laughter, cheers and applause from the audience – after which he went on to ram the contrast home with:

"The thickest part of the MacBook Air is still thinner than the thinnest part of the TZ series."

13th December 2009

Dr Cable's "medical" diagnosis of our economic problems

I've just been doing some homework preparing a course for some high-powered economists next week.

At the heart of the brief I've been given is that they want to get better at communicating complicated technical material to non-specialist audiences.

The search for suitable examples took me to my collection of clips from Vince Cable, deputy leader of the Liberal Democrats, about whom I've already posted quite a few examples and comments.

Part of what I wrote in one entitled *There's no such thing as a boring subject* (not included in this book, but available on my blog) went as follows:

> "On the subject of 'boring subjects', one of the interesting things on the British political scene in the recent past has been the rising esteem for the deputy leader of the Liberal Democrats, Vince Cable, whose star has risen on the back of his ability to sound as though he's talking more sense about complicated economic and financial topics than most of his competitors.

> "However boring and incomprehensible such subjects may seem at first sight – or when coming out of the mouths of Gordon Brown or Alistair Darling – Cable talks about them with clarity and authority.

> "And it's probably no coincidence that, unlike most of his political opponents, he's one of the ever-decreasing number of MPs who actually had a proper job outside politics before becoming a full-time politician.

> "As chief economist at Shell, making economics intelligible to colleagues who weren't trained as economists must have been a routine part of Vince Cable's everyday working life – that has now, in his 'new' life, become his strongest 'political' asset."

When it comes to making set-piece speeches, Cable is not the most brilliant exponent of the art, and his real forte is in unscripted Q-A sessions, whether on programmes like *Question Time, Newsnight* or in media interviews.

In this example, after introducing the idea that the system has suffered a heart attack, he goes on to round off the point with a three-part list – and it's worth remembering that his PhD was in economics, not medicine (or rhetoric):

Cable: This was an enormous shock to the system – a big economic heart attack – so it's not surprising that a lot of damage has been done ...

[1] ... we've got a patient that's in intensive care,
[2] it's been rescued from a disastrous heart attack
[3] but it still needs the monetary steroids.

21st December 2009

Linguistic differences and non-verbal behaviour: the mysterious case of gestures

On a recent trip to Rome, I was reminded of the fact that it's commonly believed, at least by native speakers of English, that people who speak Latin-based languages seem to gesticulate more frequently and more vigorously than we do. It wasn't that I saw lots of locals waving their hands about, but I was struck by what a lot of writing there seemed to be on the road signs on the way into town from the airport. Then, on entering the lift in the hotel, I was struck again by the length of the warning notice.

The big difference between Italian and English isn't so much the number of words as the fact that the Italian version has twice as many syllables as the English translation:

IN CASO DI INCENDIO NON USARE L'ASCENSORE USARE LE SCALE
(24 syllables)

IN CASE OF FIRE DO NOT USE THE LIFT USE THE STAIRS (12 syllables)

The point about syllables is that each one is a separate beat, so that the more beats there are in a sentence, the longer it will take to say it aloud.

This reminded me of some questions that originally occurred to me about thirty years ago as I was reading a notice about how to get into the lifeboats on a ferry between England and France – where two lines of English were translated into three lines of French.

1. Are Latin languages inherently more "long-winded" than English?

2. If so, does this create problems for turn-taking that hadn't been noticed by research originally based on tape recordings of conversations between native speakers of English?

3. If so, could a greater reliance on gestures be a practical solution to any such problems?

Combating the threat of an approaching bowl of potatoes

The reason why these questions occurred to me then was that I'd just returned from one of the first international conferences on conversation analysis at Boston University, where I'd taken part in a data session analysing a videotape of a dinner party at which a bowl of potatoes was being passed along the row of three diners on one side of the table.

A woman sitting opposite the man furthest away from the potatoes was telling him a story. When the potatoes reached the person next to him, she leant towards him and carried on with her tale. Then, a split second before the bowl reached the man being told the story, the speaker's hands suddenly came up from the table and she began to accompany her story with increasingly vigorous gestures.

The more the sequence was replayed, the more it looked as though her movements were precisely timed and choreographed with the movement of the bowl towards her listener. Leaning towards him came across as the first step in her bid to retain his undivided attention in the face of the growing threat of the approaching potatoes.

Her gestures, beginning as they did just before the bowl arrived in his hands, looked like an increasingly determined, if not desperate, effort to keep him listening.

So what? If one of the things we do with gestures is to combat threats to the attentiveness of our listeners, this raises the question of whether speakers of Latin languages like Italian, Spanish and French have more reason to use them than speakers of a predominantly Germanic-Nordic language like English?

The number of beats/syllables needed to say the words in the Italian fire warning (or the lifeboat instructions on the cross-Channel ferry) points to a reason why the problem of holding attention may be greater in some languages than others – which would give speakers of those languages more of an incentive to use gestures.

Given that conversation depends on turn-taking, the longer a turn takes, the more of a challenge it is for listeners to remain attentive until the previous speaker has finished.

We know from some of the earliest work on turn-taking by the late Harvey Sacks that, if we're going to tell a story, we have to alert people to the fact in advance – so that they can prepare themselves for having to do more listening than usual.

So, if the production of sentences in language (A) requires more beats/syllables than the production of sentences in language (B), holding the attention of listeners will be inherently more of a problem for speakers of (A) than it is for speakers of (B).

And, if gestures help to hold attention, you would therefore expect speakers of language (A) to gesticulate more than speakers of language (B).

Culture, language or climate?

The standard way of explaining why Latin speakers are alleged to gesticulate more than English speakers is on the basis of ill-defined cultural generalisations along the lines that the Italians, French and Spanish are more "emotional" and "expressive" than people in Britain, North America and Australasia.

But there's an empirical vagueness to such claims that makes me rather more convinced by the idea that it has more to do with the way turn-taking is affected by inherent differences in the length of sentences in different languages (as measured by number of beats/syllables per sentence).

Or at least I was convinced until I mentioned the theory at another conference, where a Swedish delegate came up with a rather different, but nonetheless plausible, explanation:

"It's warm around the Mediterranean, but we native speakers of Swedish have to keep our hands in our pockets because it's too cold to wave them around all the time."

Seen & Heard

4th January 2010

Do interviews ever deliver anything but bad news for politicians and boredom for audiences?

Regular readers will know that I have serious reservations about the way speeches have steadily given way to broadcast interviews as the main form of political communication in Britain.

So if you think that I might be dreading the thought of having to put up with the boredom, tedium and repetitive evasiveness that's awaiting us between now and the general election, you'd be dead right.

Masochists wanting to prepare themselves for the ordeal need look no further than Andrew Marr's interview with Gordon Brown yesterday morning.

The big story was latched on to by quite a few commentators, including the BBC's political editor Nick Robinson, who noted in his blog that:

" ... the interview was memorable ... for a slip – on election timing ... "

This reminded me of a question that first occurred to me after the 1987 general election, namely:

Has any broadcast interview ever generated any good news for a politician?

If you can think of an example of this happening, I'd love to hear from you. Meanwhile, here's a summary of the conclusions John Heritage and I reached in a paper we presented at a conference at Essex University after the 1987 election. Unfortunately I'm having to rely on fading memory, as Heritage migrated to UCLA shortly afterwards, which meant that we never got round to writing it up for publication. I do, however, clearly remember the title of the paper:

'A snakes & ladders theory of political communication'

Ladders

Our general argument was that speeches work like "ladders" that can move you up towards a winning position on the board, whereas interviews work like "snakes" that can only move you downwards.

The advantage of speeches is that politicians (and/or their speechwriters) have total control over both what they say and how they say it. Skilful deployment of rhetoric and imagery can produce punchy lines that get noticed and selected as sound bites for evening news programmes and as headlines for the next morning's newspapers.

An added bonus is that an audience of millions gets to see and hear the cheers, applause and enthusiasm coming from the local audience of a few hundreds or thousands.

Snakes

But being interviewed is like walking a tight rope. Success means getting to to the end of it without falling off – for which your reward is little or nothing in the way of positive news about what you actually said. Its only chance of becoming newsworthy is if you slip up, as Mr Brown did on Sunday, when he more or less revealed the date of the election. And slips hardly ever generate news that puts you in a good light.

In other words, our argument was that interviews are only capable of generating negative news for the politician.

Three notable examples of the Q–A format leading to negative stories about political leaders stood out during the 1987 general election.

1. Thatcher says she'll go on and on – and on

In an interview with Mrs Thatcher, Robin Day asked her if this, the third election in which she'd led the Conservative Party, would be her last election – to which she replied "No, Mr Day. I intend to go on and on".

Her two-part list was promptly extended to "on and on and on" both by headline writers and by Labour Party leader Neil Kinnock in a speech a few days later, in which he used it as the second part of a powerful contrast:

"A leader who has let unemployment go up and up and up and up should not be allowed to go on and on and on" – a line that was singled out and replayed on most prime-time news bulletins (i.e. it took him, albeit temporarily, up a "ladder" on the Snakes & Ladders board).

2. Kinnock says we'll take to the mountains to fight the Russians

Meanwhile, unilateral nuclear disarmament was still at the heart of Labour's defence policy in 1987.

When pressed on this in an interview, Neil Kinnock said that people would take to the hills and fight, thereby rendering any Soviet occupation of the UK "totally untenable" – lines that generated a huge amount of damaging publicity for him and his party (taking him down a "snake" on the board).

3. The two Davids and Ask the Alliance Rallies

The SDP and Liberal Party fought the 1987 election as the Alliance under two leaders, David Steel (Lib) and David Owen (SDP). Until close to the end of the campaign, neither of them made any set-piece speeches at all, as they'd decided to run events called "Ask the Alliance" rallies (probably because Steel was a better public speaker and Owen didn't want to be outshone by him).

The "rallies" involved members of the public reading out prepared questions to the leaders, who then ad-libbed their answers. I don't remember a single positive

Seen & Heard

quotation from either of them that made the headlines. But I do remember saying that they came across like *Gardeners' Question Time* on a bad day.

What little media interest they did generate mainly concentrated on the question of how well or badly the format was working, but reported little of what either of them had actually said.

Will 2010 be the first general election with no speeches, no rallies and no excitement?

Given the benefits that can come from making speeches to enthusiastic crowds (look no further than the success of Barack Obama's journey from nowhere), I remain completely baffled by the logic of our politicians' apparent preference for doing endless interviews rather than letting us judge what they want to say and how they want to say it to audiences at lively rallies.

After all, if you're going to play Snakes and Ladders, why on earth would you chose to spend all your time landing on snakes and avoid the ladders altogether?

The answer, I fear, is that our politicians have fallen into a bigger trap set for them by a mass media that's more obsessed with increasing their control and decreasing their costs than they are with what audiences find boring or interesting about politics and politicians. Otherwise, how could anyone get so excited about the dreary prospect of lengthy televised election "debates" between party leaders?

But accountants at the BBC, ITV and *Sky News*, of course, have every reason to get excited by the hustings being transferred to television studios. The fewer reporters and camera crews they have to send to film speeches at rallies around the country, the lower their costs will be – the net result of which looks like being the most tedious and boring election on record.

Fewer snakes and more ladders, please!

If I were still active in advising a political leader, I'd be urging him to ignore the new rules set by a misguided media and to get back on the road. And I don't mean just walking around a few schools, hospitals and shopping centres. I mean holding proper rallies, making inspiring speeches, creating some excitement and building some momentum.

The media would have no choice but to cover them, and the wider public would surely find them a bit more lively than more and more interviews in which we have to wait longer and longer, on the off-chance that someone will slip up and make it interesting enough to become news.

Gordon Brown's plotting comes home to roost again

Today's news about more plots against Gordon Brown by Geoff Hoon and Patricia Hewitt is only the latest reminder that Brown himself had spent years plotting to remove and replace Tony Blair.

A slightly more subtle reminder was the extraordinary speech he made in November "supporting" Blair's candidacy for the presidency of the European Council. "Supporting" is in inverted commas because his "support" was preceded by no fewer than seven pre-delicate hitches in quick succession.

Regular readers will know that pre-delicate hitches are things like "uhs", "ums" and false starts that often come just before a speaker says something that he/she thinks is rather delicate – e.g. when Brown was defending former Home Secretary Jacqui Smith, or when Hillary Clinton was threatening North Korea with consequences.

In this case, the question is: what was so delicate about his support for Blair that he prefaced it with so many hitches?

Was it that he was finding it difficult to "support" the very person he'd been plotting and briefing against for years?

Or was it that he, given his well-known hostility towards Blair, knew that no one would believe him – however "clearly" he said it?

Brown:

Uh-
let-let me say very very clearly that we
uh-the British

uh-government

uh-believe that

uh- Tony Blair would be an excellent

uh-candidate and an excellent person to hold the job of president of the
Council ...

18th January 2010

Martin Luther King Day – and a reminder of how to use rhetoric to convey passion

Today is Martin Luther King Day in the USA. But regardless of where we happen to live, it's a good excuse for spending a few minutes (and it only lasts 11 minutes) watching his "I have a dream" speech.

When talking about the use of contrasts and three-part lists, I'm often asked whether the use of such rhetorical techniques will somehow diminish the sincerity and passion of a speaker using them to get his or her point across.

One such example is the last few lines of his "I have a dream" speech, which concludes with two three-part lists, the first made up of three contrasts and a second one of three repeated phrases – in both of which, the third item is longer than each of the first two:

"We will be able to speed up that day when all of God's children,

black men and white men
Jews and gentiles
Protestants and Catholics
will be able to join hands and sing in the words of the old negro spiritual

free at last,
free at last,
thank God Almighty, we're free at last"

24th January 2010

TV Debate Claptrap: a warning to those cooking up rules for the leaders' election debates

Iain Dale has just reported that arguments are developing about the formats for the TV debates between party leaders during the general election.

It reminded me of the pointlessness of having rules that can't be enforced, as happened to the ban on applause (that failed miserably) during the 1984 US election debates between Ronald Reagan and Walter Mondale.

They took place a few weeks after the *Claptrap* film had been broadcast on UK television, and I'd temporarily fled the country to take up a visiting professorship at Duke University in North Carolina. While there, I was glued to the TV debates, and managed to get an article on the subject published in the *Washington Post* (one result of which was that I was later summoned to the Reagan White House to run a workshop for presidential speechwriters).

I'm reproducing the original article here as a warning to those, whether TV producers or party leaders and their aides, who might be trying to invent silly rules that won't be followed and can't be enforced.

Debate Claptrap

It didn't matter what the moderator said, the audience couldn't help applauding (*Washington Post*, 1984)

This year's presidential debates clearly demonstrated that neither rules of procedure nor moderators' warnings are capable of preventing audiences from applauding or laughing. The attempt to ban such displays of approval is presumably motivated by a fear that the mass audience of television viewers might be swayed in the direction of whichever candidate won most applause. In trying to enforce the ban, however, Barbara Walters and Edwin Newman preferred to stress the amount of valuable debating time that was being wasted by the unruly audience behaviour.

In either case, why did the procedural rules and moderators' protestations have so little effect on supporters of both candidates in the audience?

A preliminary analysis of the videotapes reveals that almost all the applause and laughter was in fact triggered by claptrap – not in the sense that the candidates were speaking nonsense, but in an older and largely forgotten sense of the word. For the Shorter *Oxford English Dictionary* informs us that claptrap is a "trick, device or language designed to catch applause."

After studying recordings of more than 500 political speeches, I can report not just that such devices are still in widespread use, but that most applause occurs in response to a very small number of verbal and nonverbal cues. When used in appropriate combinations, these work as very powerful "invitations to applaud."

Inspection of the videotapes shows that two of the most effective verbal devices were used by the candidates to make 18 of the 20 points that attracted an audience response.

One of these is a two-part contrast or antithesis of the sort made famous by Shakespeare with the lines "To be, or not to be" and "I come to bury Caesar, not to praise him." More recent examples include John F, Kennedy's "Ask not what your country can do for you. Ask what you can do for your country," and Martin Luther King Jr.'s "I have a dream that my four little children will one day live in a nation where they will not be judged by the color of their skin, but by the content of their character."

In, Louisville Walter Mondale was the first to win applause, using the following contrast:

a) I've proposed over one hundred billion dollars in cuts in federal spending over four years.

b) But I am not going to cut it out of Social Security and Medicare and student assistance and things that people need.

Later on, he prompted laughter and applause with a contrastive quotation from the past:

a) It's not what he doesn't know that bothers me,
b) but what he knows for sure that just ain't so.

Mondale's counterattack to the president's "There you go again" was formulated in terms of an overlapping contrast – the second part of a first contrast doubled as the first part of a second contrast, after the second part of which the audience applauded:

a) Remember the last time you said that? You said it when President Carter said you were going to cut Medicare.

a)-b) And you said "Oh no, there you go again, Mr. President." And what did you do right after the election?

b) You went right out and tried to cut $20 billion out of Medicare.

In the Kansas City debate, a technically simpler contrast also brought applause for Mondale:

a) Mr. President, I accept your commitment to peace,
b) but I want you to accept my commitment to a strong national defense.

Meanwhile, the same device was working equally well for President Reagan. In the first debate, his longest burst of applause came when he said:

a) I miss going to church,
b) but I think the Lord understands.

For another simple contrast, he was rewarded with laughter during the second debate:

a) I've heard the national debt blamed for a lot of things,
b) but not for illegal immigration across our borders.

And when he contrasted his own age with that of Mondale he attracted very extended laughter:

a) I will not make age an issue in this campaign.
b) I am not going to exploit for political purposes my opponent's youth and inexperience.

A second device packages political messages in lists of three, as in Hitler's famous slogan "Ein Volk, ein Reich, ein Fuehrer" (One people, one state, one leader) or in Reagan's three reasons for invading Grenada: "To protect American lives, to restore law and order, and to prevent chaos."

Contrastive and three-part elements can also be effectively used in constructing a single message, as exemplified by Winston Churchill's celebrated "Never in the field of human conflict has so much been owed by so many to so few."

In the Louisville debate, Mondale's longest burst of applause came when he used three rhetorical questions to make a point about abortion:

a) If it's rape, how do you draw a moral judgment on that?
b) If it's incest, how do you draw a moral judgment on that?
c) Does every woman in America have to present herself before some judge, picked by Jerry Falwell, to clear her personal judgment?

Having spent several years studying the workings of these and other devices involved in the applause elicitation process, I found myself feeling increasingly sorry for the Louisville and Kansas City audiences as I watched them desperately trying to sit on their hands. For they were not just supposed to stay silent while being exposed to some of the most powerful rhetorical techniques known to man, but were then chastised like naughty school-children on the relatively few occasions when the pressure to respond got the better of them.

Perhaps in future debates there should either be no live audiences or the candidates should be required to speak from specially edited scripts containing no claptrap.

14th February 2010

Piers Morgan interviews Gordon Brown: shades of Michael Aspel & Margaret Thatcher?

I've been intrigued by the way the media has been getting so wound up during the build up to Gordon Brown's appearance in a TV interview with Piers Morgan on Sunday night (and wondering what, if anything, I'll have to say in an interview about it on BBC Radio Bristol on Monday morning).

There is, after all, nothing new about embattled prime ministers taking the opportunity to appear in "soft" talk shows.

Did the the idea come from Margaret Thatcher?

Maybe Mrs Thatcher gave him the idea when she went to number 10 for tea not long after Mr Brown had arrived there – as she was the one who had pioneered the strategy in an bid to "soften" her image during the miner's strike in 1983. As Ian Hargreaves put it on the BBC website a while back:

> "Meanwhile, the politicians had their own ideas for diversifying the interview market. Bernard Ingham, Margaret Thatcher's crusty press secretary, says he was opposed to the decision to put the prime minister on Michael Aspel's ITV chat show in 1983, but was over-ruled by her image consultants.

> "But she did so well – softening the Iron Lady image assembled in the miners' strike – that even Ingham became a convert to chat show politics. Soon Mrs T was in and out of Jimmy Young's Radio Two studio as often as the *Today* programme."

For me, her appearance in Aspel & Company had at least three memorable moments:

Seen & Heard

1. Where to sit?

The first came right at the start, when Mrs Thatcher pretends that she's not sure where to sit. Yet here was someone who never went into a television studio without the advice of former TV producer Gordon Reece, who had decided that, wherever possible, her left profile should be exposed to the camera.

Also note how "dolled up" she is – which is thoroughly consistent with a point about her "unambiguously recognisable femininity" that I made in an earlier post on the evolution of charismatic woman.

2. Thatcher & Aspel were quite open about the rules of the game:

Early on in the interview, Aspel notes how unusual it is for a prime minister to appear on a show like this. Mrs Thatcher concludes her reply by saying how "very grateful" she was to have been invited – whereupon he reassures her by confirming that he's after "different kinds of answers" to those she has to come up with at prime minister's question time:

3. The audience's reaction to "I'm always on the job."

Whether or not Mrs Thatcher realised why the audience laughed and applauded when she announced that he was always "on the job"* is not altogether clear – though Aspel's sideways glance leaves little doubt that he knew perfectly well how they'd taken it.

I also suspect that her choice of those particular words may have been triggered by the fact that Aspel had just mentioned that she lives "over the job" at number 10 – in a similar way to that in which I suggested Gordon Browns gaffe about "saving the world" might have been triggered by sounds in the words he had just used.

(* Native speakers of American English may not be aware that, in British English slang, "on the job" is commonly used – depending on context – to mean "having sex").

Did *The Godfather* feature the longest pause and most blatant lie in the history of movies?

Watching *The Godfather* again the other day reminded me that the first time I saw it was when I'd just started getting interested in conversation analysis (c. 1974) – which meant, among other things, that I'd become fascinated by the way in which pauses can work in everyday conversation.

From that point of view, the most riveting scene in the movie came in the last few seconds, when Michael Corleone allows his wife to ask "just one question"about his "family business".

In conversation, pauses don't happen very often or for very long

As I've suggested in some of my books, one of the reasons why so many public speakers feel uneasy about pausing is that 99.99% of our talking lives is spent in the much more familiar world of conversation, where we collaborate with others to minimise silences – therefore avoiding the awkwardness and embarrassment that so often come with them

As a result, inexperienced presenters often find it uncomfortable, if not unnatural, to pause far more often and for much longer than they do in everyday conversation – which is one reason why some of them carry on using the conversational practice of killing off silences with frequent "ums" and "uhs".

Delay as a warning of coming trouble

The early work on turn-taking in conversation showed how a very slight delay between the end of one turn and the start of another often works as the earliest warning that the speaker is having some difficulty in producing an appropriate response.

Seen & Heard

An example of this is when you say something that limits the next speaker to making a choice between two alternatives, as when you're looking for yes/no, agreement/disagreement, acceptance/refusal, etc.

Quite often, one or other of these options is, in the jargon of conversation analysis, "preferred" – which is to say that the speaker and respondent both know perfectly well which one is expected and which one is not.

For example, in the case of invitations, acceptance is "preferred" over refusal. And that's what we're implicitly taking into account when we lead up to issuing an invitation by checking out whether or not the recipient will be able to reply with the "preferred" option (i.e. accept) if and when the invitation comes.

So a question like "are you doing anything on Saturday night?" is hardly ever heard or treated as a neutral enquiry about your plans for Saturday night. Much more usually, you'll hear it both as a signal of what the speaker has in mind (i.e. an invitation) and as providing the you with a chance to say whether or not you'll be able to take the "preferred" option (i.e. accept) before any firm invitation is actually made.

Preferred options tend to come straight away

Once an invitation has been issued, the preferred option (acceptance) is much the easier of the two options to deal with, and normally comes within a split second. But if the option taken by the invitee is not the preferred one, their refusal will be delayed and constructed very differently from an acceptance.

So, if you invite someone to dinner and they haven't started speaking within about a fifth of a second, you can be pretty sure that they're going to refuse.

And the actual refusal itself will typically be delayed beyond the initial "warning" that came with the pause, and will be pushed back towards the end of the turn so that the eventual "dis-preferred" response is cushioned by preliminary expressions of thanks and appreciation, and/or an explanation for the upcoming refusal – as in the following:

[0.5 second delay] – "Well – I'd love to – but unfortunately – I'm baby-sitting on Saturday night – so I won't be able to make it."

In this case, each of the components (between the hyphens) progressively confirms that the initial delay did indeed mean that the dis-preferred option (refusal) is on it's way (but not before suitable statements of appreciation, disappointment and explanation have been made).

The general point is that taking the option that's not preferred (refusal) is more complicated and involves considerably more time and effort than taking the option that is preferred (acceptance).

The peculiar impact when a preferred option comes after a long pause

At the end of *The Godfather*, Michael Corleone has just finished "settling family business" by delegating his minions to bump off everyone who's betrayed it. His sister has just become "hysterical" (his word) in accusing him of having had her husband murdered.

Michael's wife, Kay, has heard the argument with her sister-in-law and now wants the truth from her husband.

He knows and she knows (and we in the audience all know) that the preferred answer to her question "Is it true?" is "No". And we also know that the true answer is "Yes". If we were in any doubt that Kay suspects and fears that this is so, the long delay of eight seconds before she braces herself to whisper the key question confirms that this is exactly what she is afraid of.

But, before he eventually comes up with the preferred option, Michael delays for another eight seconds – again, far longer than would ever happen in a real, rather than a dramatised, conversation.

The suspense presumably comes from the fact that the pause implies that he might be about to select the dis-preferred option ("Yes"). The longer the silence lasts, the more it implies that this is where he's going – as he would, after all, need plenty of time to work out an apology, explanation, justification and/or whatever else might be required to cushion the journey towards the dreaded "Yes".

His blatant lie lets those of us in the audience know for sure that the respectable college graduate and war hero at the start of the film has gone forever, and that Michael Corleone has now fully committed to a career of crime and deception.

Kay's apparent acceptance and relief when he goes for the preferred option makes us feel sorry for her and appalled that even his long-suffering wife is now included in his web if deceit.

Then, when she sees his murderous underlings paying homage to him as the new Godfather and shutting the door on her, the expression on her face leaves us wondering whether she's finally got the point.

4th March 2010

Michael Foot's memorable oratory

For me, news of the death of former Labour Party leader Michael Foot brought back memories of the days when I was doing research for my book *Our Masters' Voices*, which included a section comparing the speaking effectiveness of him and Mrs Thatcher during the 1983 general election.

In those days, British television companies still showed quite a lot of speeches on their news programmes and it had been easy enough to collect examples of Mrs Thatcher using the main rhetorical techniques and video clips of her being applauded by enthusiastic supporters.

But, although Michael Foot had a reputation for being a very effective orator, it was almost impossible to find any comparable video clips of him using the same techniques, let alone receiving much in the way of applause. In fact, in some of the clips discussed in my book, he'd come across as uncharacteristically stumbling and long-winded.

A style that failed to meet the demands of the media

The problem was that Mr Foot was at his best when speaking without a script. But, early in the 1983 campaign, the media had started to complain that there was too much of a gap between the advance press releases of his speeches and what he actually said from the platform. To make life easier for reporters, he took to reading out the text of the pre-released speeches word for word – a style of delivery with which he was quite unfamiliar.

To make matters worse, Michael Foot didn't have very good eyesight – and no one in the Labour Party had thought of equipping him with a teleprompter. As a result, he spent most of his time glued to his scripts, hardly ever looking up at the audience and his delivery was much more hesitant than when he was free to speak without a text.

The day his advisors ignored a free tip

At some stage, his advisors must have become worried enough about how he was coming across for one of them to phone me asking for help. When I asked what kind of fee they had in mind, I was told that they assumed I was a Labour supporter who would be happy to do it for nothing.

When I refused, the voice the other end of the phone pressed me further "But surely you could just give us at least one tip without us having to pay anything?"

"OK" I said "tell him to get some rimless spectacles."

The reason was that Mr Foot used to wear very thick horn-rimmed glasses, which made his eyes almost invisible to viewers, especially when he was looking down at a script.

But they knew best, and Michael Foot's stumbling campaign carried on unchanged – not that I'd be foolish enough to claim that my generous advice, however accurate it may have been, could have saved him or his party from the disastrous result that followed.

9th March 2010

Murder most foul: story-telling in conversation

When sorting through old videotapes, I sometimes stumble across something speaker-related that prompts a post that's relevant to the main themes of these articles.

But today's post is a bit different on two counts: it's not only the first time I've featurred any of my relations, but it also comes from the oldest speaker yet posted on the blog.

In 1981, my brother held a party to celebrate the 100th birthday of our paternal grandfather (who lived on for another five years after that). When most of the guests had gone, the camcorder was left running with a view to picking up some "oral history" about the family and how farming had changed since he'd left school to work full time on the land in 1893.

Murder?

By far the most startling revelation came when he launched into a story about a neighbouring farmer who, according to him, had murdered his brother (in an incident we later discovered had been passed off as a shooting accident).

Although it came at the end of a party, you shouldn't think that his narrative was influenced in any way by drink (other than tea). In fact, he used to boast that he hadn't been in a pub since 1898 – and hadn't drunk any alcohol then (or since). And on this occasion, in line with our childhood training, any evidence of domestic alcohol and tobacco consumption had been hidden away before he came anywhere near the house.

Stories take more than one turn to deliver

Anyone interested in conversation analysis will note that it's a fine example of an early observation by the late great Harvey Sacks about the way story-telling works in conversation, namely that stories take more than one turn to deliver.

So, before getting down to telling his story, JA prefaces it by giving us notice to expect an extended sequence of talk from him on the same topic ("I can tell you something else about ...") – after which DA's turns punctuate the story with regular "continuers" (e.g. "Yes") and occasional understanding checks (e.g. questions).

It's also interesting to see how, even at such a great age, a speaker still conforms to and can perform pretty well within the basic constraints of turn-taking.

To make this gripping tale easier to follow, there's an approximate transcript below (the video clip can be found on my blog).

> JA: I can tell you something else about -uh – that farm that joins – does it join you?

> DA: Yes

> JA: what we called Mollets

DA: Yes, Mollets.

JA: The brothers fell out.

DA: Yes.

JA: And one brother killed the other – and the inspector went to see this farm.

DA: Yes.

JA: Because he'd said it about – that he'd killed him or he had died

DA: Yes.

JA: And do you know what the farmer said when he said to him about it?

DA: What?

JA: "I saw him do it!"

DA: (laughs): He saw him do it himself?

JA: No – his brother killed his brother.

DA: Yes, but he reckoned he'd killed himself?

JA: (Aye) I don't know what the inspector or whoever he was who went to see him – but he'd be somebody but (????) if he shut up then, wouldn't he?

DA: (laughs)

JA: And they got over it some way or another but I never knew how – at least if I did I've forgot – but (?I haven't?) forgot that he did it – You see his brother – I think – him 'at got killed was the eldest. Well t'next man he was more of a gentleman, you see, he- this first one – worked – and he liked riding about on a horse.

DA: Yes

JA: And he thought I expect that he was a bit (of a waster) – and he would -uh – boss's brother – thats how the tale was when I was young.

DA: (Aye)

JA: But I never forgot it – never shall do.

(Background noise)

JA: (???) from Monk Fryston station to that farm – and he used to – this brother that he killed, he liked drink you see – he used to call at t'pub for a pint I expect – or else something else that he drank – but (?it was easy?) in them days – aye ...

12 March 2010

Sales, showbiz and speaking

I've sometimes been mystified by the willingness of large companies to squander huge amounts of money on sales events without bothering to spend a little extra on preparing key speakers to make the most of such occasions.

One of the most extreme examples of this came at the UK launch of some major new products by a famous American multi-national corporation.

Sales by showbiz

They had hired one of the country's best-known radio and television presenter (daily rate: £15,000.00) to chair a discussion with their directors from the stage of one of London's West End theatres (daily rate: £ quite a lot) – from where 'the show' was transmitted live to several more theatres around the UK for others to see on cinema screens (daily rate: £ quite a lot more).

They had also hired me (daily rate: £ very little) to go to one of these distant venues and report back on how it came across to the local audience.

All went well until just before the coffee break, when the TV presenter introduced the company's marketing director to say a few words to bring the first session to a close.

The director was suddenly beamed up from his seat on the stage to appear on

the screen, where he'd been filmed on a balcony above the factory floor where we could see the new products being assembled in the background.

With his eyes glued to a teleprompter, and an expression on his face serious enough for a funeral oration, he spoke in a flat and regular monotone that sounded like an audition for the the voice-over part of a speaking robot in a science fiction movie.

The verbatim transcript of his final 'few words' went as follows:

" ... I hope you're all as excited by these new products as I am."

Audience entertainment?

The 400+ viewers in the theatre where I saw it exploded into a collective and extended fit of laughter, before adjourning for coffee in a thoroughly jovial mood.

Although I'd be the first to admit that humour can be a powerful weapon in the armoury of public speakers, I don't think this kind of hilarity was quite what the company had in mind for this particular point in the proceedings.

Luckily for me, it made the job of writing the report they were paying me to write that much easier, as I was able to make the very obvious point that, if your directors are going to say that they're excited about something, it's worth spending a few extra pounds on getting someone (e.g. me) to train them to sound as though they really are excited.

Why "Ha-ha-ha"?

As for why the audience laughter went "Ha-ha-ha", rather than other options like "Ho-ho-ho" or "He-he-he", it was almost certainly because they were latching on two of the last three vowel sounds in the marketing director's final words – i.e. the 'a' sounds in "... as I am".

Or, for more on the subject, you can download the original paper by Gail Jefferson – 'On the Poetics of Ordinary Talk', *Text and Performance Quarterly*, 1996, 16(1), 1-61).

15th March 2010

Brown may plan to "keep going" but Mrs Thatcher never said she'd go "on and on and on"

Yet again, something said in an interview, has landed a politician in a bit of trouble – providing further support for my "snakes and ladders" theory of political communication.

Gordon Brown's announcement on *Woman's Hour* that he intends to "keep going" even if he loses the election has, not surprisingly, prompted commentators like Iain Dale to hark back to an interview in the 1987 general election when Mrs Thatcher is alleged to have said that she intended to go "on and on and on". I say "alleged to have said", because she never actually said it: what she actually said was "I hope to go on and on" – which became a headline on BBC Television News.

Thatcher's snake gives Kinnock a ladder

This is not, of course, the only example of a famous quotation being expanded (or contracted) into a three-part list – one of the most famous contractions being Churchill's "blood, sweat, toil and tears", which is most frequently quoted as "blood, sweat and tears."

If Thatcher's "on and on" was a nice example of how interviews are the snakes in the game of snakes and ladders (by generating negative headlines for the interviewee), Neil Kinnock was quick to use it to jump on a ladder in a speech (ladder because speeches are more likely to work in the speaker's favour). In this case, he contrasted two repetitive lists of three:

"When Britain has a Prime Minister

that has allowed unemployment and poverty and waiting lists and closures and crime to go up and up and up,

that is a Prime Minister that must not be allowed to go on and on and on."

Thatcher adopts "on and on and on"

By the time the Conservatives came to launch their 1987 election manifesto, "on and on and on" had been so widely publicised in the media that even Mrs Thatcher felt able to use the revised three-part phrase in a slightly different and light-hearted context:

> "I intend to do my level best to win a third term and for that we shall work, to coin a phrase, on and on and on every day until the end of polling day."

16th March 2010

How NOT to introduce a speaker

About 20 seconds into a clip from the Liberal Democrats' Spring conference at the weekend, you'll see a fine example of how not to do an introduction.

Clap on the name

As far as the structure of the sequence is concerned, it's a reasonable example of how to use the "clap on the name" technique to elicit applause (for more on which, see my books):

(1) Identify or hint at the identity of who's being introduced
(2) Say a few words about him/her
(3) Name him/her [Audience applauds]

Be positive and confident about who it is

But it really isn't a very good idea to spend stages (1) and (2) raising questions or doubts about the person you're introducing, or to sound less than 100% sure who it is.

Normally, the "clap on the name" technique works so that the audience is able to come in before you get to the end of saying the person's name – which has the added advantage of making it sound as though they're all so pleased to see him/her that they can't wait until you've finished to start clapping.

But, in this case there's a delay of a whole second before the applause gets under way – which was almost certainly prompted by the hesitancy shown in leading up to the announcement of his name (and/or possibly even because the audience was still mulling over the controversial implications of the first sentence):

> CHAIR: I'd like to introduce you conference to *probably one of the very few MPs* in British politics at the moment *who is genuinely trusted* by the British public (**What?** – **1**: Is he only "*probably*" one of them, 2: Are there only "*very few*" of them, and 3: Where does that leave all the other LibDem MPs?).

> It's – the – shadow – Treasury – uh – shadow Chancellor of the Exchequer rather (**What?** Doesn't she know who their most famous MP is or what his job title is?), Vince Cable.

17th March 2010

Using "clap on the name" to introduce or commend someone

This is a sequel to yesterday's post on *How NOT to introduce a speaker*, and discusses some more examples of the "clap on the name technique" in action.

Michael Parkinson is introducing the next guest on his chat show.

(1) Identify or hint at the person's identity:

> "... her latest film, "In the Cut", is dark and erotic."

(2) Say a few words about him/her:

> "She's a writer who becomes involved with a detective investigating a serial killer. Ladies and Gentlemen"

(3) Name him/her:

> "Meg Ryan" [Applause/cheers].

The second example illustrates how the "clap on the name" technique doesn't just work for introductions, but is also just as effective when you're congratulating or commending someone.

At the 2004 Democratic National Convention, Barack Obama commends John Kerry:

(1) Identify or hint at the person's identity:

"Our party has chosen a man to lead us"

(2) Say a few words about him/her:

"who embodies the best this country has to offer, and that man is"

(3) Name him/her:

"John Kerry" [Applause/cheers].

30th March 2010

Vince Cable shows how "Yah-boo politics" can win victories for the Lib Dems

I've just been watching last night's Channel 4 broadcast of the Chancellors' Debate, and was fascinated to see that Vince Cable was the only one of the three spokesmen who prompted applause from the audience during his closing statement (see transcript below).

A victory for yah-boo politics

It proved something I've always argued, namely that yah-boo politics works just as well for the Lib Dems as it does for the other main parties – in spite of the Lib Dems' long-standing "holier than thou" claim to be the only party that doesn't lower itself to using yah-boo tactics.

Seen & Heard

During Paddy Ashdown's leadership of the party, I often found myself arguing against such an approach, for the simple reason that we knew that 84% of the bursts of applause in political speeches are triggered by two particular types of message (or a combination of the two):

> Boasts about our side: 40%
> Attacks or insults aimed at opponents: 34%
> Combined boast + attack: 10%
> (*Our Masters' Voices*, pp. 34-45).

So, if you're really serious about refraining from yah-boo politics, you're voluntarily reducing your chances of winning applause by more than a third.

Liberal yah-boo moments from the past

This is not to say, of course, that the Lib Dems have always (or ever?) been consistent in practising what they preach when it comes to avoiding yah-boo politics. After all, Vince Cable's most famous line during his temporary leadership of the party was his yah-boo remark about Gordon Brown becoming more like Mr Bean than Stalin.

More than 30 years ago, during the 1979 general election, Liberal leader David Steel was also not averse to it, as you can see from this neat example of how to use a puzzle with contrasting solution to say yah-boo to both the other parties at the same time:

> Puzzle: There are two Conservative parties in this election.

> Solution: (A) One is offering the continuation of the policies we've had for the last five years.
> (B) And the other is offering a return to the policies of forty years ago.

> [Applause]

Cable's latest yah-boo moment

In his closing remarks at the end of last night's debate, Vince Cable again showed how to use this "plague on both your houses" approach to craft a yah-boo sequence that wins a positive response from the audience.

As with the Steel example from 1979, it showed that a rhetorical advantage for

LibDem politicians is that there is always plenty of scope for making simple contrasts between the two main parties – and, in this case, Cable adds to the rhetorical impact of that by listing three dreadful things that each of them is alleged to have done – all of which are offered as the start of a solution to the puzzle with which he opened the sequence.

Then, as he moves towards making a favourable contrast between the LibDem's and both the alternatives, he's interrupted by one of the evening's few bursts of applause:

Puzzle: The question is who can you trust to do it?

Solution: (A1) The Labour government led us into this mess
(A2) they've done severe damage to pensions and savings
(A3) they've wasted a vast amount of money on over-centralised public services.

(B1) The Tories presided over two big recessions in office
(B2) they wasted most of the North Sea oil revenue
(B3) they sold off the family silver on the cheap

Now they want to have another turn to get their noses in the trough and reward their rich backers.
The Liberal Democrats are different ...

[Applause]

... the Liberal Democrats are different.

16th May 2010

It was Brown's last minute speeches wot might have won it – if only he'd done it sooner

One of my complaints before and during the election was the way in which speeches have played an ever smaller part in UK general elections and media coverage of them.

I was therefore fascinated to hear former Labour deputy leader Roy Hattersley on this week's *Any Questions?* (BBC Radio 4) echoing various other commentators by singling out the last three days of the election as the point at which Gordon Brown finally came into his own:

> Hattersley: What I'm utterly certain of is that had Gordon Brown behaved, for instance, as he behaved during the last three days of the campaign when he was himself, had he behaved like that for three weeks, let alone three years, the election outcome would have been quite different. But that was the only occasion I saw the real Gordon Brown I knew and the tragedy is he didn't become that earlier.

And what was so different about those last three days?

Answer: He made two traditional barnstorming speeches at large rallies.

I rest my case – but very much doubt whether any of the Labour leadership candidates declared so far is capable of doing likewise.

21st May 2010

Hillary Clinton warns North Korea of "consequences" (again)

It's nearly a year since North Korea announced it had exploded a nuclear weapon as powerful as the one that destroyed Hiroshima – which prompted US secretary of State Hillary Clinton to warn them: "There are consequences to such actions."

After the sinking of a South Korean ship by the North Koreans, she's on about "consequences" again.

Pre-delicate hitches

Last year, I made the point that her warning about consequences was punctuated by a large number of pre-delicate hitches.

What's interesting about Mrs Clinton's latest dire threat to the North Koreans – "provocative actions have consequences" – is that there are so many hitches (i.e. ums, ers and pauses) after she issues the warning.

Post-delicate hitches?

This raises the question of whether conversation analysts should be turning their attention to analysing a new and possibly related phenomenon, namely post-delicate hitches. Or do they simply indicate that the US Secretary of State knows perfectly well that the Americans' "best actions moving forward"' will be exactly the same as they were last year – i.e. nothing much?

7th July 2010

Rhetoric, neutrality and controversy in the Queen's speech to the United Nations

In previous posts, I've highlighted the Queen's mastery in displaying neutrality when making speeches. Yesterday another fine example was on show as she addressed the General Assembly of the United Nations – where members have heard some pretty controversial speeches from other heads of state, and for many of whom the very idea of a politically neutral speech must be quite strange.

But as a constitutional monarch of 16 countries and head of a commonwealth of 54 countries, the Queen's challenge was, as usual: how do you say anything of relevance to such a diverse audience without appearing to take sides?

The answer is that you take sides with positive achievements of the organisation and its worthy values – with which all member states can agree or, at least, to which they can all pay lip service.

Then you deliver it in a flat monotone to avoid sounding too passionate about anything in particular – and especially anything verging on the controversial.

The most controversial line?

Although few, apart from supporters of Al Qaeda, could take exception to her singling out "the struggle against terrorism" as one of the two "new challenges" facing UN member states, her inclusion of climate change as the other one was arguably the most controversial thing that she said – running, as it did, the risk of offending all the climate change deniers around the world.

Best lines?

One line that stood out for me must also have stood out for her speechwriter, as it featured a quotation from a UN Secretary General that's survived for more than fifty years, namely a medical metaphor, to which was added an apt extension:

"Former Secretary-General Dag Hammarsköld once said that 'constant attention by a good nurse may be just as important as a major operation by a surgeon'. Good nurses get better with practice; sadly the supply of patients never ceases."

I was also impressed by the idea of "waging peace".

And her opening line – "I believe I was last here in 1957" – was presumably meant to be humorous.

The Queen's use of other rhetorical techniques

The speech also included quite a few neatly constructed contrasts, such as:

(A) "... many of these sweeping advances have come about not because of governments, committee resolutions, or central directives – although all these have played a part –

(B) but instead because millions of people around the world have wanted them."

(A) "When I was first here, there were just three United Nations operations overseas.

(B) "Now over 120,000 men and women are deployed in 26 missions across the world."

"In my lifetime, the United Nations has moved from being

(A) a high-minded aspiration to being
(B) a real force for common good."

There were quite a few three-part lists:

(1) "You have helped to reduce conflict,

(2) you have offered humanitarian assistance to millions of people affected by natural disasters and other emergencies,

(3) and you have been deeply committed to tackling the effects of poverty in many parts of the world."

"... it is my hope that, when judged by future generations,

(1) our sincerity,

(2) our willingness to take a lead,

(3) and our determination to do the right thing, will stand the test of time.

The challenge now is to continue to show this clear and convening leadership while not losing sight of your ongoing work to secure

(1) the security,

(2) prosperity

(3) and dignity of our fellow human beings."

And there was also one example of a combined format, in which the first part was a list of three:

(A) "... many of these sweeping advances have come about not because of

(1) governments,

(2) committee resolutions,

(3) or central directives – although all these have played a part –

(B) but instead because millions of people around the world have wanted them."

8th July 2010

The rise of Chomsky and the fall of grammar

In a recent post by Iain Dale, entitled *Its Grammatikal, Innit?*, he tells us that an earlier tweet about poor grammar (Why is it that so many people in their twenties have v little understanding of English grammar or basic sentence construction? Aaaaaaagh.) had provoked a huge response.

When I saw his tweet, I shared his frustration about declining standards of English grammar. But I was rather disappointed to see him using this to launch a generalised attack on "progressive" educationalists on his blog – because I don't think it comes from progressiveness so much as from the way news from the frontiers of different disciplines (e.g., in this case, linguistics), get watered down over a period of time before it reaches the syllabus of applied courses like those provided for trainee teachers.

Dilution and dissemination

In a limited way, I know this from my own experience, because I saw some of my own early research into the sociology of suicide being watered down to the point of being included in some of the A level syllabuses – and never quite knew whether to be annoyed by the oversimplifications or pleased to see my work reaching a wider audience.

I also know from my own experience that Iain Dale's point about the way learning a foreign language (as he did) helps you to understand the workings of grammar in your own native tongue. My late wife was head of modern languages in a comprehensive school during the 1980s, and was continually at war with the English Department about the fact that their reluctance to teach grammar meant that she and her colleagues had to spend huge amounts of time introducing pupils to verbs, nouns, adjectives, etc. before being able to teach them French and German.

Education is not a "pure" academic discipline

The trouble is that education is not a pure discipline built on its own body of knowledge and research. So the absence of much in the way of pure educational theory drives lecturers in education departments (and former teacher training colleges) into the market for material from other disciplines, like psychology, sociology and linguistics, that can be borrowed, diluted and adapted for the benefit of aspiring teachers.

Enter linguistics

In the 1960s, a new discipline concentrating on language in general, rather than any particular language, began to take off. But to convince universities and their paymasters that it was worth establishing a new academic department, you need a few distinguished theorists whose work can be cited to establish the credibility and legitimacy of the discipline in the face of competing demands for scarce funding.

Enter Chomsky

For linguistics, the ideas of a professor called Noam Chomsky were just what they'd been looking for. The fact that he worked at an institution as prestigious as MIT was an added bonus when it came to demonstrating that there was some pretty serious stuff at the heart of the emerging discipline.

And so it was that Chomsky became the central orthodoxy that dominated the new linguistics departments that were springing up around the Western world from the 1960s onwards.

The diluted version of Chomsky

At the heart of his theory was the claim that humans are born with an innate ability to master grammar, and this is what explains the extraordinary mystery of language acquisition. This was rather bad news both for empirically inclined researchers and for what was to happen to the training of teachers and, ultimately the teaching of English grammar in our schools.

Bad news for researchers

For those of us naive enough to believe that observing how people actually speak, interact and use language might be a good idea, our work could be written off by the Chomskians before we'd even started – because he'd decreed that language could be understood without bothering to dirty your hands with detailed empirical investigations.

Even worse news for grammar in the teaching of teachers and children

By the time the diluted Chomskian orthodoxy had reached university education departments and teacher training colleges, the news was that "grammar was innate" and wired into the human brain. So, if it was innate in all of us, what possible point could there be in teaching it to youngsters who'd already been born with an understanding of grammar?

Of course, this might not be quite what the master had actually meant or intended. But it has, I believe, played a critical and disastrous part in relegating grammar to the sidelines of teacher training – and in explaining why so few people in their twenties and thirties have so little understanding of English grammar and sentence construction.

Misspeaking, mistaken and misleading

According to Downing Street sources, David Cameron "misspoke" when he said that Iran has nuclear weapons.

Misspeaking

Until Hillary Clinton came up with the word "misspeak" – when trying to explain away her (false) claim to have landed in Bosnia under sniper-fire – I'd never heard the words "misspeak", "misspoke" or "misstatement" before. And I remember being vaguely amused at the way both she and an Obama aide used the new word to create some quite neat contrasts, which were reported in *The Independent* as follows:

> "I think that, a minor blip, you know, if I said something that, you know, I say a lot of things – millions of words a day* – so **if I misspoke it was just a misstatement**," she said.

> "But an Obama spokesman, Tommy Vietor, noted she made her claims in a scripted speech. 'When you make a false claim that's in your prepared remarks, **it's not misspeaking, it's misleading**.'"

By Mr Vietor's criteria, David Cameron can at least invoke in his defence the fact that this was not a scripted speech.

Mistaken

But an even bigger mistake than the PM's gaffe arguably came from the Downing Street "source" who decided to borrow and use this newly invented word, even though it had been created for such a dubious purpose and did little or no good for Mrs Clinton's reputation.

After all, as it said in *The Independent*, she was "well ahead in most polls" at the time but her misspoken words had "eclipsed coverage of her scheduled appearances and threatened to undercut her foreign policy experience message".

Misleading

All of which is to warn Mr Cameron and his aides that, when it comes to explaining away a mistake or misdemeanour, misguided memos can cause miscellaneous mishaps, mistakes, misconceptions and misfortune, not to mention quite serious misgivings about your "foreign policy experience message".

* "Millions of words a day"?

Mrs Clinton's claim to have been saying "millions of words a day" was also an example of "misspeaking". Assuming she was working an 18 hour day at the time and spoke continuously during her waking hours at 150 words per minute (i.e. half-way between the speed of conversation and speech-making), 2 million words (i.e. "millions", plural) would require a speaking rate of 1,852 words per minute. Or, to put it another way, delivering 2 million words at a more normal speed of 150 words per minute would take 222 hours – i.e. 12 eighteen-hour days of non-stop speaking without pausing for a moment.

6th August 2010

Another example where 100% of the communication is "non-verbal"

Regular readers will know that I'm not over-impressed by experts who exaggerate the importance of body language and non-verbal behaviour, and especially those who continue to spread the Mehrabian myth that 93% of communication is non-verbal.

But there are exceptions where 100% of the communication is indeed non-verbal, as in the case of a World Cup referee sending a player off for not having hit an opponent in the face that I posted a few weeks ago .

A more elegant example where 100% of the communication is non-verbal is to be found in the way conductors interact with the orchestra during a concert.

No doubt the Mehrabianistas would want to put a percentage on how much of the communication is coming from Simon Rattle's facial expression as compared with movements of his hands (left, right and/or together), body, mouth, eyebrows, face, etc.

But how you'd go about arriving at such measurements is quite beyond me, and I'd be most interested to hear from anyone who could enlighten me on the matter. Meanwhile, I'll just have to make do with watching (and listening to) the music.

20th September 2010

Objects as visual aids: UK Speechwriters' Guild Conference, 2010

When Brian Jenner, founder of the UK Speechwriters' Guild asked me to do a 10-15 minute presentation at this year's annual conference, the challenge was to try to put into practice the advice of one of my heroes, the late Professor Sir Lawrence Bragg, one of whose tips for lecturers was:

> "There should be one main theme, and all the subsidiary interesting points, experiments, or demonstrations should be such that they remind the hearer of the theme. As in a picture, so in a lecture, the force of the impression depends upon a ruthless sacrifice of unnecessary detail."

The "one main theme" I selected was something I've blogged and written about before, namely how the use of an object as a visual aid can sometimes have an impressive impact when it comes to getting a point across to your audience.

There were (of course!) three reasons why it struck me as a promising topic for a short talk at this particular conference.

1. It was potentially relevant for an audience of speechwriters, most of whom would have had conversations, if not arguments, with their clients about whether to use PowerPoint or some other type of visual aid.

2. Being able to show the audience actual examples makes it a subject that's much easier to speak about than to write about (as I'd discovered when writing about visual aids in my books on speech-making and presentation).

3.   It would give me a chance to give an implicit demonstration of a subsidiary theme that I'm also quite keen on, namely that short video clips are another type of visual aid that can help to get your point across with clarity and impact.

1. "Peace on our time"

The picture of Neville Chamberlain holding up the piece of paper he and Hitler had just signed in Munich seemed a suitably famous example to feature on the opening title.

2. Holding up a boring paper

But the first time I realised that anyone could use a piece of paper to strike an instant chord with an audience was in the speech Ann Brennan gave at the SDP Conference in 1984 (for a fuller story of which, see the *Claptrap* series of posts).

Her "one main theme" was that the new party was failing to communicate with working class voters who'd become disaffected by the Labour Party. So we wrote a line that involved her holding up the background paper for the debate on equality in which she would be speaking.

It prompted immediate laughter and applause from the audience.

3. Paddy Ashdown holds up a newspaper

The next time I saw the impact a piece of paper could have was five years later on the tenth anniversary of Margaret Thatcher's premiership in 1989.

Someone in Paddy Ashdown's office had unearthed a copy of the *London Evening Standard* from 1979 that carried a front page headline announcing that she would quit after ten years. So he held it up during Prime Minister's Question Time in the House of Commons and asked if she intended to keep her promise.

The instant reaction was was laughter and uproar from MPs; the delayed reaction came with action replays of the sequence on prime-time TV news programmes later that evening.

But we also learnt something else – don't overdo it. A week or two later, he held up another newspaper during PMQ, only to be reprimanded by the Speaker for making such a blatant attempt to grab the headlines again.

4. Senator Scott Brown holds up a newspaper

The same technique goes down just as well with American audiences. Scott Brown had just won the election to take over as Senator for Massachusetts following the death of Edward Kennedy. The audience is already chanting enthusiastically, but their chants turned into cheers and applause as soon as Brown held up a newspaper with the headline "He did it".

5. Examples of other objects (1) a glass

Using an object can involve things as simple as holding up a glass and asking whether it's half-full or half-empty.

6. Examples of other objects (2) currency notes

A year before the 1979 UK general election, when still leader of the opposition, Mrs Thatcher came up with a successful photo-opportunity by using a pair of scissors to cut through a £1 note to illustrate how much the pound had depreciated since Labour came to power.

I've seen economists make some neat points whilst waving notes about. I once worked with a client in Spain who had a stunning impact on his audience by setting fire to a 200 Peseta note to open his presentation.

7. Steve Jobs pulls a rabbit out of a hat

I blogged about this sequence a while back. The things that stood out were how the audience reacted when he (a) picked up the envelope, (b) took the MacBook Air out of it and (c) held it up in the air.

8. Bill Gates releases some insects from a box

In a TED talk on malaria and education, Bill Gates claimed to release some mosquitos from a box in front of him.

9. Archbishop of York cuts his dog collar into pieces

During an interview on Andrew Marr's Sunday morning BBC TV show, Archbishop John Sentamu stripped off his clerical collar and cut it up into pieces to illustrate what Robert Mugabe has done to the people of Zimbabwe – a sequence that was replayed many times on the main news networks later that day.

10. Government minister throws his microphone on the table

At the 1982 Conservative Party conference, Robin Day interviewed John Nott, who had been Secretary of State for Defence during the Falkland's war and had announced that he'd be resigning in the near future to join a merchant bank. When Day refers to him as a "here today gone tomorrow" minister, Mr Nott announces that he's fed up with this interview, pulls off his microphone and throws it down on the table.

On the longer term impact of this sequence, there were two interesting footnotes. One was that *Here Today, Gone Tomorrow* resurfaced nearly ten years later as the title of John Nott's autobiography. Then, a few weeks ago, the sequence was featured in a *Daily Telegraph* article on the "Top-ten Television Moments of the Eighties".

11. More mundane objects can also work

A few years ago, I worked with a client who had built a very successful business manufacturing metal clips that hold lamps in place above streets and motorways. He'd been invited to speak about the fatal, legal and financial consequences that could result if any of the thousands of such products failed. He started his presentation to an audience of lawyers at a conference on product liability law by holding up one of the clips and explaining that everyone there had benefited from them, had driven under them but almost certainly didn't know what they were. By the time he got to providing the solution to his puzzle, the audience was fully attentive and listened closely to the rest of his presentation

12. The swinging ball of death

The final clip I used came from one of the Christmas lectures for children by Professor Chris Bishop at the Royal Institution.

What surprised and fascinated me when I played this at the conference was that the rising "woooooh" noise from the children and their response when the ball stopped just short of the speaker's head was echoed, with precision timing, by the conference audience as they watched the clip.

13. Conclusion: showing what you mean

As I noted at the beginning of this post, I'm a big fan of one of the founders of the Christmas Lectures for children and what he had to say about communicating science to wider audiences. It's to be found in a short booklet – *Advice to Lecturers* – published by the Royal Institution and consisting of writings by Lawrence Bragg and Michael Faraday, whose ability to take lay audiences to the frontiers of science used to fill lecture theatres until there was standing room only.

So I ended by quoting some lines from Bragg. Writing about how the interest of many distinguished scientists as first aroused by the Christmas lectures for children, he says:

> "In recalling their impressions they almost invariably say not 'we were told' but 'we were shown' this or that."

A few lines later, he adds:

> "The final result of the popular talk is measured by the extent to which the audience recalls it afterwards, and this fixation of the image is effected by arousing an emotional response of interest and thrill."

Chris Bishop's swinging ball of death achieved this both with the audience in the Faraday lecture theatre and, if the noises they made are anything to go by, with the audience in Bournemouth last week – demonstrating also that the traditions set by Faraday and Bragg are still alive and well at the Royal Institution.

For speechwriters, the moral of the story is that it's worth giving at least a few moments of thought as to whether there might be a suitable object that could bring "interest and thrill" to the audiences for whom they are writing.

21st September 2010

Delayed applause at a key point in Nick Clegg's conference speech

The way in which journalists monitor applause in political speeches and use it as a basis for assessing the effectiveness or otherwise of a speech is something that's fascinated me since writing *Our Masters' Voices* more than 25 years ago. So I checked to see what columnists in *The Guardian* which had, after all, backed the Lib Dems at the election, thought of the Deputy Prime Minister's speech yesterday at the Liberal Democrat Conference.

Nor, given what I'd seen of it, was I surprised to find "...they gave him polite applause but no more than that" from Jackie Ashley and "...it was telling that the silences came in the wrong places" from Julian Glover.

Apart from the fact that there were quite a few places where the audience refrained from applauding lines that should have been applauded, I was also struck by the fact that there were also quite a few instances of longish delays before the audience managed to get their hands apart.

Applause should be instant or early

The point about delayed applause is that, when the script and delivery are working well together, it should happen within a split second of the speaker finishing a sentence.

That's why contrasts and three-part lists are so effective, because they project a clear completion point where everyone knows in advance where the finish line is and that it's now their turn to respond.

Interruptive applause

Better still is to get the audience to start applauding early, because it gives the impression that they're so enthusiastic and eager to show their agreement that they can't wait – and the speaker ends up having to compete to make himself heard above the rising tide of popular acclaim.

One way to do that is to use a three-part list, in which the third item is longer than the first two.

Delayed applause

In conversation, silences of anything more than about a fifth of a second before a next speaker starts to speak usually mean that some sort of trouble is on its way (refusals, disagreements, etc.).

In political speeches too, silence before the applause starts is not only noticeable, but also tends to create a rather negative impression – and the longer it lasts, the worse the impression is.

22nd September 2010

Delayed applause for the coalition in Vince Cable's conference speech (at exactly the same point as in Nick Clegg's)

After the Deputy Prime Minister's leader's speech at the Liberal Democrat's conference, I posted a clip in which the audience delayed for two seconds before applauding when he said that the party could not be expected to be taken seriously if they had not joined in a coalition government.

I also pointed out that a delay of anything more than one fifth of a second is likely to be heard by viewers/listeners as significant.

But today there was an even longer delay of three seconds before they applauded after Vince Cable, deputy leader and Secretary State for Business in the coalition government, said this about the coalition government:

"we must make sure that it's good for the Liberal Democrats as well."

Evidence of weak support for the coalition by Lib Dem activists?

There are two reasons why this extended delay was potentially even more significant than the one in Clegg's speech:

1. It was not only the third "it's good for" in a row, but was announced as the final one in the list by the word "and ... "

2. It only attracted a pitiful four seconds of applause.

Audiences regularly applaud after the third item in a three-part list – and 4 seconds is only half the "normal" duration of 8±1 seconds for a burst of applause.

23rd September 2010

More lessons from Vince Cable's speech

A few weeks ago, I blogged, not for the first time, about the Business Secretary's speeches under the heading: If you can't remember Vince Cable's best lines, nor can he!

And there were some pretty good lines in yesterday's speech at the Lib Dem conference that both got the audience going and were picked up by the media.

Yesterday, I blogged about what struck me as the oddest moment in the speech, when the audience took three seconds to get their hands apart on being told that we must make sure that the coalition is good for the Liberal Democrats as well – echoing as it did an extended delay before the applause started at a similar point in Nick Clegg's conference speech.

Today, I've been intrigued by a few more potentially instructive details.

1. Applause for the 3rd item in a 4-part list

His opening reminded me of a speech from years ago by Neil Kinnock, who produced a sequence of five consecutive rhetorical questions – and the audience applauded after the third one.

> "I've come here today to account to you for the work I've been carrying out in the coalition government. I've managed to infuriate the bank bosses, I've acquired a fatwah from the revolutionary guards of the trade union movement, I've alarmed the *Daily Telegraph* with a progressive graduate payment, [applause builds] I've got. And I've upset some very rich people who were trying to dodge British taxes, I've concluded that [applause]..."

Here, Cable's script lists four of his achievements since coming to office – and the audience comes in after the third one. Notice also that he moves to "I've concluded that" immediately and with no gap after completing the fourth item, but that the audience interrupts his attempt to continue with another burst of applause – creating the (positive) impression that they're so enthusiastic that showing approval is more important than letting him continue to his concluding punch-line:

"I've concluded on the strength of that, that I must be doing something right."

2. Why did 'yah-boo' contrasts prompt delayed applause?

During the election, I blogged about how Vince Cable had shown that 'Yah-boo politics can win victories for the Lib Dems' during the TV Chancellors' Debate.

Although contrasts are among the most reliable ways of triggering applause, especially when used to construct an attack on opponents, there were at least two examples in yesterday's speech where they didn't work quite as well as they could have done.

In the first one, it may have been because the key word in the second part of the contrast – "hindsight" – wasn't delivered clearly enough. On first hearing, I thought he said "unsight" or "insight", and had to check the text of the speech to discover that it was actually "hindsight". If the audience in the hall had the same problem, it's hardly surprising that it took a while for the penny to drop.

In the next example, he's also attacking the Labour Party, but there's another two seconds pause between the end of the second part of the contrast ('plan A') and the applause getting under way.

As for why this delay happened, two factors may have played a part. One is that, after ending the first part of the contrast ('plan B') with rising intonation, it would have worked better if he'd used more decisively falling intonation to finish off the second part.

The second is that, when using a teleprompter, the eyes stay looking up in the air, implying that the speaker is going to carry on – and can create ambiguity in the minds of the audience as to whether or not he's finished. This was quite a problem for Mrs Thatcher when she abandoned hard copy on a lectern in favour of reading from an teleprompter (after which, her applause rate fell significantly).

All of which is to suggest that Mr Cable could move his performance up a notch or two with a bit more practice at reading from teleprompter screens.

6th October 2010

Delayed applause, poor speechwriting & delivery strike again in George Osborne's speech

This year's curious trend of party conference audiences delaying applause at points where you'd have expected an instant or early response was on show again in George Osborne's speech at the Conservative Party conference.

In the first example, they waited more than a second before showing their approval at being in government again after so long in opposition – and then failed to keep it going for the standard 8±1 seconds.

This looked less like the activists being less than enthusiastic in their response than a result of poor speech writing and poor delivery, aided and abetted by poor use of the teleprompter.

Poor speech writing

Having set up the puzzle of what's the good and bad news, Osborne started with the key point – "we are in government" – and left the negative thought of the country being on the brink of bankruptcy to the end:

"The good news is that we are in government after 13 years of a disastrous Labour administration that brought our country to the brink of bankruptcy."

Had he put the negative first and the positive second, the audience would have been ready to applaud as soon as he got to "we are in government" (and possibly even before that):

The good news is that, after 13 years of a disastrous Labour administration that brought our country to the brink of bankruptcy, we are in government.

Delivery and teleprompter troubles

There were also two indicators that he'd come to the end of the sentence missing. There was little in the way of emphatic downward intonation on the final syllables.

Add to that the fact that his eyes remained gazing up into the air rather than returning downwards to look at the script on the lectern, and the uncertainty about whether or not he'd finished was amplified.

Later on, when it came to one of his best lines, the same problems messed up a neat piece of imagery (that provided a solution to the puzzle about what they'll say at the next election) – greeted by another delay and a meagre 5 seconds of applause.

Practical implications

If you watch the whole speech (on my blog), you'll see numerous other examples of the same problems, which have two rather obvious implications:

1. For teachers and students, it's a useful resource for analysing how and why things can go wrong in speeches.

2. For George Osborne, his speech writers, speech coaches and anyone else trying to improve the performance of a client, it's a rich source of data on how and how not to speak effectively.

21st October 2010

Osborne takes a leaf out of Gordon Brown's bluffer's guide to budget speeches

If George Osborne's objective yesterday was to pack so much detail into his spending review statement and rattle through it so quickly that no one had time to take much of it in, it must be heralded as a great success: clearly he learnt a lot from having to listen to so many budget speeches by Gordon Brown.

Reading so quickly means that you can't help stumbling on a few words here and there, and makes it too much of a risk to look up from your script very often or for longer than a split second or two. So all Mr Osborne was able to manage were slight glances away about once every 34 words.

On the three occasions when David Cameron raised his right had to his mouth, I couldn't help wondering whether he was trying to hide or suppress a yawn. And there were a number of moments when it began to look as though Nick Clegg was about to nod off, if he hadn't already done so.

25 October 2010

Are BBC PowerPoint-style news reports going from bad to worse?

The increasing use of PowerPoint-style presentations by BBC Television News programmes is something that's been bothering me for quite a while.

We've known for years that there's much about the modern slide-dependent presentation that audiences detest (*Lend Me Your Ears*, 2004, Chapters 4-5). We know that it's wasting the UK economy billions of pounds a year. What I want to know now are the answers to four important questions:

1. Where did the BBC and its television news producers get the idea that it would be a good idea to stand their reporters next to screens a few yards away from the evening's news reader showing slides to the millions watching at home (many of whom will already have quite enough of being on the receiving end of slide-driven presentations during the working day).

2. Has the BBC done any research at all into what viewers think of such "presentations"?

3. If "yes", can we see the results, please?

4. If "no", why not?

Bigboard?

Last week, I learnt a new word from BBC *Newnight*'s economics editor Paul Mason, who made the following announcement on Twitter: "OK – am getting ready to go on *Newsnight* to do bigboard about the regressive impact of the SR2010 ... "

"Bigboard"? Or did he mean "Bigbored"? Is this the name of the all-singing-all-dancing graphics package that BBC presenters use in stead of PowerPoint, I wondered. So I tweeted Mr Mason to ask him, and he was gracious enough to tweet a reply: "No – there's no gfx package it is all done by our gfx artists from scratch."

But which comes first, the script or the graphics?

As there were only a few hours to go between his tweet and *Newsnight* going on air, this got me wondering whether he writes the script before the gfx artists go to work on it, or vice-versa? In any event, I thought, a Bigboard presentation sounded like something not to be missed.

There seemed to be a few "innovations" that I hadn't noticed before:

Innovation (1) A lectern

Whereas BBC reporters usually stand next to the screen during their slide shows, *Newsnight* has invested in an expensive looking circular lectern for the presenter to rest his hands on. Yes, there is a glass of water and some sheets of paper on it, but Mr Mason doesn't use either of them during his presentation and the sole purpose of the lectern is apparently to provide something for him to lean against.

Innovation (2) Camera angle zooms in from on high

As he starts replying to Gavin Esler's question, the camera cuts away to a different angle from somewhere up on the studio ceiling, before gradually zooming down towards him and the video clips that are starting to materialise on the screen behind him.

Innovation (3) Silent movies replace bullet points

In most BBC PowerPoint-style news presentations, the main focus is on bullet points that variously appear, disappear, whizz around the screen and/or explode before our very eyes.

What made this stand out as different was that 16 (yes, sixteen) silent film clips were crammed into the 45 seconds (at a rate of one every 2.8 seconds) it took for Mason to get to his first and only bullet-point slide in the sequence.

So what?

A major problem associated with bullet points (and other slides with nothing but writing on them) is that the audience's attention is split between (1) trying to read what's on the screen at the same time as (2) listening to and following what the speaker is saying and (3) looking repetitively from speaker to screen and back again.

All too often, there is the added distraction of trying to to work out what the connection is between what you're reading and what you're hearing (*Lend Me Your Ears*, Chapter 4), which is one reason why pictorial visual aids tend to be much more helpful to audiences than written ones (*Lend Me Your Ears*, Chapter 5).

Although BBC news producers and designers seem oblivious to the hazards of slide-dependent presentations, there are others elsewhere in the corporation who are perfectly well aware that slide-dependent presentations can make life difficult for audiences: otherwise, why would their website magazine section have asked me to write a short piece on *The problem with PowerPoint* to mark the software's 25th anniversary last year?

But pictorial material on its own is no guarantee of success and can sometimes be just as distracting as slides made up of words and sentences as, for example, when the visuals don't illustrate or exemplify a point that's being made. Above all, whatever it is that the speaker is showing to the audience should make it easier for them to understand the message.

How did these clips relate to the commentary?

The sixteen consecutive clips that appeared while Paul Mason was talking did none of these things, and I can't believe that I was the only viewer who found it distracting trying to work out what the connection was (if any) between what we were watching and the commentary – especially when his reference to Nick Clegg was suddenly followed (illustrated?) by film of Iain Duncan Smith:

1. Two people walking along a pavement

2. Iain Duncan Smith talking to someone on a street corner

3.   Children on a balcony

4.   Two people outside a building with litter in foreground

5.   Four young men looking out of a window

6.   Two people looking at a building

7.   Building in a sloping grass field

8.   Window with white tube hanging out of it

9.   One end of a building with road barrier in foreground

10. Empty balcony

11. Iain Duncan Smith meeting some people

12. Man at with a flip chart

13. Iain Duncan Smith at a table with two men

14. Different camera angle on Iain Duncan Smith and people at a table

15. Another camera angle on Iain Duncan Smith and people at a table

16. Deserted balcony gets blanked out by brightly coloured slide

If the minds of viewers start to focus on finding some sense or orderliness in the disjointed images they are watching (and how they relate to the words coming from the person they are supposed to be watching and listening to at the same time) there's a very high probability that the points being made by the speaker will pass them by.

This is exactly what happened to me when I saw this sequence for the first time – and a single viewing is, of course, all that the vast majority of viewers (other than the few of us with fingers on the "record" button) ever do get to see.

Glimmer of hope from IpsosMORI?

The concluding slide with the latest news from Britain's top polling company left me wondering why on earth the BBC doesn't commission IspsosMORI to do some independent research into what viewers actually think of this style of news presentation. While they were at it, they could also check on whether there's been any decline in audience ratings for news programmes since BBC journalists started reporting from slide screens at the other end of the studio.

The cost of such a project would surely be far less than the BBC's daily spending on the production of ever-more elaborate news-related graphics (not to mention expensive and pointless furnishings like designer lecterns).

At a time when the BBC is also having to prune its budget, here's a chance for them to save millions of pounds worth of licence fees a year – with the added bonus of making their news output easier to follow and less distracting than they are at present.

31st October 2010

You can fault Harman's "ginger" jibe, but you can't fault her rhetoric

Whatever you might have thought about hearing the politically correct Harriet Harman referring to Danny Alexander as a "ginger rodent", the offending sequence was a technically very effective example of how to use the Puzzle-Solution technique to trigger applause.

It's based on the very simple principle that, if you say something that gets the audience wondering what's coming next, they'll listen more attentively and, if it's a good "solution", they'll applaud it.

Combining two rhetorical techniques

It can work even better if you use the second part of another rhetorical technique – the contrast – to set up the puzzle.

And that's what happened in this case: the first part of the contrast refers to something they all love – the red squirrel – and the second part contrasts it with something (yet to be named) that they never want to see again.

Setting it up in this way enables the audience to anticipate where it's going early enough to start clapping when she's only half-way through the puzzle – so that she has to deliver the solution against a rising tide of applause:

[A] Many of us in the Labour Party are conservationists and we all love the red squirrel.

[B] Puzzle: But there is one ginger rodent that we never want to see again in the Highlands:

Solution: Danny Alexander.

Or a contrast can provide the solution to a puzzle:

An alternative way of combining these rhetorical techniques is to pose a puzzle and then solve it with a contrast, as in this example from Margaret Thatcher at the start of the 1987 general election:

Puzzle: From the Labour Party expect the iceberg manifesto.

Solution:
[A] One tenth of its socialism visible.
[B] Nine tenths beneath the surface.

18th November 2010

0% of viewers remember all the points made in a BBC PowerPoint-style news presentation

Last night, I discovered that after dinner speeches don't always take place after dinner. I'd been invited to talk about PowerPoint to the Council of the Management Consultancies Association between the starter and the main course, with a Q-A session scheduled to take place after the diners had finished eating their main courses.

As after-dinner speeches are normally expected to be vaguely entertaining, it was a chance to combine a bit of amusement with some opportunistic research into

Seen & Heard

something that, as regular blog readers know, is one of my recurring obsessions – namely the increasing use of PowerPoint-style presentations during British television news programmes.

So I ended my talk with a clip from a BBC Television News broadcast on the financial crisis, in which business editor Robert Peston gives us a 36 second presentation from the other side of the studio.

Research design

The diners were given no advance warning that, about half-way through the main course, they would be issued with a short quiz aimed at testing their retention of Peston's words of wisdom.

MCA Council Dinner Quiz

1. How much is the rescue deal going to cost the government?
2. How much is that as a proportion of GDP?
3. How much a year will it cost each tax-payer?
4. How does Peston describe the recovery in bankers' willingness to lend?
5. What reason does he give for that?

Rules

1. No conferring.
2. To be completed before the end of the main course.
3. In the event of a tie, the result will be decided by the judge.

Results

As there was only one prize (a signed copy of *Lend Me Your Ears*), I had to allow for the possibility that everyone might score 100% – which I did by preparing a few tie-breaker questions.

It came as something of a surprise, even to me, that none of the 40 or so participants was able to answer all 5 questions correctly.

Only three of them (7.5%) managed to answer 4/5 correctly – so it didn't take long for the tie-breaker questions to produce a winner.

So what?

I wouldn't want to give too much weight to a research design that was intended partly as entertainment and partly to illustrate one of the themes of my talk. But I do think it's interesting that 92.5% of an audience of highly educated professionals – with far more experience of watching PowerPoint presentations than most ordinary viewers of BBC Television News programmes – were only able to remember three (or fewer than three) of the main points in Peston's report/presentation.

19th November 2010

Was the royal engagement interviewer more nervous than his interviewees?

It was quite a coup for Tom Bradby, ITN's political editor, to be favoured by Prince William and Kate Middleton for the first interview after the announcement of their engagement.

The couple also did viewers a favour by sparing us from having to watch either of the Dimbleby brothers, let alone rival BBC or *Sky News* political editors, Nick Robinson or Adam Boulton, doing the job.

Who was the most nervous of them all?

But I was surprised to see various interviews with Mr Bradby about his encounter with them, in which he told us how nervous the couple had been during the interview – because there were a number of places where he seemed more nervous than either of his interviewees.

This was especially evident in the way he giggled as he put some of the more "delicate" questions.

Take, for example this one about whether they plan to have lots of children – to which Prince William's response is rather more assured than Bradby's question.

More giggles, a few pauses and hesitations came from Mr Bradby when he asked Miss Middleton about what it had been like meeting the Queen for the first time – to which her reply is rather more fluent than his question.

These are only two examples of something evident in quite a number of Mr Bradby's questions during the interview and on which I've blogged about before, namely what conversation analysts call "pre-delicate hitches".

Taken together, they gave the impression that he was much more nervous and less confident than he usually is when interviewing politicians.

20th November 2010

Prince Charles knew that what he said about Camilla becoming Queen was extremely delicate

Yesterday, I blogged about how the pre-delicate hitches in some of the questions put to Prince William and Kate Middleton by ITN's Tom Bradby could be heard as indicating that he was rather more nervous than his interviewees.

Little did I expect that more pre-delicate hitches from Prince Charles were about to feature in a big news story on both sides of the Atlantic.

Newspapers don't often print detailed transcripts of what someone said in an interview. But several of the reports of the way Prince Charles answered the much publicised question from NBC's Brian Williams – about whether Camilla would ever become Queen – provided rather more detail than usual, accompanied as they were by dots along with comments to the effect that he'd been "hesitant" or "caught off guard".

Daily Telegraph

> Asked by NBC's Brian Williams if the Duchess would become queen, the
> Prince, who seemed taken aback by the question, said: "That's, well…we'll
> see, won't we? That could be."

Although aides insisted the Prince had been caught off guard and there had been "no change" in the official position, the comment will be seen by many as an indication of his inner thoughts.

Daily Mirror

In a shift from previous statements, the Prince of Wales did not contradict an American interviewer who asked: "Does the Duchess of Cornwall become Queen of England, if and when you become the monarch?" Until now, the official position has been that the Duchess of Cornwall would have the title Princess Consort.
Hesitating, the prince replied: "That's well ... we'll see won't we? That could be."

The Guardian

During an interview with the American network NBC, due to be aired tomorrow, Charles did not correct the presenter of NBC's Dateline programme, Brian Williams, when he asked: "Does the Duchess of Cornwall become Queen of England, if and when you become the monarch?" The prince hesitated, then replied: "That's well ... we'll see won't we? That could be."

More hitches than a few dots

If you watch the video clip, you'll see the dots used in these news reports hardly do justice to the extraordinary number of pre-delicate hitches – i.e. at least eleven of them – that led up to his most widely reported sentence: "that could be":

"Wehh -uhhh-that's-umm that's (1 second pause) well (0.5 second pause) let's see won't we. But-uhh (1 second in-breath) Ummm (0.5 second pause) that (0.5 second pause) could be."

Hardly surprising, then, that his hesitancy featured in news reports. But one interesting question is whether "the comment will be seen by many as an indication of his inner thoughts" (*Daily Telegraph*), or whether it became headline news because of the way he led up to and made the comment – as is implied by the inclusion of dots in the rather inadequate media transcripts.

Whatever the answer, research in conversation analysis suggests that Prince Charles was displaying an awareness that he knew perfectly well that he was about to say something that would be heard by others as very delicate indeed.

22nd November 2010

Thanks to Margaret Thatcher, 20 years on from her resignation ...

When I was doing the research that led to my first book on public speaking (*Our Masters' Voices*, 1984) Margaret Thatcher was the leading British politician of the day and provided me with much of the data analysed in the book – for which I was and still am extremely grateful.

Later on, when I was writing speeches for former Lib Dem leader Paddy Ashdown, she provided much raw material for lines that were more or less guaranteed to get rapturous applause.

But those were only two of my debts to her. Another was that I've often summed up my professional life by saying that it came about as a result of being both a victim and a beneficiary of Thatcherism.

Victim of Thatcherism

This was because of the appalling damage her governments inflicted on higher education and research in the UK, not to mention what they did to my standard of living or the two years of insecurity that came to a head in 1981 – when her Education Secretary Sir Keith Joseph commissioned Lord Rothschild to investigate my then employer (the Social Science Research Council) with a view to making a case for closing it down.

Luckily, he didn't oblige, concluding that it would be a "gross act of intellectual vandalism" to do so. The compromise accepted by Thatcher and Joseph was to delete the word "science" and elevate the importance of their favoured discipline with a new name: the Economic and Social Research Council.

Beneficiary of Thatcherism

A few years later, the benefit from Thatcherism came when Nigel Lawson's budget of 1988 reduced the top rate of income tax to 40%. That was the moment when and the reason why I decided to risk leaving the groves of academia to become a self-employed consultant and author.

To that extent, I can claim to be living proof that the official economic case for Thatcher-Reagan tax reductions, namely that they would unleash entrepreneurial zeal, worked in at least one case.

The cricketing simile that put an end to her innings

To mark the twentieth anniversary of Margaret Thatcher resignation as prime minister, I have taken another look at the speech that fired the starting gun for what turned out to be a rather quick sprint to the end – coming as it did only 21 days later.

In his speech on resigning as Deputy Prime Minister, Sir Geoffrey Howe, who wasn't renowned as a brilliant speaker, deployed a vivid cricketing simile to describe what it had been like working with Mrs Thatcher.

> "It's rather like sending your opening batsmen to the crease, only for them to find, the moment the first balls are bowled, that their bats have been broken before the game by the team captain."

The speech ended with a fairly explicit invitation to other discontented colleagues to stand against her for the leadership:

> "The time has come for others to consider their own response to the tragic conflict of loyalties with which I have myself wrestled for perhaps too long."

Three weeks later, she resigned.

There was a rumour at the time that this particular sequence was actually written by Sir Geoffrey Howe's wife – a claim that, so far, I've never managed to verify

25th November 2010

Sarah Palin's North Korean slip of the tongue: what we heard and what we'll make of it

Sarah Palin: "We gotta stand with our North Korean allies"

For American politicians, talking about North Korea seems to be a bit of a minefield.

When Hillary Clinton threatened North Korea with "consequences" for its misconduct, she prefaced her dire warning with a large number of pre-delicate hitches.

Now we have Sarah Palin telling us that she wants to "stand by our North Korean allies".

As she's also trying to convince her fellow Americans that she's a credible presidential candidate, it's hardly surprising that her gaffe was not only noticed, but has also become a big news story around the world.

But however much her opponents may be hoping that it will damage her reputation, the most likely explanation of it is that it was a rather common type of "slip of the tongue" – i.e. what the late Gail Jefferson, one of the founders of conversation analysis, described as a "category-formed" error.

Sound-formed errors

Two years ago, a similar gaffe from Gordon Brown attracted widespread media attention when he claimed to have saved the world.

However, as I pointed out at the time, there were four "w" sounds in the sentence that ended with "world", which he quickly corrected to "banks". In other words, it looked like a fairly typical example of what Jefferson had described as a "sound-formed" error, namely one that was triggered by a repeated sound in the words spoken just before the wrong one came out.

Category-formed errors

A similar type of conversational "error" described by Jefferson was what she called the category-formed error. This is when the word that comes out means something that's related to the one intended – a common example of which involves selecting a word that means the exact opposite of what we meant, e.g. right instead of left, hot instead of cold, black instead of white, etc.

Viewed in these terms, Palin's use of North for South therefore sounded like a fairly typical example of a category-formed error.

Freudian slips or slips of the tongue?

The trouble is, of course, that media commentators (and other experts) love to find deeper meaning in such errors, regardless of how they were formed. As Jefferson pointed out in her original paper, many alleged Freudian slips turn out to be sound-formed or category-formed errors.

But, as I discovered when doing a radio interview on Gordon Brown's "saving the world" gaffe, the media isn't very interested in a such mundane explanation of slips of the tongue when there are alternative that are "deeper", more sensational or more damaging.

Once it's out, it's anyone's

In case opponents of Mrs Palin think that I'm trying to offer her a neat way of getting off this particular hook, I should mention that there is also some encouraging news for them from one of the other founders of conversation analysis, the late Harvey Sacks – who used to say about talk: "Once it's out, it's anyone's".

He didn't just mean that you can't "un-say" words after they've already been said, but that they're available for anyone to analyse and interpret in whatever way they like. And that is precisely what the media is doing in this particular case.

27th November 2010

Ed's weekend Miliramblings

Yesterday, I was struck by a line in an interview with Ed Miliband by Nicky Campbell on Radio 5 live, in which he said something that seemed a bit short in the precise and decisive departments:

> "I think I can fairly sort of certainly say to you now, Nicky, that's unlikely to be the biggest priority for the country."

Part of that interview was trailing the speech he was going to make today at Labour's National Policy Forum. So stand by, I thought, for a bit more precision and clarity in his first major speech since paternity leave.

Just after Mr Miliband had started speaking, I noticed that *Sky News* reporter Alistair Bunkall (@AliBunkall) had suddenly got busy on Twitter whilst listening to the speech – with a series of tweets that included the following:

- Miliband speaking without notes. Multiple accusations that govt is arrogant.

- Miliband. There are 5 things we (Labour) need to do.

- 1. "Need to reconnect. Talk to people" Must be one of the most over-used phrases.

- 2. Need to give a voice to Labour Party members. Will help create better policy.

- Finally a spot of clapping. Thought the audience might have dropped off..

- Sorry, lost track, I can't count. Apparently must-do number 2 is the need to change the economy.

- Miliband: "We have to under-promise and over-deliver." Is that a subtle address to the criticisms of lack of substance?

- Miliband jokes about Cameron going 2 arctic with huskies early in his leadership. But it got Cameron headlines & Miliband needs some of that.

- Summary: Miliband wants Lab Party to reform and focus on economy, climate change and liberties. Party must hold conversation with voters.

I was intrigued that a professional television news reporter was losing track of the five-part structure Miliband had announced and didn't include all of them in his summary. Maybe the structure would be easier when reading rather than listening – so I turned to the transcript.

Clearer for readers than listeners?

But the written version also seemed to be a bit lacking in the precision department – and actually sounds, at least to this reader, rather rambling and incoherent as you're reading through it. Keeping track of the five-part structure announced at the start is quite hard work and involves having to re-read some of the segments to check whether he's on to a new point or still on the previous one.

As you'll see from the following outline of the structure as it unfolds, things really start to go astray after the 4th one starts with a "But". And is the "one other thing" the fifth or an extra one that he's added to the fifth?

"So I want to talk to you about the five things that I think we need to do ...

"First of all we have to be a party rooted in people's lives ...

"Secondly we have to change our economy and we have to understand how we need to change our economy ...

"Thirdly we need to change our approach not just to markets, but to government as well ...

"But fourth we also need to think about not just the relationship of the individual to the market and the relationship of the individual to government but also the thing that probably matters most to all of us in this room, the relationships between individuals ...

"There's, one other thing which is the way we do our politics ...

(Miliband's summary of the 5 points)

"We've got to change in terms of the way we are rooted in people's lives, and you are essential to making that happen. We have to change in the way we think about our economy, the way we think about government, the way we think about community and indeed in the way we think about politics too."

Two tips for Mr Miliband

1.   Stop trying to copy the walkabout "script-free" style of speaking that played such an important part in David Cameron's surprise victory in the Tory leadership beauty parade. The PM is pretty good at it, but most politicians are not.

2.   Do some homework on how to structure a speech so that your audience will find it easy to follow, on which Chapter 9 of my book *Lend Me Your Ears*: *All You Need to Know about Making Speeches and Presentations* might be as good (and cheap) a place to start as any.

1st December 2010

Child of Thatcher or son of Brown: the power of contrast strikes again

After Wikileaks had revealed that William Hague had described himself and other top Tories as "children of Thatcher", it had been widely expected that Labour leader Ed Miliband would mention it during today's Prime Minister's Question Time.

Less expected, perhaps, was that David Cameron had not only anticipated it too, but had also come ready with a neat contrast up his sleeve in case it came up.

And so it was that the PM's "I'd rather be a child of Thatcher than son of Brown" was instantly picked up in the TV studios, made mass appearances on Twitter and will no doubt be the only line that get's quoted or remembered from today's proceedings in the House of Commons.

For students of rhetoric, it was sheer delight to see the power of the contrast striking yet again.

You can find out more about the different types of contrast and how to use them in *Lend Me Your Ears* (especially pp.182-190). Or you can see a variety of video clips, transcripts and discussion in the selection below.

Shades of Nye Bevan and Oscar Wilde?

Cameron's performance today reminded me of a couple of stories about Aneurin Bevan and Oscar Wilde that are relevant to anyone who wants to excel as an ex tempore speaker.

Renowned as a brilliant parliamentary speaker, Bevan apparently didn't leave everything to chance. His preparations for speaking in debates apparently included anticipating the most likely Tory heckles and composing witty ripostes, just in case they happened.

I also heard it said of Oscar Wilde, originator of so many famous quotations, that he would go to parties equipped with a list of witticisms in his pocket that he could trot out if the opportunity arose.

Whether or not either of these is true, I don't know, but they do point to a practical tip that David Cameron already seems to be putting to good use.

11 December 2010

Naughtie's gaffe: "C", "K" & "U" sounds or "Freudian slippage"?

I've been a bit late catching up on news of James Naughtie's "slip of the tongue"on BBC Radio 4's *Today* programme last week because I was away on holiday when it happened.

But I did hear about it and started wondering, as I did on hearing of Gordon Brown's claim to have "saved the world", whether it would turn out to be yet another case of an "error" being triggered by sounds of nearby words.

Now I've been able to listen to it, I can report that this is exactly what appears to have happened. As you can see from the transcript and hear in the audio-clip below, the hard "c" or "k" sound came just before and twice in quick succession immediately after the dreaded "slip" – and, when a speaker is reading, he can see sounds and rhymes coming up before he's actually read out some of the earlier words (including the "u" sound that also comes both before and after the error):

"First up after the news we're going to be talking to Jeremy Kunt-Hunt the culture secretary about broadband ..."

As such, it was a fairly ordinary example of what the late Gail Jefferson described as a sound-formed error (as too was Gordon Brown's "saving the world" gaffe).

But, as I noted of Sarah Palin's recent North Korean slip of the tongue – an example of the related category-formed error – "The trouble is ... that media commentators (and other experts) love to find deeper meaning in such errors, regardless of how they were formed. As Jefferson pointed out in her original paper, many alleged 'Freudian slips' turn out to be 'sound-formed' or 'category-formed' errors."

And on Radio 4 last Monday, it hardly took an hour for just such an expert to pop up in the very next programme, Andrew Marr's *Start the Week* – where one of the guests, David Aaronovich of *The Times*, was there to plug a series of programmes he'd made on ... er... Freudian Slippage:

"C" , "K", "U" – or "Freudian slippage"?

Although I've always been mystified by the extraordinary intellectual influence of a theory as thin on empirical backing as Freud's (unless it really is just that id, ego and superego amount to a particularly impressive example of the persuasive power of three-part lists), there's one thing about all the reports I've read about Mr Naughtie's gaffe that makes me wonder whether there might be more to all that sexual gobbledygook than I'd thought.

After all, everything I've seen about the story in the media refers to the four-letter word in question as C*** and not, as I did in my transcript above, as Kunt.

Could this, I wonder, along with the coughing and sniggering to be heard in the two audio clips, be firmer evidence of "Freudian slippage" than anything said by Mr Naughtie last Monday morning?

What made Brian Hanrahan's famous contrast so memorable?

"I counted them all out and I counted them all back."

There's hardly a media report today on death of distinguished BBC journalist Brian Hanrahan that doesn't refer to his famous line from the aircraft carrier *HMS Hermes* during the Falkland's war in 1982.

Not only did he use repetition and contrast, but he followed it up with a list of three adjectives to describe the mood of the pilots, who were "unhurt, cheerful and jubilant."

There's interesting report in today's *Guardian*, which includes the following:

> "He used that form of words to get round military censorship of media reports – and it became the title of his book about the conflict, co-written with fellow correspondent Robert Fox ...

> "He was on the aircraft carrier *HMS Hermes* during the Falklands war when the first air strikes started taking place on Port Stanley in May 1982. Naval officials placed severe restrictions on what he could report, particularly in respect of the numbers of sorties flown by the Harrier jets.

> "Fox told the BBC today that in order to get round the restrictions, Hanrahan colluded with the 'raffish Old Etonian intelligence officer' Rupert Nichol, who told him that they had both seen the same number of planes going in and coming back, and 'that was the way he should go'. Hanrahan turned the idea into the line he used on his broadcast.'

Why so memorable?

Hanrahan's contrast had already become memorable by the time I was writing a chapter on the way in which rhetorically formatted statements are likely to get noticed and quoted (Ch. 5: 'Quotability') for my book *Our Masters' Voices*, which came out two years later.

Seen & Heard

And the question of what makes a particular speech, or a particular line from a speech, memorable is one that has fascinated me ever since. In a post a couple of years ago, I ventured the suggestion that it helps if it strikes the right chord with the right audience in the right place at the right time – all of which are arguably true of this line from Hanrahan.

In another post, I noted that memorable lines, such as the most famous one from John F. Kennedy's inaugural speech, aren't always recognised as "memorable" straight away.

Indirectness v. Directness

I still think, however, that part of the answer to why rhetorically formatted lines are so effective at grabbing the attention of audiences is that they tend to be less direct ways of saying things that, if said directly, would hardly have been noticed.

Consider, for example, whether Hanrahan's line have been so widely reported and remembered if he'd selected a more direct way of reporting the same thing, such as "All the planes returned safely"?

I very much doubt it, just as I doubt whether anyone would have noticed if Margaret Thatcher had said "No one is going to make me change my economic policies" rather than her most memorable contrast "You turn if you want to. The lady's not for turning."

The idea that indirectness works better than directness is consistent with other research into conversation, which suggests that, in many and perhaps most contexts, there is a preference for saying things indirectly rather than directly.

As I said of these examples from Hanrahan and Thatcher in *Our Masters' Voices* (pp. 162.163): "these more direct modes of communication leave nothing whatsoever to the imagination and little or no effort is required to be able to see the point" – and of the less direct options "... to identify and appreciate the point being made, people have to put their brains to work. The increased mental effort involved in decoding interlocking contrasts and lists may increase the chances that particular message will remain in listeners' minds ..."

Miliband does well with instant rebuttal + 3 things that Alan Johnson does know

I didn't see the whole of Ed Miliband's press conference this morning, but did see quite a lot of comments on Twitter suggesting that he did better in the Q-A session after his formal statement than in the statement itself.

As I'd already questioned his effectiveness in "face-to-camera" pieces a few days ago, I was intrigued enough to see whether any of the news channels had posted anything from the Q-A session yet. The BBC instantly obliged with a short clip, that is indeed rather interesting.

Seen & Heard

Welcoming smiles from Ed Miliband?

When Joey Jones from *Sky News* refers to Shadow Chancellor Alan Johnson's weekend gaffe, Mr Miliband grins. Not so much "nervous" grins, I suggest, as an "I know what you're talking about, I'm a good sport with a sense of humour, I expected that and what's more I've got a prepared answer up my sleeve" sort of grin. And that's what he had: an instant rebuttal contrasting Johnson favourably with Chancellor Osborne, explained by three things about the economy that the former does know about.

Instant rebuttal as a useful weapon for interviewees

In conversation, answering "No" to a question that's looking for a "Yes" – instantly and without any delay, "ums", "ers" or other particles indicating that a "dispreferred" answer is on its way – doesn't happen very often.

But it really comes into its own when you want to ensure time to give reasons why you are disagreeing so immediately. As soon as you've done it, the floor is still yours for a while, as your questioner will expect and wait for you to explain why you don't agree before he/she speaks again.

If you then package your message as a contrast between Chancellor and Shadow-chancellor and explain it with a brief list of three things that the latter does know, you're likely to come across as decisive, articulate and confident. It might even persuade or convince some of your listeners that you're right.

A promising day for Miliband

On the basis of this specimen, at least, I can see why the Twitterati thought that Miliband did better in the Q-A session than in the statement that preceded it. More generally, it may be evidence that he and his communication team are beginning to get the hang of things.

19th January 2011

50 years since John F Kennedy asked not ... Which lines were noticed on the day?

This post is one of a series (the first of which you can find on my blog) marking the 50th anniversary, on 20th January 2011, of President John F. Kennedy's inaugural speech.

My first book on public speaking described the main rhetorical techniques that trigger applause in political speeches (*Our Masters' Voices*, 1984), the story of which can be found in the *Claptrap* series.

Quotability

It included a chapter on "Quotability", which looked at how the lines that get applauded are much more likely to be noticed and reported in the media that those that don't – and that a tiny minority of these are remembered long enough to end up in dictionaries of quotations.

Given the central role of Barack Obama's oratory as he emerged from nowhere via the DNC in 2004 through an inspiring election campaign to become US president, I was intrigued to see various commentators complaining that his inaugural speech wasn't up to his usual standard. For one thing, the critics said, it was a bit short on memorable quotes compared with JKF's masterful effort back in 1961.

This intrigued me enough to check back on the front pages of two leading American newspapers, the *New York Times* and the *Washington Post* to see which lines from Kennedy's inaugural speech had been quoted on their front pages the following day (21 January 1961).

To my surprise, the answer was none of them, even though quite a few of Kennedy's inaugural lines lines not only made it into dictionaries of quotations, but will be aired again this week as the media get into the swing of commemorating the speech's 50th anniversary.

The audience got it right

But if you look at the lines that were applauded by the audience who where actually there on the day, you'll see that they did a rather better job than some of the media when it came to spotting the lines that were eventually to become "memorable".

Those in Washington that day were sufficiently moved by eleven of the things Kennedy said to react with a positive physical response (applause). And, I predict, you'll certainly have seen many or most of them before – in which case, it supports the point made about the connection between clapping and quotability in *Our Master's Voices*.

The power of contrasts

Given the emphasis in my teaching and writing on the effectiveness of different types of contrast in the armoury of rhetorical techniques, an added bonus for me is that contrasts featured in about half of the examples that were applauded – including some of the most famous quotations of all.

Where did the tiger come from?

In the midst of Kennedy's flourishes of imagery in some of these lines, there's one that still puzzles me. The audience would presumably not have applauded if they hadn't both understood and approved of what he meant when he said "those who foolishly sought power by riding the back of the tiger ended up inside."

But to my British ears, it's always struck me as the oddest metaphor in the speech and my attempts to find out where it came from have so far been unsuccessful. If any readers can enlighten me, it would be great to hear from you.

P.S. More on the tiger

Thanks to the reader who replied with this email:

"I think Kennedy was alluding to Churchill's remark: 'the dictators ride to and fro on tigers they dare not dismount and the tigers are getting hungry.' I wish I could find out when and where he said it. I wonder if it was a speech in the USA."

20th January 2011

50 years since John F Kennedy asked not ... modelled for the media

Now that the BBC website has gone live with an article and notes I wrote on the speech, I feel free to reproduce one of the points made in it.

The following section from the piece on the BBC website commends Kennedy for following "the first rule of speech-preparation: analyse your audience".

If you wonder where that came from, I have to confess that that I was immodest enough to have taken it from my own books *Lend Me Your Ears* (pp. 280-286) and *Speech-making and Presentation Made Easy* (pp. 34-37).

First inaugural designed for the media?

Impressive though the rhetoric and imagery may have been, what really made the speech memorable was that it was the first inaugural address by a US president to follow the first rule of speech-preparation: analyse your audience – or, to be more precise at a time when mass access to television was in its infancy, analyse your audiences.

In the most famous fictional speech of all time, Mark Antony had shown sensitivity to his different audiences in Shakespeare's Julius Caesar by asking his "Friends, Romans, countrymen" to lend him their ears. But Kennedy had many more audiences in mind than those who happened to be in Washington that day.

His countrymen certainly weren't left out, appearing as they did in the opening and towards the end with his most famous contrast of all: "Ask not ... " But he knew, perhaps better than any previous US president, that local Americans were no longer the only audience that mattered. The age of a truly global mass media had dawned, which meant that what he said would be seen, heard or reported everywhere in the world.

At the height of the Cold War, Kennedy also had a foreign policy agenda that he wanted to be heard everywhere in the world. So the different segments of the speech were specifically targeted at a series of different audiences:

"Let every nation know, whether it wishes us well or ill"

"To those new nations whom we welcome to the ranks of the free"

"To those in the huts and villages of half the globe"

"To our sister republics south of the border"

"To that world assembly of sovereign states, the United Nations"

"Finally, to those nations who would make themselves our adversary"

The following day, there was nothing on the front pages of two leading US newspapers, *The New York Times* and the *Washington Post* to suggest that the countrymen in his audience had been particularly impressed by the speech – neither of them referred to any of the lines above that have become so famous.

The fact that so much of the speech is still remembered around the world 50 years later is a measure of Kennedy's success in knowing exactly **what** he wanted to say, **how** best to say it and, perhaps most important of all, **to whom** he should say it.

More on JFK's target audiences

In fact, Kennedy aimed his speech at twice as many audiences as those mentioned in the above extract from the BBC website. You can listen to edited clips in the video at the top of the page on the blog.

VIPs on the platform & US citizens

Vice-president Johnson, Mr Speaker, Mr Chief Justice, President Eisenhower, Vice-president Nixon, President Truman, Reverend clergy, fellow citizens…

Everyone in the world

Let the word go forth from this time and place, to friend and foe alike, that the torch has been passed to a new generation of Americans…

Let every nation know, whether it wishes us well or ill …

Allies

To those old allies whose cultural and spiritual origins we share …

Emerging nations

To those new states whom we welcome to the ranks of the free ...

Third world

To those people in the huts and villages of half the globe struggling to break the bonds of mass misery ...

Latin America

To our sister republics south of our border ...

North & South America

Let all our neighbors know ...

United Nations

To that world assembly of sovereign states, the United Nations ...

Communist countries

Finally, to those nations who would make themselves our adversary ...

US citizens

And so, my fellow Americans ...

Citizens outside the USA

My fellow citizens of the world ...

US + Non-US citizens of the world

Finally, whether you are citizens of America or citizens of the world ...

Postscript: Kennedy's fashion legacy

Apart from putting much effort into what he wanted to say to whom, JFK also put quite a bit of thought into what the inaugural would look like in the global media. Jackie Kennedy's white coat was deliberately selected to ensure that she would stand out on a platform mainly populated by men in dark clothes.

And, the heavy snow in Washington the day before didn't prevent him from appearing without an overcoat or a hat. The former was made possible by his decision to wear thermal underwear – which presumably kept him warm enough not to bother wearing a hat.

This may have been all very well for him, but his hat-free head kicked off a new era for men in the Western world, in which routine hat wearing went out of fashion – look at any picture of a football crowd before 1961, and you'll see that the men all wore hats or caps. As a result, half the population has been condemned to being colder in winter than we'd have been without Kennedy's fashion legacy.

So, however much I may admire his rhetoric, I am definitely *not* an admirer of his lack of headwear.

2nd February 2011

More three-part lists and a touch of management speak from Obama on Egypt

From his five minute speech yesterday, it was yet another three-part list that was singled out from President Obama's statement about Egypt to become the most widely quoted line in the news headlines:

> "An orderly transition must be meaningful, it must be peaceful and it must begin now."

I say "yet another" because I've commented before on Obama's frequent use of three-part lists, of which there were 29 in his ten minute victory speech in Chicago.

And yesterday's headline was only one of six such lists in his five-minute statement, the others being:

1. "Over the past few days, the American people have watched the situation unfolding in Egypt."
2. "We've seen enormous demonstrations by the Egyptian people."
3. "We've borne witness to the beginning of a new chapter in the history of a great country, and a long-time partner of the United States."

"And throughout this period, we've stood for a set of core principles.

1. "First, we oppose violence ...
2. "Second, we stand for universal values ...
3. "Third, we have spoken out on behalf of the need for change ... "

1. "Furthermore, the process must include a broad spectrum of Egyptian voices and opposition parties.
2. "It should lead to elections that are free and fair.
3. "And it should result in a government that's not only grounded in democratic principles, but is also responsive to the aspirations of the Egyptian people."

"I want to be clear:

1. "We hear your voices.
2. "I have an unyielding belief that you will determine your own destiny and seize the promise of a better future for your children and your grandchildren.
3. "And I say that as someone who is committed to a partnership between the United States and Egypt."

1. "That truth can be seen in the sense of community in the streets.
2. "It can be seen in the mothers and fathers embracing soldiers.
3. "And it can be seen in the Egyptians who linked arms to protect the national museum."

Management-speak?

However smooth the rhetoric written into this hastily prepared statement (produced, as it was, very soon after Mubarak's speech in Cairo) might have been, I was surprised to hear the inclusion of a participle that's been featuring more and more in management presentations over the past few years, namely the use of "going forward" when speakers are talking about the future:

"And going forward, I urge the military to continue its efforts to help ensure that this time of change is peaceful."

"And going forward, the United States will continue to stand up for democracy and the universal rights that all human beings deserve, in Egypt and around the world."

Personally, I find it almost as irritating and distracting as the growing preference for using "ahead of" when the speaker or writer (journalists being the worst offenders) actually means "before"- and I recommend people on my courses to avoid using either of them.

Unless President Obama really does want to sound like an MBA graduate who's just swallowed a dictionary of management jargon, I think it's time he had a word with his speechwriters. And, while he's at it, he might like to remind them that one "furthermore" in a speech is one too many.

2nd February 2011

You don't need to speak Arabic to tell that Mubarak isn't much of an orator

I'm grateful to Martin Shovel for asking me via Twitter (@MartinShovel) earlier today: "Where's your much anticipated rhetorical analysis of Mubarak's latest speech?"

The short answer is that there are some things for which I lack the time or inclination (or both).

But Martin's question did take me back to something I blogged about last July, when Fidel Castro had just given his first TV interview since his "retirement." That had reminded me of a rather obvious point I'd made in a heading above a picture of the young Castro in my book *Our Masters' Voices* (1984, p.4):

> "Skillful public speaking can be readily recognized even in those whose politics we may disagree with, and whose languages we do not understand."

What fascinated me then – and still does – is the fact that we don't have to be able to understand Spanish or German to be able to recognise that Castro and Hitler were highly effective orators.

The opposite is also the case: you don't have to be able to understand Arabic to be able to tell at a glance that Egyptian President Mubarak is a long way from the Premier League when it comes to public speaking.

The rise of the ineffective orator

Much the same can be said of other second and third generation revolutionary leaders. Compared with Nelson Mandela, Thabo Mbeki was a bit short in the communication skills department. So too were Stalin, Khrushchev and Brezhnev in comparison with Lenin (and I don't speak Russian, either).

The point is that, once a new order is established, behind the scenes committee work, plotting, befriending the right people, bumping off or otherwise disposing of rivals, winning support of the right factions and organisations, etc. become far more important than being able to appeal to a mass audience of people whose votes will determine your rise or fall.

Nor, if you can get to the top job – like so many leaders of Arab nations outside Egypt – by being the favoured relation of the previous head of a ruling family, do you have to worry about anything so tiresome as being able to move, persuade and inspire mass audiences.

Although I've no idea how effective an orator President Nasser, the first leader of the new Egypt, was, I'll bet he was a good deal better at it than his ousted predecessor (King Farouk).

Aprés Mubarak?

It now looks as though Hosni Mubarak's plan to take a leaf out of the Assad family book in Syria – by handing over to his son – is about to be thwarted. So, if Gamal Mubarak is still hoping to see his father's dream come true, he may well be in the market for some professional coaching.

Martin Shovel – and other likely UK suppliers of such services – may like to note that, according to *The Sun*, Gamal and his family have already decamped to his modest little £8.5 million pad in Knightsbridge. For his phone number and other contact details, I'm sure that the Murdoch family and/or News International will be able to oblige ...

9th February 2011

In praise of parliamentary rowdiness

Following today's Prime Minister's Question Time, Patrick O'Flynn, chief political commentator at the the *Daily Express*, made an interesting point on Twitter about the Speaker's attempts to deter MPs from booing, heckling and cheering so vigorously (via @oflynnexpress):

> "Bercow overdoing the 'calm down' stuff on PMQs. Many of us think ideas must be aggressively scrutinised and don't hate the rumpus."

I don't hate the rumpus either – but for rather more technical reasons that have to do with providing incentives for our representatives to pay attention to what each other is saying during parliamentary proceedings.

Rowdiness and the debate about broadcasting parliament

My research into speaker-audience interaction started fairly soon after broadcasts from the House of Commons first began (radio only) in 1975. In the debates leading up to it, I remember being amused and baffled by arguments from the opponents along the lines that it shouldn't be allowed because the rowdy behaviour of MPs would set a bad example to the young.

My interest in audience responses to different forms of public speaking had already reached the point of realising that the central problem for listeners to speeches was that the primary incentive for paying attention in conversation (i.e. the threat that you might have to start speaking any second now) is massively eroded for audiences: once you know that you won't get a chance to speak for the next 10 or 20 minutes, staying awake can become a serious problem.

As I've written elsewhere: "The reason why applause in political speeches seemed a promising place to start was because it provides instant and unambiguous evidence that listeners are (a) awake and paying close attention and (b) approve strongly enough of what's just been said to show their approval of it (by clapping hands, cheering, etc.)."

Rowdiness as a powerful incentive to pay attention

In *Lend Me Your Ears* (pp. 32-33), I touched on the issue of negative audience responses as follows:

"... the apparently rowdy behaviour of British Members of Parliament during debates in the House of Commons may have some rather more positive benefits than its negative public image would suggest. After all, if the odds of being called upon to speak are as poor as one in several hundred, there's so little chance of getting the next turn that you might as well go to sleep. But the tradition of cheering, booing and heckling not only provides an alternative way of expressing a view, it also give members more of a reason to listen. To be effective, booing and cheering require a degree of precision timing that can only be achieved by paying attention closely enough to be able to identify statements worth responding to."

Rowdiness and democracy

If, like me, you think it's rather a good idea for our representatives to pay close attention to what others are saying in parliamentary exchanges, getting our MP's to "calm down", as recommended by Mr Speaker Berkow, would be a rather bad idea.

And, if you don't believe me, go and watch some legislative assemblies in other countries where there is no tradition of audience participation. If you do, you'll be as amazed as I've been on quite a number of occasions by what I saw: when one person is speaking, most of the others spend most of their time going through their brief cases, sorting out papers, reading them and generally showing no sign whatsoever of listening to anything said by anyone else.

In the face of such indifference from other members, the speakers themselves typically deliver their speeches with marginally less passion and conviction than a weather broadcaster reading out the latest shipping forecast.

Further reading: Clayman, Steven E. 1992 "Caveat Orator: Audience Disaffiliation in the 1988 Presidential Debates." *The Quarterly Journal of Speech* 78: 33-60

25th February 2011

The target audience for a perfect Oscar winner's speech

In the run-up to the Academy Awards a few years ago, a Sky TV publicist asked me to have a go at writing "the perfect Oscar acceptance speech". My initial reaction was that it had already been done – by Alfred Hitchcock, who, on being awarded the Irving G. Thalberg Award in 1967, went up to the microphone, said "Thank you" and walked off the stage.

I also knew that I couldn't compete with the brilliant advice to winners offered by Paul Hogan in his Oscars warm-up act in 1986:

> "Winners, when you make your speech it's a good tip to remember the three 'G's: be gracious, be grateful, get off."

Who's my audience?

As I say in my books, the first step in preparing a speech or presentation is to analyse the audience. But one thing that stuck me on reviewing some of the horrors of the past was that, in so far as winners have any audience in mind, it's a rather small and narrow in-crowd. Sometimes their endless lists of names are aimed at their relations, sometimes at film industry insiders – who, unlike most of the millions watching at home, have presumably heard of some of those who get a mention.

So I decided that it would make a change if a winner actually addressed and thanked the fee-paying audiences, whose hard-earned cash decides which films succeed at the box-office – i.e. the millions of (or, according to Paul Hogan, billion) viewers watching the Oscar ceremony on television, rather than the few thousand celebrities who happen to be in the audience.

The most important audience of all?

I wouldn't say that what I came up with was "the perfect Oscar acceptance speech", but at least it was reasonably short, started with a touch of modesty and ended by paying tribute to the most important audience of all:

Being nominated for an Oscar is a bit like being told that Father Christmas might possibly bring you a present – but you mustn't get too excited because the odds are that he'll give it to someone else.

So when I heard my name read out, I was struck by a mixture of shock and disbelief. At my age I didn't expect to learn that there really is a Father Christmas after all.

So thank you to the Academy for making a dream come true.

Thank you to everyone involved in (insert name of movie). This (holds up Oscar) is as much for you as it is for me. Because without such a rich pool of talent, there'd have been no dream, no nomination and no award.

And thank you to the real stars in our universe – the millions on the other side of the screen who pay to see our movies. You are the ones who keep the heart of our industry beating. And without you, none of us would be here tonight.

So from all of us to all of you, thank you for letting us carry on doing what we love doing best.

However, if the audience that really matters is made up of the millions watching at home, incoherent emotional outbursts can be far more entertaining than a half-decent speech – a point well understood by Paul Hogan in what was arguably even more impressive than Alfred Hitchcock's exemplary performance 20 years earlier.

9th March 2011

Using video in a presentation: 7 steps to success

Over the last few days, I came across a couple of things that have prompted this post. The first was that I found myself giving a few tips to a Twitter follower on how to use video in a presentation.

The second was reading an interesting post by Lily Latridis on the *Fearless Delivery* blog, entitled *Video in a Presentation can be a Big Mistake*. At first sight, the title got me worried – as I hardly ever give a talk without using video clips to illustrate key points about public speaking and presentation.

It also reminded me that, when I first started using videos, we were still using Betamax rather than VHS – since when I've used them in hundreds, if not thousands, of presentations. What's more, I'm fairly sure that it hasn't been "a Big Mistake" – unless feedback, course evaluations and repeat bookings are a completely misleading guide to audience reactions.

Fortunately, my initial sense of dread on seeing the title disappeared as soon as I'd read the post, as it turned out that the types of video Lily Latridis was warning against and the purpose for which they were being used were both very different from the the short clips used in my own presentations (which mainly consist of 10 second excerpts from speeches illustrating different rhetorical techniques).

In fact, I found myself agreeing with pretty much everything Lily Latridis had to say about the types of videos she was talking about – and suspect that she might well agree with something I wrote about the use of videos in the section on different types of visual aids in my book *Lend Me Your Ears* (pp. 117-174):

"When using video, it's usually best to keep the clips short and the 30 second television commercial is a useful guide to optimal length. If you play longer clips, the danger is that the audience will start to feel that they're at a film show rather than a presentation. Once that happens, you may well find yourself losing the impetus, and have problems getting them back into the mood for listening to a talk. And, if it was a lively well-produced piece of video, there's the added risk of coming across as dull and amateurish compared with what they've just been watching' (LMYE, p. 152).

In retrospect, I realise that I could (and probably should) have included more practical advice on how to use video in presentations. So here, with thanks to Lily Latridis and my other Twitter contact for inspiring this postscript, are some tips from my own experience of discovering that video doesn't always have to be a big mistake.

Seven steps to success

1. Select clear examples

Many of the illustrations in scientific and medical text books are selected from hundreds of pictures in order to give the clearest possible example of whatever it is that's being described. The same principle should also be used in selecting video clips, as your audience has to be able to see/hear what you've told them to look out for instantly and at a glance (and without prompting doubt or irrelevant questions).

2. Use more than one clip to illustrate the same point

If you're making a point about the regularity with which speakers use a particular technique, you need to show more than one example of the same thing in action. By the time they've seen a third one, they'll have got the point, and you don't need four, five or six to convince them.

3. Think twice about who and what to include

When I first started teaching how to use rhetoric, I quickly discovered that, however effective an orator may have been, there were certain politicians and public figures who aroused such strong political reactions (e.g. Hitler, Ian Paisley, Arthur Scargill, Tony Benn, etc.) that their inclusion distracted audiences away from whatever technical point I was making.

So, whilst I still think it's important to show that the same techniques work in the same way irrespective of the party represented by a speaker, I've found it necessary to exclude certain speakers from my demo tapes over the years.

A related lesson I learnt very early on was to concentrate on showing clips by effective speakers and to make minimal use of ineffective ones. Hopeless speakers may demonstrate how not to do it, but the trouble is that what was boring in the first place is no less boring for the audience you're inflicting it on in the second place via a video.

4. Blank the screen out between each video clip

One of the (many) advantages that Betamax had over VHS was that, when you pressed the "Stop" button, it stopped exactly where you stopped it and the screen blanked out until you pressed "Start", when it carried on with the next clip you wanted to play. But do that with a VHS machine, and the tape would back up and, on pressing "Play", you'd get a replay of part of the previous clip – which was, to say the least, extremely annoying and distracting (both to me and my audiences).

As the market forced us to use VHS, my initial solution was to press the "Pause" button and then release it when I was ready to play the next example. The trouble was that having a still picture up on the screen while introducing the next one was a needless distraction for the audience. So I started to insert a few seconds of darkness on each demo-tape to encourage the audience's attention away from the screen and back to me until I was ready to "un-pause" it and show the next exhibit.

Now that we have to use DVD players or laptops, I still make sure that the screen goes blank between each clip.

5. To embed or to edit?

As regular readers of my blog will know, I often include video clips to illustrate points being made in a particular post. The easiest way to do this is to "embed" videos from YouTube or some other website. But the trouble with this is that the originals are often far too long and/or there's only a short excerpt from it that I want to comment on.

So you either have to tell readers how far to scroll in to see the point of interest (which I find quite annoying when looking at other blogs) or you can edit out everything else and produce a shorter clip of the relevant sequence.

The tips I found myself giving via Twitter the other day started by responding to someone who wanted to use video in a presentation and had tweeted a question asking if you can extract video from a DVD on to a Mac, to which I replied "Yes, I do it all the time but can't explain how in 140 characters."

As others have also asked me where I get clips from and how I edit them, it might be useful to outline how to go about it.

6. Where do you get videos from?

Thirty years ago, we had to record from live television – which produced very long video tapes and extremely time-consuming editing of short clips on to a demo-tape (using two VCRs). Today, we can either do the same by recording directly on to DVDs or select from the thousands of videos on the internet.

If you have a Mac, you'll be equipped with iMovie which, compared with Windows video-editing programs like Pinnacle, is far more reliable and much easier to use. Once you've edited a video, you can instantly convert it into whatever format you need (e.g. high quality DVD or lower quality for the web or email).

7. Useful software

If you want to copy movies from a DVD to your computer, you'll need a program like HandBrake that enables you to rip a DVD into QuickTime or other format that can be handled by iMovie.

If you've downloaded an FLV movie (e.g. from YouTube), Emicsoft FLV converter will convert it into an MP3 or other format that you can import into iMovie.

And anyone who thinks that this sounds like rather a long-winded process should remember that in the pre-digital age it could take anything up to two whole weeks to produce a half-decent demonstration tape.

Today I can create a new one from scratch in an hour or less – unless, of course, I need to fast-wind my way through hundreds of hours of videotapes before converting a long-lost clip to DVD before even being able to begin on the steps outlined above.

14th March 2011

Could Clegg improve his impact with better speechwriting and rehearsal?

As is explained in my books and illustrated by numerous video clips posted on my blog, the contrast is one of the most important and reliable rhetorical devices for triggering applause in speeches. So it can often be instructive to look at "deviant cases", where they don't work quite as smoothly as they could or should have done, to see what went wrong and what, if anything, we can learn from them.

There was at least one such example during the Deputy Prime Minister's speech winding up yesterdays conference of the Liberal Democrats in Sheffield yesterday after a simple past/present contrast:

Clegg: "We cherished those values in opposition. Now we're living by them in government."

But, the applause didn't start straight away and, when it did, after his first "So yes", it sounded somewhat lukewarm (i.e. not only delayed, but also lasting well below the "standard" burst of 8 ± 1 seconds):

It could, of course, be argued that this merely reflected the audience's ambivalence about their party's involvement in the coalition government. But there were at least two technical errors without which it could have induced a much more prompt and longer-lasting response.

1. Better scripting?

Instead of using a pronoun ("them") to refer to "those values" in the second part of the contrast, the speechwriters could have made the sequence work better by repeating "those values", so that it read as follows:

"We cherished those values in opposition.

Now we're living by those values in government."

2. Better rehearsal?

A second reason why the audience delayed before applauding was that Clegg didn't stop immediately after the second part of the contrast, but rushed on to continue with "so yes-". This may have been because he was too glued to the words coming up on the screens and was "teleprompted" onwards, or because he hadn't rehearsed it enough beforehand – or perhaps a combination of the two. In any event, a rather crucial line only managed to prompt a delayed and lukewarm response, leaving him looking vaguely perplexed as to what to do next, other than repeating the same two words waiting there on the screens.

So what?

You might think that this hardly mattered on a day when the news was dominated by the Japanese earthquake. And you'd be dead right, were it not for the fact that this particular sequence was one of the few that actually did make it on to the prime-time news bulletins last night and, via ITN, on to YouTube.

29th March 2011

Memorable speeches in Berlin revisited

Before leaving for a few days in Berlin last week, I posted a note about my first visit to the city in 1964, one year after John F. Kennedy's "Ich bin ein Berliner" speech and more than twenty years before Ronald Reagan challenged Mr Gorbachev to open this gate and tear down this wall.

On arriving home, I heard Ed Miliband making a not very successful attempt at delivering a memorable speech, in which he sought to identify with the likes of Martin Luther King and Nelson Mandela and the suffragettes.

Coming so closely together, these two events got me thinking again about something I've blogged about before, namely the question of what makes a speech memorable? Of the speeches mentioned in that particular post, I noted:

"... what, if anything, did these particular speeches have in common that made them stand out as more memorable than most?

"The best I've been able to come up with is that, in each case, the speaker managed to hit the jackpot by saying something that struck just the right chord with just the right audience in just the right place at just the right moment in history – which means that it's more or less impossible to predict 'memorability' with any certainty in advance of any particular speech – though I did wonder whether this was what Barack Obama had in mind when he tried unsuccessfully to speak at the Brandenburg Gate when visiting Berlin last year – given the previous Berlin successes of Kennedy in 1961 and Ronald Reagan's 'Tear down this wall' in 1987."

Right chord, right audience, right place, right time

Given that Ed Miliband's speech at the weekend arguably failed to hit the mark on any of these counts, it's hardly surprising that it didn't get a very good press – and, though I don't often make predictions, I'd say that there's not much chance of its going down in history as "memorable" – unlike those by Kennedy and Reagan in Berlin, both of which scored highly on all of these attributes.

Since my last visit to the city in 1964, it had changed almost beyond recognition. Being able to wander around the Brandenberg Gate, Checkpoint Charlie and some of the remaining segments of the wall (without fear of being noticed or harassed by armed guards) is quite a moving experience if you'd seen what it was like just after the wall had been built.

As a speeches anorak, I found lines from Kennedy and Reagan coming back to me and kept wondering what it must have been like to have been there listening to them speak in the shadow of the wall. On arriving home, I watched both of them again and wasn't disappointed.

If you're too young to remember them or have never seen them, a few minutes looking at them will be time well spent.

John F. Kennedy, 1963

Although some have claimed that John F. Kennedy's "Ich bin ein Berliner" means "I am a doughnut" and that JFK should have said "Ich bin Berliner", my German friends assure me that both options are equally acceptable ways of saying "I am a Berliner."

Three technically impressive points are worth noting:

1.   His final line repeats and harks back to his first use of it at the beginning of the speech – always an impressive technique for creating a neat impression of overall structural unity (*Lend Me Your Ears*, pp. 292-293):

> "And, therefore, as a free man, I take pride in the words 'Ich bin ein Berliner.'"

2.   The first appearance of "Ich bin ein Berliner" came as the second part of a past-present contrast, further strengthened by the contrast between Latin and German versions of the "proudest boast":

> "Two thousand years ago – Two thousand years ago, the proudest boast was 'civis Romanus sum.' Today, in the world of freedom, the proudest boast is 'Ich bin ein Berliner.'"

3.   The repetition of "Let them come to Berlin", concluding with more words in German, was greeted by repeated cheers and applause from the audience. Had "Ich bin ein Berliner" not struck such a powerful chord, the speech might well have become known as the "Let them come to Berlin" speech – just as the repetitive use of "I have a dream" by Martin Luther King became the name of another great speech in Washington two months later.

Ronald Reagan, 1987

The most famous lines were by no means the first impressive parts of the speech. Other points worth noting included:

1.   The target audiences had been clearly analysed in advance (Step 1 in preparing a speech or presentation, *Lend Me Your Ears*, pp. 280-286): "Our gathering today is being broadcast throughout Western Europe and North America. I understand that it is being seen and heard as well in the East. To those listening throughout Eastern Europe, I extend my warmest greetings and the good will of the American people. To those listening in East Berlin, a special word: Although I cannot be with you, I address my remarks to you just as surely as to those standing here before me. For I join you, as I join your fellow countrymen in the West, in this firm, this unalterable belief: Es gibt nur ein Berlin. [There is only one Berlin].

2.   **Powerful imagery:** "those barriers cut across Germany in a gash of barbed wire, concrete, dog runs, and guard towers."

3.   **Powerful use of contrasts:** "President Von Weizsäcker has said, 'The German question is open as long as the Brandenburg Gate is closed.' Well today – today I say: As long as this gate is closed, as long as this scar of a wall is permitted to stand, it is not the German question alone that remains open, but the question of freedom for all mankind."

6th April 2011

What does a 147 word sentence sound like?

Looking for suitable video clips for a presentation at the UK Speechwriters' Guild conference on "We do, do God" later this week took me back to the Archbishop of Canterbury's lecture on Sharia law three years ago.

Although it aroused a great deal of media interest and controversy at the time, I very much doubt whether many of the commentators managed to read or watch all the way through – both of which you can have a go at doing on my blog. If you do, you might like to ask yourself the question that I couldn't get out of my mind while going through it, namely:

Is this the most boring and incomprehensible lecture you've ever heard?

To be fair, I ought to be grateful to the Archbishop for providing part of the script (and the biggest laughs) in a comedy sketch written just after he'd given the lecture. The extract that achieved this was the following sentence made up of 147 words:

"The rule of law is thus not the enshrining of priority for the universal/abstract dimension of social existence but the establishing of a space accessible to everyone in which it is possible to affirm and defend a commitment to human dignity as such, independent of membership in any specific human community or tradition, so that when specific communities or traditions are in danger of claiming finality for their own boundaries of practice and understanding, they are reminded that they have to come to terms with the actuality of human diversity – and that the only way of doing this is to acknowledge the category of 'human dignity as such' – a non-negotiable assumption that each agent (with his or her historical and social affiliations) could be expected to have a voice in the shaping of some common project for the well-being and order of a human group."

But, when we know that the average sentence length in effective speeches is sixteen words, how on earth could anyone justify including one that's more than nine times longer than that?

After reading and listening to it quite a few times, I'm still none the wiser about what it means. And you don't have to go very far through the rest of the lecture to find plenty of similar examples of long-winded incomprehensibility.

Was the appointment of Dr Williams a Papist plot?

A friend of mine believes that it was no coincidence that Tony Blair was thinking about converting to Roman Catholicism when he elevated Rowan Williams to the top Anglican job, and that his selection of such a hopeless communicator was proof that Blair was serving as a secret agent for the Pope with a view to bringing the Church of England into disrepute.

At the time, I thought it rather a good joke, but the more I've seen of the Archbishop's communication skills since then, the more I'm beginning to wonder whether there might be more than a grain of truth to the theory.

24th May 2011

Will Obama's speech tomorrow match up to Reagan's Westminster masterpiece in 1982?

A speech to an audience of politicians and a miscellany of the great and the good in Westminster tomorrow poses a very different challenge to the one President Obama faced in Dublin yesterday, where he spoke to a crowd in the open air.

Not for the first time, he finds himself up for comparison with Ronald Reagan, whose speech to both houses of parliament in 1982 was a tour de force of the kind that earned him the title of "the great communicator".

The last time President Obama followed so closely in Reagan's footsteps was in Normandy on the 65th anniversary of the D-Day landings. Compared with his predecessor's masterpiece from the cliffs at Pointe du Hoc on the 40th anniversary of D-day, Obama's speech was so disappointing that a former Reagan speechwriter compared it unfavourably with Gordon Brown's speech on the same occasion.

Rhetoric and applause

At one point, Reagan prompted a sustained and extended burst of applause. Not surprisingly, given that it took place during the Falklands war, it was when he spoke about "lumps of rock and earth so far away".

But just look at how he did it: the second part of a first contrast becomes the first part of a second contrast that's packaged as a three-part list – hardly surprising that such a combination of rhetorical techniques prompted early applause that went on for longer than the "standard" burst of eight seconds:

Distant islands in the South Atlantic young men are fighting for Britain.

[A] And, yes, voices have been raised protesting their sacrifice for lumps of rock and earth so far away.

[B] [A] But those young men aren't fighting for mere real estate.

[B][1] They fight for a cause

[2] for the belief that armed aggression must not be allowed to succeed

[3] and the people must participate in the decisions of government.

27th May 2011

President Obama's speech at Westminster awarded a B-

President Obama opened his speech with a quip about the "very high bar" of the occasion:

> "I'm told the last three speakers here have been The Pope, Her Majesty the Queen, and Nelson Mandela, which is either a very high bar or the beginning of a very funny joke."

As regular readers will already know, it was another "very high bar" that really interested me: how would it compare with Ronald Reagan's speech to both houses of parliament in 1982?

Taking rhetoric, content and delivery into account, I'd have given the original great communicator a straight A and a B- for his successor .

Certainly there were a few highs (and lows), on which more below. But first, some reactions from the British media seemed to point towards a B- rather than an A:

Media moans

"Obama's historic speech fails to soar" – Mark Mardell, BBC website.

"partly platitudinous" – Steve Richards, *The Independent*.

"failed to raise the roof" – George Parker, *Financial Times*.

"failed to live up to his own high standards" – Andrew Grimson, *Daily Telegraph*.

"less moving than we had expected.. more of a hand-stitched tapestry than a speech" – Simon Hoggart, *The Guardian*.

Simon Hoggart was arguably on to something, and was by no means the only commentator to suggest that Obama tried to cover too much ground.

As Andrew Grimson put it in the *Daily Telegraph:* "The presidential text sounded as if it had been worked on so hard and conscientiously by a vast team of helpers that it had lost all savour, and been reduced to a series of orotund banalities, of the sort which can be heard at every tedious Anglo-American conference: 'Profound challenges stretch out before us … the time for our leadership is now … Our alliance will remain indispensable.'"

And a similar verdict from Mark Mardell, the BBC's North American editor: "It didn't quite work. It was flat and lacked soaring passion. That is part of the Obama conundrum. Sometimes this tremendous orator doesn't pull it off. It is often when the argument is over-constructed and the raw emotion can't burst through the stretched logic ... This felt like an attempt to mix too many elements. Flattering Britain, promoting the essential relationship, American exceptionalism, Britain's role in creating it, universal values. They were all there, but like oil and water stayed stubbornly apart".

Applause?

Quite a few commentators suddenly became expert observers of audience reactions and tried to make something of the fact that, apart from standing ovations before and after the speech, the president was only applauded once.

Needless to say, none of them noticed that it came after he'd used a rather neat contrast – which, as readers of my books and this blog will know, is one of the most reliable rhetorical devices for prompting applause:

[A] "it's possible for the sons and daughters of former colonies to sit here as members of this great Parliament

[B] "and for the grandson of a Kenyan who served as a cook in the British Army to stand before you as President of the United States."

Nor did any of the instant experts seem to know that Ronald Reagan also only received one burst of applause when he spoke to parliament in 1982 – which came after he'd deployed an even more powerful rhetorical technique than a contrast on its own.

Obama still lacks Reagan's teleprompter mastery

Both presidents majored on foreign policy. But, separated as the two speeches were by more than a quarter of a century, comparing their respective treatments of international issues of the day is no easy task.

But on their respective delivery of the speeches, Reagan's ability to read a speech as though he wasn't reading at all was second to none (not to mention his brilliance at carrying on as if nothing had happened when a teleprompter lets you down) – and it's one area where Obama still needs to do more homework/practice.

It's also something of which American communications expert Bert Decker has been very critical over the last few years and his blog on "Obama, Teleprompters and Authenticity" is well worth a read.

Highs and lows

1. The USA isn't the world's only democracy

If there's one thing that irks me about speeches by American presidents (and other US politicians), it's their tendency to overstate the case for their country being the first, finest or only example of freedom and democracy in the world.

So the positive highlight of the speech for me was to hear him openly recognising that Britain has not only played a part in the development of liberal democracy but also qualifies as such in the eyes of Americans (or at least of this American president).

2. Don't overdo your references to Churchill (and use with care)

Obama had plenty to say about and quote from Churchill (as did Reagan in 1982) – which is, of course a sure-fire recipe for any American politician who wants to strike a few chords with a British audience. But I thought he rather overdid it and made the mistake of using some not particularly well-known lines, which rather gives the game away that they'd been lifted from dictionaries of quotations. And, when it comes to quoting more famous lines from Churchill, you really do need to get the context right.

It's all very well for Obama to say "Hitler's armies would not have stopped their killing had we not fought them on the beaches and on the landing grounds; in the fields and on the streets." But Churchill's "fight on the beaches" speech dates from 1940 – before the USA had joined in – and, in anticipation of an expected invasion, the beaches, landing grounds, fields and streets he was talking about were those of Britain, not Normandy, Northern France, the Netherlands or Germany.

3. Management speak

I've noticed in some of President Obama's other speeches that he or his speechwriters have tended to let bits of awkward management jargon – like "going forward" – creep into his scripts.

Going forward was thankfully absent from this one, but there were a few other lines that could have benefited from rewriting.

There were at least two examples of putting things in place:

> "In the last century, both our nations put in place regulatory frameworks..."

> "... we must keep working through forums like the G20 to put in place global rules of the road to prevent future excess"

Words like "moreover" tend to work (slightly) better in documents written for readers than when used in spoken English (and reminded me of former PM John Major):

> "Moreover, even when the free market works as it should"

And I'm not very keen on the current trend for turning nouns into verbs (nor am I quite sure what an "Afghan lead" is:

> "we are now preparing to turn a corner in Afghanistan by transitioning to Afghan lead."

"Empowering" is also becoming more and more widespread as an all-purpose way of being vague in presentations and speeches both by managers and politicians:

> "we should empower the same forces that have allowed our own people to thrive"

Nor was I very impressed by his echo of a vague threat that's been used a few times in recent years by Hillary Clinton:

> "those who flaunt their obligations will face consequences."

6th June 2011

Why has British political oratory been banished to the sidelines?

My recent blogpost on the decline of oratory prompted an open letter from David Murray, Editor of *Vital Speeches of the Day*, with three questions that I ought to have a go at answering:

An Open Letter to Max Atkinson

Dear Mr. Atkinson,

In the latest post on your excellent blog plainly-enough named *Max Atkinson's Blog,* you applaud a writer from *The Independent*, for echoing your long held view that, in England anyway, the once-celebrated art of oratory is going to hell in a hand basket.

Scribbled Steve Richards, to your standing ovation:

"In the UK an important political art is no longer practised, even though the skill brings politics to life in an era of determined apathy. The demise is neither mourned nor noticed and yet the absence makes for duller politics – politics at a distance.

"This is the first generation of national politicians without a single orator, a single mesmerising speaker. There is not one who can cast a spell. Tony Blair was the last great speaker, an underestimated orator who never delivered a dull speech. Blair could make a lacklustre text and sometimes a silly one come to inspiring life."

Your only quibble with Richards' piece is your disagreement with its claim that the decline in oratory was sudden. "There were already signs of it in the title of the paper I gave at the Essex conference after the 1983 general election, namely 'The 1983 election and the demise of live oratory.'"

Max, I have three questions: First, why do you think oratory is declining so? Second: Do you see this decline as a British thing, or do you see this in the States too? Finally: Doesn't it give you the least bit of pause (as it does me) when you see the world declining at the same steady rate as you?

I'll look forward to hearing from you, Sir.

Sincerely,

David Murray, Editor, *Vital Speeches of the Day*

I found it easier to respond to these in reverse order:

3. Doesn't it give you the least bit of pause (as it does me) when you see the world declining at the same steady rate as you?

Who says I'm "declining"? If so, I haven't noticed (yet).

2. Do you see this decline as a British thing, or do you see this in the States too?

A similar trend has been evident in the USA where, "between 1968 and 1988, the length of excerpts from speeches shown on American television news programmes during presidential campaigns fell from an average of 42 seconds in 1968 to 9 seconds in 1988".

But (a) These days, we're lucky if we get to see even as much as 9 seconds from political speeches on British television news programmes. (b) Don't forget that candidates in US presidential elections do still give speeches at large rallies around the country – extracts from which still reach a mass audience via the broadcast media.

In the UK, however, leading politicians have more or less given up on speaking at such events – which is hardly surprising given that the best they can hope for is to be faded into the background while a commentator tells us what they're saying or treats the speech as background wallpaper while talking about something else.

(c) The fact that Obama (like Reagan before him) could emerge from nowhere on the back of one speech at a party convention to become president suggests that the speeches still matter far more in the USA than in the UK. Interestingly, however, it was a single ten minute speech in a "beauty parade" of candidates at a Conservative Party conference that enabled a rank outsider (David Cameron) to become the front-runner in the most recent Tory leadership stakes, a fact that our media commentators curiously seem to have forgotten about.

But Cameron's success may just have been a rare exception that proved the rule. From the little we see of US politics over here, my impression is that the importance of live oratory over there hasn't declined to anything like the same extent as it has done here in the UK.

1 . Why do you think oratory is declining so?

A fuller answer will have to wait until I've updated *Our Masters' Voices* (1984), but the shortest answer I can come up at the moment is that it probably results from a tacit agreement (or perhaps even a conspiracy) between British politicians and the media that suits both of them just fine.

(a) Not my fault!

In my less modest moments, I used to think that it might have had something to do with me. In the last chapter of *Our Masters' Voices*, I'd speculated about the impact of "televisuality" on political communication, suggesting that Ronald Reagan had become known as "the great communicator" because he understood that a chatty conversational style of delivery works better with television audiences than more traditional theatrical oratory (he had, after all, been a movie rather than a theatre actor).

But I never suggested that the effectiveness of a conversational delivery on television pointed towards the greater effectiveness of televised interviews. In any case, although it sold quite well for a book on politics, sales were never enough to justify such a megalomanic fantasy.

(b) An edict from television editors?

At some stage, probably during the late 1980s/early 1990s, television editors and producers must have decided that speeches made bad television, whereas interviews made good television. For any politician who might have doubted this, the tipping point probably came with the Labour Party's disastrous Sheffield rally in 1992, after which being interviewed by a journalist, regardless which one it happened to be, must have seemed a much safer and softer option.

(c) Supported by print media editors?

Last year, Michael Crick, political editor of BBC *Newsnight*, made the interesting point that British newspapers had also more or less given up on publishing extended reports on speeches:

'Your concern about us using real-life speeches less and less is a very valid one. It applies to Parliament too, when we ignore debates in favour of interviews outside. I try and resist producers on this when I can ... and of course none of the newspapers run extracts from Parliament any more either, though all the qualities did up until about 15 years ago'.

(d) What's in it for the media?

Replacing speeches with interviews as the main form of televised political communication had the advantage of being convenient and cheap for the television companies. Bringing politicians into a London studio saved all the hassle and expense of having to send outside broadcast crews to distant corners of the country to fit in with inconvenient schedules and locations that had been determined by the different political parties.

The change also gave the broadcasting media more control of other things as well. They could now mediate the news far more than they had ever been able to do in the past. In effect, they acquired the power to decide what counted as political news and how to report it.

Meanwhile, some of the leading television journalists had become highly paid celebrities in their own right, endowed with so much 'authority' that programmes could be organised around a Paxman or a Dimbleby – leaving any politician wanting to be seen and heard by a wider audience with little choice but to fit in with schedules and formats dictated by the media.

This takeover of political coverage by television journalists is arguably getting worse and becoming institutionalised within some of the broadcasting organisations. For example, during President Obama's recent visit to London, a Labour MP told me that one young (and very up-and-coming) BBC television reporter had explained to him that her job wasn't to report what politicians said but to interpret what they had meant "for the benefit of the viewers".

(e) What's in it for politicians?

One of the problems politicians faced with the advent of television was much the same as that faced by comedians who tried to make the transition from music hall to the small screen. Before television, you could tell the same jokes to different audiences in different places every night of the week. But once your act was broadcast to a mass audience, you needed new material every week for every show you did.

So for politicians, agreeing to subject themselves to endless television and radio interviews must have seemed a small price to pay for being let off the hook of having to prepare new speeches day after day during a 3-4 week general election campaign.

(f) What's in it for the public?

In short: boredom, waffle, evasiveness and the removal of any sense of enthusiasm and excitement from politics. I've often asked, but never found out, what evidence the media has for believing that interviews make better television than speeches.

Ten years ago, I was asked to write an introductory chapter in a collection of *Great Liberal Speeches* (edited by Duncan Brack, Robert Ingham and Mark Pack, Politico's Publishing Ltd) – in which I touched on where I think the problem (or at least part of it) lies:

"... it is perhaps time that the broadcasters themselves gave some thought to the impact on audiences of their preference for showing countless extended interviews with politicians during elections, rather than more or longer excerpts from speeches. These quasi-conversational confrontations between top politicians and top interviewers may be easy to organise and convenient to schedule. However, whether they make better television than excerpts from speeches is debatable. Their quasi-conversational nature limits the time available to develop any particular point to seconds rather than minutes. Like the conversationally worded speech, memorable lines or displays of passion or enthusiasm from the speaker are few and far between.

"Once in this conversational cockpit, many politicians proceed, with breathtaking regularity, to flout one of the most basic conversational rules of all, namely that questions should be followed by answers. Treating questions as prompts to say anything they like, or opportunities for yet another evasion of an issue, have become part of the routine repertoire that is inflicted daily on viewers and listeners. If politicians seriously believe that viewers and listeners lack the intelligence to see at a glance when they are being evasive, they can hardly complain when people conclude that they are patronising or arrogant. If they think that audiences will be impressed or inspired by the tortuous circumlocutions in which so much of their evasiveness is expressed, they should not be surprised when people conclude that they are out of touch with the way real people tick. We hear that politicians are becoming worried about their low esteem in the eyes of the public, and about growing voter apathy. Perhaps they should consider whether one factor might be that the way they speak in interviews is at best bland or boring, and at worst evasive and downright irritating.

"Yet the broadcasting establishment still seems to be committed to the view that interviews, however sterile and tedious they may be, make better television than excerpts from well crafted passionately delivered speeches. If they ever get round to reassessing their policy, one piece of evidence to which their attention should be drawn is the fact that editors and publishers of books do not seem to find televised interviews interesting, inspiring or provocative enough to merit the publication of collections of Great Interviews, whether Liberal or of any other kind. Rhetoric and oratory may well have had a bad press in recent years, but readers of this book will surely be thankful that it consists of speeches rather than transcripts of interviews. They can therefore look forward to reading carefully developed arguments in language robust enough to have survived the immediate moment of delivery to become a form of historical literature."

7th July 2011

James Murdoch backs Rebekah Brooks, but not without pausing every 2 seconds

"Apparently, James Murdoch went to the School of Lawyerish Non-speak, and passed with high honors!"

Denise Graveline (@dontgetcaught) via Twitter, yesterday.

I've blogged before about something that conversation analysts call "pre-delicate hitches".

Hitches are things like pauses, "ers" and "ums", restarts of a word that had been aborted, etc. They tend to occur at points in a conversation where you're leading towards a topic or a word (or it could be news, gossip, a swear word, obscenity, joke, etc.) that's likely to come across as rather delicate, controversial or even offensive to whomsoever you happen to be talking to.

The general argument is that we use such hitches to let our hearer(s) know that we know that they too might find what we're saying rather delicate.

One pause every two seconds

So I wasn't at all surprised to see that James Murdoch's backing of Rebekah Brooks yesterday (a delicate topic if ever there was one) was punctuated by 24 pauses in 48 seconds – although, like Denise Graveline (above), I was fairly appalled by his use of transparent and proactive "lawyerish non-speak".

Apart from the high pause rate in this particular clip, I also enjoyed "I am satisfied" and "I think", neither of which sounded as confident or certain as he perhaps should have done under the circumstances. Note also the slight hesitation "are-are.." before coming up with his assessment of her standard of ethics and conduct as "very good".

The question put to Murdoch was the interviewer's second attempt to get an answer:

"My question was is it really conceivable – you're asking people, in looking people in they eye and saying 'look, she and others in her position did not know that you were paying out enormous sums of money to these people' and what I'm saying is 'is that really conceivable?'"

After delaying for about 1 second, Murdoch starts to reply (slash marks in the transcript below indicate pauses of different duration):

Murdoch: "I am satisfied ///that Rebekah//her leadership of this business//and her//standard of ethics/and her standard of conduct/throughout her career//are-are very good/and I think/ what she's shown and what what we have shown//with our actions//around/transparently and proactively working with the police//Recall/it's the///process of information discovery//that we went through//proactively and voluntarily/that actually started these investigations /to be opened again by the police//earlier this year//It's the proactive and transparent handing over of information to the police/to aid them in their inquiries around payments to the police and things like that actually/she has led/and this company has led."

10th July 2011

News of the World bows out by hacking into George Orwell – and misrepresenting what he said

The final editorial of the final edition of the *News of the World* began by making out that George Orwell was a fan of the newspaper.

"The wife is already asleep in the armchair, and the children have been sent out for a nice long walk. You put your feet up on the sofa, settle your spectacles on your nose and open the *News of the World*."

These are the words of the great writer George Orwell. They were written in 1946 but they have been the sentiments of most of the nation for well over a century and a half as this astonishing paper became part of the fabric of Britain, as central to Sunday as a roast dinner.

- "the sentiments of most of the nation for well over a century and a half"?
- "part of the fabric of Britain"?
- "as central to Sunday as a roast dinner"?

Er – no, no and no!

I haven't ever seen – and can't think of – a single shred of evidence that would support any of these bizarre boasts – and you certainly won't find any if you read the rest of the editorial.

Plagiarism?

More intriguingly, the reference to Sunday roast dinner looks as though it was lifted from what Orwell said in the very next sentence after the one they quoted:

' ... and open the *News of the World*. Roast beef and Yorkshire, or roast pork and apple sauce, followed up by suet pudding and driven home, as it were, by a cup of mahogany-brown tea, have put you in just the right mood ... '

Was Orwell really a fan of the *News of the World*?

Even more intriguingly (or should that be "even more typically/predictably"?), the editorial gives the impression that Orwell was a fan who was recommending the *News of the World* – and conveniently omits any reference to why he was planning to open the said newspaper:

"In these blissful circumstances, what is it that you want to read about? Naturally, about a murder ... "

Nor, unsurprisingly, is there any mention of the fact that Orwell's interest was in murders that "... have been re-hashed over and over again by the Sunday papers... "

When I read the whole article by Orwell, I was staggered at how appropriate it was that the *News of the World's* final editorial was such a fine example of the newspaper quoting someone so selectively, self-servingly and, fundamentally, misleadingly.

On this evidence, and as we'd have said when I was too young to be allowed to read the *News of the World*, it looks like a case of "good riddance to bad rubbish."

Yet, according to the surprising number of supposedly serious journalists who have devoted so much energy on Twitter bemoaning its passing, it seems that I may be missing something.

15th July 2011

What went wrong with BBC Newsnight's latest attempt to involve a studio audience?

A couple of nights ago, BBC's *Newsnight*, advertised in advance as involving a live studio audience, attracted quite a lot of negative comments on Twitter, both during and after the programme. The main complaint was that the audience was rather unforthcoming and that even Jeremy Paxman seemed to be having trouble getting any of them to say very much about the phone-hacking scandal.

Never blame the audience

When things go wrong in a presentation or speech, my advice, like that of many presentation trainers, is never blame the audience – because there's no such thing as a bad audience. And I think the same goes for TV news and current affairs programmes that try to get an audience involved in a discussion.

In fact, on this occasion, I can even claim to have been wise before the event. After an earlier tweet from Newsnight on Wednesday, I'd tweeted: "Oh dear, @BBC*Newsnight* trailing 'live studio audience' tonight – expect hopeless chairing and zzzzz ... "

This was based on having seen many such programmes, in which the presenter shows little or no technical appreciation of how turn-taking works and how the implicit rules change according to how many people are involved – and how someone's ability to perform in a TV interview is not unrelated to their experience of being interviewed (or lack of it) – for more on which, see Clayman & Heritage, *The News Interview: Journalists and Public Figures on the Air* (Cambridge University Press, 2002).

A multi-patched quilt

So what we got the other night was a patchwork quilt of a programme with far too many patches in it. In keeping with the modern myth that no one is capable of paying attention for more than a few seconds at a time, it kept switching at regular intervals between six quite distinct elements – of which the various attempts to involve the live audience, who were the only TV novices on the show, made up a mere sixth of the total:

1. Paxman + *Newsnight* political editor (1+1)
2. Paxman + cabinet minister (1+1)
3. Paxman + pundits (1+2)
4. Paxman + MPs (1+3)
5. Paxman + Audience (1+25)
6. Video footage from day's events.

The numbers in the brackets highlight the different sizes of group featured on the show – differences that inevitably involve different turn-taking rules – and depend for their success (or otherwise) on the participants, and especially the chair, having at least some tacit awareness of what they are.

The frequent flitting backwards and forwards between each of them made life difficult even for as experienced a presenter as Jeremy Paxman, let alone the inexperienced live audience. And, of all these permutations, ensuring effective turn-taking in such a large group is by far the most difficult.

Add to that the fact that the poor old audience kept being interrupted by cutaways to yet another few seconds of video film or by Paxman turning away to ask "what do you think, Danny?" and the attempt to pack such a miscellany of interviews, film footage and "discussion" into 45 minutes, and is it any wonder that they came across as rather less than forthcoming?

I wasn't at all surprised that such a format didn't work. But the last people I'd blame for that would be the audience in the *Newsnight* studio ...

17th August 2011

Yvette Cooper's precisely timed response to a contrast from Ed Miliband

I noted a while back in a post showing how a member of the audience anticipated the answer to a rhetorical question by David Cameron that television editors are sometimes very helpful in providing detailed data on the interaction between a speaker and audience. In that particular case, the camera switched from speaker to audience just before he delivered the answer to his question – with which a woman in the audience was already agreeing before he actually got there.

In the House of Commons, some members of the audience are routinely visible behind the person who's speaking, as seen during Ed Miliband's speech in the debate about last week's riots.

What's interesting is that it shows just how quickly some listeners can and do respond when a speaker uses a rhetorical technique – in this case a contrast, with repetition and alliteration – to make a point:

> [A] "To seek to explain
> [B] is not to seek to excuse."

Yvette Cooper, behind Mililband's right shoulder, starts nodding in agreement before he gets to the end of the word "excuse" – at which point the MP sitting behind her starts to nod too.

In *Our Masters' Voices* (1984) I suggested that contrasts work to trigger applause (and other positive reactions) because the first part enables listeners to anticipate and identify precisely when the speaker reaches the end of the second part.

What I liked about this sequence, apart from Ed Miliband's neat contrast, was the way in which we can actually see Ms Cooper's positive response getting under way a split second before he's finished saying the word "excuse".

Footnote

This was also the first speech I'd heard from Mr Miliband since his nose operation and all the speculation about whether its real aim was to change his voice or to cure his sleep apnoea, which had made me curious to see if he sounded any different than he did before the operation.

As far as I could tell, his voice sounded exactly the same, but I do hope that the operation will have given his wife and children some relief from his alleged snoring – I say "alleged" because I too am regularly accused of the same offence, even though no one in the family has ever managed to produce any evidence (other than hearsay) in support of their complaints.

22th September 2011

Clegg's conference speech: 1 plus & 2 minuses

Having grumbled previously about Nick Clegg's past attempts to imitate David Cameron's walkabout apparently unscripted style of delivery, I was delighted to see that he stood at a lectern for yesterday's speech. If you want to look more like a statesman than a management guru, that's the way to do it, even if you do forget to pretend that you're reading from the hard copy text in front of you.

Minuses

1. Faces in the background

Fashionable though it has become for our party leaders to make speeches with some of the audience sitting behind them, I cannot for the life of me see what the point of it is.

During the 1992 election, John Major took to speaking in the round and, if I ever manage to unearth my videos of people yawning and dozing in the background, I'll certainly post them on the blog.

Back in the 1970s and 80s, party leaders used to speak from a platform, surrounded by colleagues – until, that is, Harvey Thomas (former impresario for Billy Graham's UK crusades) got involved in staging Conservative Party conferences, where Mrs Thatcher was set apart from the rest so that any signs of audience dissent or doziness couldn't be seen by viewers at home.

Neil Kinnock quickly followed suit – and with very good reason. I have another video from one of his earliest leader's speeches, in which Dennis Skinner and Joan Maynard (aka "Stalin's aunty") sat behind him eating sweets, shaking their heads and generally looking very cross.

There may not have been any such damaging distractions from those who sat behind Mr Clegg yesterday, but the possibility was always there.

Nor did it do a very good job in accomplishing the only defence for it I've ever heard, namely to demonstrate the ethnic and gender diversity of the party's supporters. I could only see one black face and not as many female faces as there should have been.

2. An unfortunate contrast

The power of the contrast in the armoury of rhetorical devices available to speakers was strongly evidenced by the fact that Clegg's recurring "not easy, but right" line was widely noticed and reported by the media as the leitmotif of the speech.

But, given the alternative meanings of the word "right" in the English language, and especially in the world of politics, it hardly seemed an appropriate choice. If you're suspected by some of your supporters (and enemies) of selling out to go into coalition with a right-wing party, "right" is, at best, an ambiguous word to use in such a context – and that too was spotted and has been commented on in the media.

Whether or not this was deliberately intended by Clegg and/or his speechwriters, I do not know. But I'd have gone for a safer option like "not easy, but necessary", "not easy, but unavoidable" or "not easy, but no choice."

On the other hand, if speeches have become as unimportant in UK political communication as I suggested in the previous post, maybe none of this nit-picking matters very much at all ...

2nd October 2011

The snake (interview) that did for Nixon's reputation and the ladder (speech) that had saved it

The Frost-Nixon interview as the ultimate snake

Was it, I wonder, pure coincidence that BBC2's schedule last night included some archive footage of the original Frost-Nixon interview, followed by the film version of the events surrounding and leading up to it?

After all, the party conference season, with its mix of extended interviews with politicians, very short clips from their speeches and much longer clips from media commentators telling us what they're talking about, has yet to grind to a close.

From my point of view, having started the season by asking why our politicians are so willing to play snakes and ladders under media rules that give them little chance of landing on anything but a snake, the chance to see the Frost-Nixon film could hardly have come at a more appropriate time.

Here was a disgraced American president who thought himself smart enough to run rings around a talk-show host and salvage his reputation – only to be lured into landing on about as damaging a snake as David Frost and his media colleagues could ever have dreamt of.

The Checkers speech as the ladder that saved his career

A quarter of a century earlier, claims that vice-presidential candidate Nixon might have misappropriated campaign funds almost forced his withdrawal as President Eisenhower's running mate.

What saved him was not an interview, but the carefully crafted "Checkers speech" (still ranked as the 6th greatest political speech on the American Rhetoric website).

Interestingly, both the name it became known by and much of its powerful impact derived from a simple anecdote about his children and a little cocker spaniel dog.

I think our current politicians could do worse than to watch both – and reflect on what a single interview and a single speech did for Nixon's political reputation.

Were they to do so, they might think again about what, if anything, they are gaining from their tacit collusion with broadcasters about the relative merits of interviews and speeches as alternative ways of communicating their messages (and conveying positive/negative images of themselves) to a wider public.

4th October 2011

Swim or sink with the president of the European Commission

Preparing for a speechwriting course in Brussels this week, I thought it would be nice to include an example of a 'local' using some of the main rhetorical techniques in one of my demo tapes.

Such are the wonders of YouTube that it took less than a minute to find a little gem from the president of the European Commission, José Manuel Barroso, which had been singled out for replaying in a news report on his "state of the union" speech:

Reporter: He said Europe has to move forward towards matching its monetary union with a real economic union among its member states:

Puzzle: This is Europe's moment of truth.

Solution: Europe must show that its more than 37 different national solutions.

Contrast (with swimming metaphor + alliteration): We either swim together or sink separately.

Not surprisingly, this selection of key rhetorical techniques worked well enough for it to be singled out by the media as a sound bite – but it didn't mpress everyone.

Guess who doesn't want to be seen clapping

British readers may be interested to note that, of the five MEPs shown just before Mr Barroso starts speaking, the only one who doesn't join in with the applause is none other than Nigel Farage, leader of UKIP (the UK Independence Party).

Whether or not you're one of his supporters or opponents, it has to be admitted that his behaviour here is admirably consistent with his long-standing antipathy towards the EU.

6th October 2011

Cameron's too good a speaker to be following Mrs Thatcher into the teleprompter trap

A couple of years ago, I posted some video clips showing how Margaret Thatcher's speech-making became less effective when she stopped using hard copy scripts and started reading speeches from teleprompter screens.

A few months later, I realised that I'd been mistaken in thinking that David Cameron was having problems reading from screens – as it turned out that he wasn't using an Autocue or any other form of teleprompter at that time.

Cameron follows Thatcher down the same hill

But yesterday Mr Cameron had not only taken to using a teleprompter for his leader's speech, but was also encountering the same kinds of difficulties that diminished Mrs Thatcher's effectiveness all those years ago.

When using a script on a lectern, she would return her eyes to the text, clear her throat and close her mouth after making an applaudable point, leaving no one in any doubt that the time had come for them to get their hands apart. But, when reading from teleprompter screens, her head stayed up gazing into space, with the result that her applause rate fell dramatically.

And there were some rather long sections in Mr Cameron's speech yesterday where the lack of applause was noticeably absent. You can see see two examples of him falling into the same trap as Mrs Thatcher. In both cases, he sets up what's coming as an applaudable point. But in both cases, nothing happens for so long (2-3 seconds) that he's already carried on again by the time it finally does – at which point he has to break off.

Also in both cases he seems to acknowledge the glitch with a slight nod, indicating, perhaps: "yes, it is your turn and you should jolly well have started a bit sooner than that"?

Given that Cameron is more effective than most of his contemporaries at speaking from scripts on a lectern, I'd advise him to ditch the teleprompter forthwith. Or, if his aides have cooked up some reason that's convinced him it's a good idea, they should also convince him that he's going to need a lot more practice if he's to get anywhere near his effectiveness with old-fashioned scripts (or, for that matter, with no script at all, as in the 10 minute speech that clinched the leadership for him at the beauty parade in 2005).

10th October 2011

50 years of Private Eye: a story of retail, rejection and recognition

It's supposed to be a sure sign of growing older when you start thinking that police officers and doctors are getting younger. Another is when you realise that more and more significant anniversaries are taking place of events you think of as recent memories. For me, the latest reminder of this is the news that it's 50 years since the fortnightly satirical magazine *Private Eye* was first published. Not only do I remember it well, but I was also an early salesman and have been a subscriber and (very occasional) contributor ever since.

Retail

Selling the *Eye* outside university cafeterias was my first serious business venture. Lord Gnome had rightly seen students as a promising source of potential readers and had invited volunteers to join his sales force.

Once a fortnight, all I had to do was to go down to the station and collect my 60 copies of the latest edition, then priced at 1/6d (one shilling and sixpence, or 7.5 pence in new money) – for which I had to pay 1/- (one shilling, or 5 pence in new money) each, leaving a net profit of 30 shillings (£1.50 in new money) per fortnight.

These days, 75 pence a week may sound like a pittance. But when pubs sold a pint of beer for the equivalent of 7.5 pence, it was riches indeed.

Rejection

For years, I tried unsuccessfully to get *Private Eye* to publish my hilariously funny (?) cartoons, only to be bombarded with rejection slips suggesting that I should send them to *Punch* magazine (now coming up to the 10th anniversary of its demise in 2002).

I also rather regret that nothing I've written has ever made it into "Pseuds' Corner", even though I know that such acclaim can have embarrassing consequences. Someone (and we haven't forgotten who you are) had successfully submitted a sentence from an article about conversational turn-taking that one of my best friends had published in a learned journal.

When I told him that I was rather envious because nothing of mine had ever got into "Pseuds' Corner", he warned of the dire consequences such recognition can have. It had been published a few days before he was due in Cambridge to serve as external examiner in a PhD viva. As he put it "they already think we're mad enough to be doing conversation analysis in the first place, without being able to rub it in by waving *Private Eye* at me before the meeting started."

Recognition

It wasn't until the mid-1980s that I finally managed to extract a cheque from Lord Gnome for a photograph that I'd taken of the village sign outside a village in Northamptonshire that bore the legend "Silverstone – please drive slowly."

Even then, it had seemed like another rejection for the many months it failed to appear in the "I Spy" feature, making me grumpier by the fortnight. Then, to give them their due, it turned out that they hadn't binned it after all, but had merely been waiting, with the journalistic flair we expect from *Private Eye*, to publish it the week before that year's British Grand Prix at Silverstone.

More recently, the *Eye* published another photograph I'd taken of a fly-posted planning notice from Mendip District Council – at a time when they were wasting unspecified amounts of council-tax payers' money on a campaign against fly-posting notices of forthcoming village events on "items of street furniture", i.e. MDC jobs-worthy jargon for telephone and electricity posts.

15th October 2011

Two engaging women speakers from British politics – and two models for powerful women?

During the Labour Party conference last month, I raised the question of whether some of the party's leading women, such as Yvette Cooper, Caroline Flint and Harriet Harman, are better speakers than the party's current generation of leading men.

Shirley Williams

On hearing the 81 year old Shirley Williams speaking at the Wells Literary Festival the other night – along the lines of the above from a similar speech she made at the Stratford-upon-Avon Literary Festival – I realised that there's nothing particularly new about effective women speakers holding their own with their male contemporaries and rising to the higher reaches of the Labour Party (and later, in her case, within the SDP and Liberal Democrats too).

Long before Williams and the three male members of the "gang of four" had broken away from Labour to form the SDP, she had been a cabinet minister in the Wilson and Callaghan governments. And, from quite early in her political career, she was sometimes mentioned as a possible first woman Labour leader and even as a possible first ever woman prime minister.

Although these both eluded her, she's still not only a very engaging speaker, but also one who's retained an energy to rival many, if not most, speakers who are very much younger than she is. During her brief stay in Somerset this weekend, she was making speeches and taking questions from 1930-2130 on Friday night and from 0930-1130 and 1230-1400 on Saturday (i.e. for about 50% of the waking hours she was here).

As if that wasn't enough, she was planning to spend her train journey back to London reading a few more hundred pages of the health bill and its amendments in the current House of Lords debate in which she is playing a very active part.

Barbara Castle

Twenty years older than Shirley Williams was another leading figure in Harold Wilson's Labour government, the late Barbara Castle. I haven't been able to find any clips of her speeches on YouTube – where there seem to be more of Miranda Richardson playing her in the film *Made in Dagenham* than there are of the real Mrs Castle – but some of us are old enough to remember that she too was a much better than average public speaker.

Castle, Williams and the Thatcher solution

In *Our Masters' Voices*, I suggested that Margaret Thatcher had found a solution to the professional woman's problem of being damned if they behave like a man and damned if they behave like a woman by being tough and decisive in her actions while being uncompromisingly female in her external appearance – and that this was summed up by the nickname the "Iron Lady", capturing as it does both "strength" and "femininity".

In this respect, Barbara Castle, regarded in her day as being as tough, glamorous and well-dressed, came much closer to the Thatcher model for women politicians than Shirley Williams ever did.

The Williams alternative

At the time of writing *Our Masters' Voices*, I remember suggesting somewhere that Mrs Williams represented a rather different available role-model for women in politics than the one offered by Thatcher and Castle: the "intellectual", "blue-stockinged", "untidy", "verging on scruffy" stereotype of the female Oxbridge don (or Women's Institute lecturer).

As for whether she consciously developed such an image, there are at least two pieces of evidence that she is certainly aware of it in retrospect. One is that she actually referred, without any prompting, to her erstwhile reputation for having untidy hair during the talk she gave on Friday night.

Clothes + fashion = frivolous waste of time peddled by supercilious saleswomen

The other evidence comes in the first chapter of her autobiography, *Climbing the Bookshelves* (of which I'm now the proud owner of a signed copy), where she reveals that she already had little or no interest in clothes and fashion by the time she was 10 years old. Comparing herself with her mother, she writes:

> " ... she did allow herself some moments of frivolity. She loved clothes and used to take me with her while she tried on the elegant polka-dotted silk dresses and emphatic hats of the 1930s. A new hat or pair of gloves could lift her spirit for days. It was a pleasure I did not share. After the first ten minutes of each encounter with a supercilious sales lady, I began to think about ponies and tricycles, and to resent the waste of my time. These early experiences immunised me against both shopping and fashion. For years I bought the first thing that looked even vaguely as if it might suit me, though often it didn't."

21st October 2011

Effective broadcasters aren't always effective public speakers: the case of Melvyn Bragg

In his autobiography, the late Professor A.J. Ayer, noted that he'd been surprised to discover, when appearing long ago on BBC Radio's *The Brains Trust*, that broadcasting was very different from lecturing – in that it worked perfectly well for him and the other participants to speak at their normal conversational speed.

Last night, on the way out of Wells Cathedral after a lecture by Melvyn Bragg, I overheard a conversation between two other members of the audience that went as follows:

A: "There was too much to be able to take in."
B: "And he kept rambling off the subject with too many digressions."

I resisted the temptation to intervene with the strangers to express my complete agreement that he had indeed tried to cover far too much ground in a lecture that was also sadly lacking in structure and direction.

To these complaints, I would have added: "He also spoke far too quickly for a lecture, and especially one that went on for far too long" (i.e. 90 minutes).

Lecturing v. broadcasting

Bragg is, of course, a very experienced award-winning broadcaster – whose *South Bank Show* was seen as so crucial to London Weekend Television's franchise bid (after the 1990 Broadcasting Act) that he was one of a small group of staff who were paid multi-million pound "golden handcuffs" to keep them with the company during and after the bid.

But, unlike Professor Ayer, he doesn't seem to have realised that lecturing calls for a rather different pace than broadcasting – not least because listeners are up against the problem of trying to stay awake and pay attention to a far longer stream of talk than is ever the case in any of his television or radio programmes (or in everyday conversation, where the average length of turns at talk is about 8 seconds).

For radio listeners, eavesdropping on conversations, even intellectual ones like those on Bragg's *In Our Time* on BBC Radio 4, is easy enough. But he needs to learn that pausing much more frequently, and for much longer than you would ever do in a conversation (or on radio), is crucial to effective public speaking – and that includes lecturing.

In conversation, native speakers of English talk at a rate of about 180 words per minute, whereas the speed of effective public speakers is 120 words per minute (for more on which, see *Lend Me Your Ears*).

In a clip from a lecture by Melvyn Bragg marking Darwin's bicentenary at the Natural History Museum (where the acoustics sound remarkably similar to Wells Cathedral), the pauses are so infrequent and so short that his rate of delivery is just over 161 words per minute – i.e. much closer to conversational/broadcasting speeds than to the ideal for effective public speaking.

31 October 2011

Professional broadcasters should beware of saying "um" and "er"

The previous post on a famous broadcaster who speaks more effectively on television and radio than when he's lecturing (Melvyn Bragg) reminded me that there are also some professional broadcasters who punctuate their reports and interviews with rather more "ums" and "ers" than they should.

Someone I've noticed doing this is Adam Boulton, political editor of *Sky News*. On turning to YouTube for possible examples, even I was surprised that I had to look no further than the very first clip I came across, in which there were 37 "ums" and "ers" in 150 seconds – at a rate of about one every 4 seconds.

Sounds of Silence: Ums and Ers

• Needless noises?

A normal feature of conversational speech is the way we punctuate much of what we say with ums and ers. But, for audiences trying to listen to a speech (or broadcast) this can become a major source of irritation, because presenters who retain their normal conversational umming/erring rate come across as hesitant, lacking in confidence, uncertain of their material and badly prepared.

• Don't worry – I've started

In conversation, one of the commonest places for ums and ers is right at the start of a new speaker's turn, where we use them to avoid what might otherwise be heard as a potentially embarrassing silence – by indicating: "I'm not being impolite or disagreeable but am about to respond any second now". But some public speakers (and broadcasters) make a habit of starting almost every new sentence with an um or an er, of which they're typically completely unaware of until they hear themselves on tape – when most are appalled by the negative impact they must have had on their audience.

• Hold on – I haven't finished yet

Another place where we often um or er in conversation is when we suddenly find ourselves stuck for a word or name we need to be able to carry on. We know that, if we simply stay silent while searching for the word, someone else will use the pause as a chance for them to speak, thereby preventing us from finishing whatever it was we were about to say. So saying um or er is a simple and effective device for letting everyone know that you haven't finished yet and that it's still your turn.

• When pause-avoidance loses its point

If the primary functions of ums and ers in conversation are to avoid silences and reduce the chances of being interrupted, they lose their point in presentations and broadcasts. After all, presenters are not competing to hold the floor in the same ways as in everyday conversation and, once in full flow, they certainly don't need to keep reminding us that they've just started a new sentence. As a result, umming/erring rates that would be perfectly normal and hardly noticed in everyday conversation stand out as needless distractions when heard from the mouths of presenters.

In defence of Mr Boulton?

In the particular clip I found, it could be argued that Adam Boulton's umming/erring reflects his uncertainty in the face of two things that are new to him: (1) the gadget he's showing to the interviewer (and us) and (2) giving a televised *Tomorrow's World* style demonstration that's far removed from his natural habitat of political interviewing and reporting.

But the reason I started looking for a video clip of him in the first place was that I'd often noticed (and been surprised by) the frequency of his umming and erring in his regular contributions on *Sky News*. Nor, would it appear, am I alone in having done so – as his was one of the names mentioned on Twitter yesterday after I'd invited people to guess the identity of the umming/erring television news presenter about whom I was planning a blog.

14th November 2011

Presentation tip: beware of flip charts on wheels

In previous posts (and books), I've written favourably about writing on blackboards and flip charts. But on Saturday, in the middle of a lecture to 200+ people, I suddenly realised that there was a rather important point that I'd failed to mention, namely: if the flip chart has wheels, make sure you LOCK THEM before trying to write anything on it.

Disaster averted

As the chart began falling backwards, the screen (on which I was about to show video clips on which the rest of my lecture depended) started to follow suit. Total disaster was only kept at bay by the weight of the curtain behind the stage and the quick reflexes of one of the organisers, who pushed the flip chart back on to the stage and locked its wheels.

A stunt worth repeating?

The huge amounts of laughter prompted by its sudden reappearance have now raised the question of whether such a stunt might be worth developing (and rehearsing) for use on another occasion?

I'm pretty sure that my blood pressure isn't up to risking it again – but, if anyone else would like to try it for themselves, I'd be delighted to hear whether it achieves a similarly positive impact.

22nd November 2011

700th blog post: English and the problem of communicating with foreigners

First, a very big thank you to everyone who came up with ideas after my Twitter appeal about my 700th blog post. There were so many good ones, plus some funny and some verging on the obscure, that I was initially tempted to reproduce the list and leave it at that.

I'll resist the temptation to blog in French, as suggested by Phil Waknell and Marion Chapsal. But the question of how we ever manage to communicate effectively with people who speak different languages is an interesting one, especially for native speakers of English who tend to assume that everyone else speaks it too.

"Simplification" isn't always the answer

The first time I ever spoke at a conference where most of the audience were non-native speakers of English, I quickly became aware that they weren't understanding much of what I was saying. So I started to make it simpler – or so I thought.

In retrospect, I realised that my pitiful attempt to make things "simpler" had led me to use more and more slang and colloquial expressions than I would ever normally do in an academic lecture. These may have made it easier for the native speakers of English to understand, but had made it far more more difficult for everyone else.

Translate jokes or tell the audience to laugh?

A former colleague of mine, who was a fluent speaker and teacher of Russian, used to be hired to do simultaneous translation for visitors from the (then) Soviet Union at major civic events. One of his problems was that the speeches by "locals" often included jokes that he found quite impossible to translate.

His solution was to say in Russian something along the lines of "he's just told a joke that I can't translate into Russian, so you had all better start laughing – NOW" – which apparently worked well enough for the locals to think that their guests had both understood and appreciated the joke they'd just heard.

Does it matter?

With so much hanging on recent meetings between Euro-zone leaders, not to mention other important "conversations" taking place elsewhere in our ever more "globalised" world, a question that comes to mind is: how much should we worry about our reliance on simultaneous translation and/or the pretence that everyone speaks or understands English as well as we do?

23rd December 2011

Is there still time to learn from a video of yourself speaking to an audience?

Browsing through YouTube the other day, I was surprised – and not sure whether to be flattered or annoyed – to come across a clip from a lecture I gave in Copenhagen last year.

Yes, I may have spent decades making, collecting and commenting on videotapes of other people speaking. But, like so many others, I don't much like watching myself in action – which raises the question of why I've decided to draw attention to it with this post?

The short answer is that it made me realise how very few clips I've ever seen of myself actually speaking to an audience. So it gives me a chance to treat my performance as data and to analyse where there might be room for improvement – if it's not too late for that.

It also gives anyone else a chance to do the same – and especially those of you who've had to put up with my feedback on your efforts during courses or coaching sessions. It only seems fair to let you have a chance get your own back on me.

For what they're worth, here are a few of the things that occurred to me.

Pluses & minuses?

Eye-contact with the audience was better than I'd expected, and I was gratified to hear a few laughs from the audience so close to the start of the lecture, when getting their attention is so crucial.

The pace of the delivery also rather surprised me. I don't know whether I pause as often or for as long as I do here when I'm speaking to native speakers of English, but did wonder whether it was rather too slow and ponderous. I was, however, very conscious that almost everyone in this particular audience was a native speaker of Danish.

Mumbling monotone?

There were moments of mumbling that took me back to my first attempts at lecturing more than forty years ago. I was aware then that even the remnants (?) of a Yorkshire accent can come across as flat and monotonous to those who come from anywhere else, and that sounding a bit livelier was something that I was always going to have to work hard at – on this evidence: "still room for improvement."

Where's his jacket?

In a previous blog post, I recalled a course that I'd attended more than 4o years ago:

> " ... while I was being video-taped doing a lecture on a course for new
> university lecturers, the studio lights were so hot that I took my jacket off.
> At the feedback session, it became a matter for discussion: the tutor

stopped the tape with the words, 'Here's a speaker who really means business.' Though nothing could have been further from the truth, the realisation that some people might see it that way has made jacket removal a routine prelude to almost every lecture I have ever given since then."

I still don't know whether speaking in shirtsleeves gives the impression that I "really mean business". What I do know that it helps to keep the sweat under control, which makes me feel marginally more comfortable than would otherwise be the case.

Nor, until or unless someone makes a very strong case that I shouldn't do it, is it something that I plan to do any differently in the near future.

Retirement beckons?

And a near future is all that's left to one who's already qualified for the old age pension and a bus-pass. Gone are the days from a distant past when I used to worry that audiences would think me too young to be taken seriously.

Today, the problem has become the opposite: how are you to know if and when an audience thinks that you're past your sell-by date and really ought to pack it in forthwith?

On the basis of this video clip (aided and abetted by the bias of my own eyes and ears) he doesn't look or sound too much like an old fogey (yet).

But will he ever know when to stop and how will he ever know when that time has arrived – unless he starts to forget crucial points he was planning to mention, falls off the stage or comes across as a doddering old fool?

For all he knows, he may be already there – and might even have been there for quite a while.

So maybe the answer should come from the world of sport – where the sensible few retire before they start losing (or get dropped from the team) – in which case, the safest option may be to call it a day sooner rather than later ...

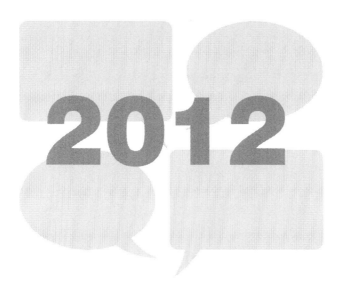

14th January 2012

A gentleman who is for turning: snakes or ladders weekend for Ed Balls?

Thanks to a speech to the Fabian Society and endless interviews by Ed Balls, this weekend has been alive with the sound of turning in the mainstream media, blogs and on Twitter.

Under a headline "This is new all right. It just isn't enough", John Rentoul of the *Independent on Sunday* tells us "Ed Balls caught up with where the Labour Party should have been 16 month ago. It was an important moment ... ".

The *New Statesman* is rather less optimistic, with an article by Owen Jones telling us "Ed Balls' surrender is a political disaster".

And, perhaps not surprisingly, the unions aren't too pleased by what looks like a rather sudden U turn from Mr Balls – see *Unions criticise Ed Balls's pay freeze* comments on the BBC website.

Snake, ladder or both?

For me, I find myself wondering how the speech and interviews by Mr Balls fit in (or not) with the snakes and ladders theory of political communication, which proposes that interviews work like snakes for politicians (by attracting negative news coverage) and speeches work like ladders (by attracting positive news coverage).

But here we have an example of a politician staying consistently "on message" – and a highly controversial one at that – both in a speech and related interviews.

There's no doubt that a message has got across (though to how many over a weekend?) and, given how little of the speech was actually to be seen or heard on broadcast news programmes, this probably had more to do with the interviews than his Fabian Society lecture.

However, whether it's had (or will have) a positive or negative outcome for Mr Balls and the Labour Party, only time will tell.

16th January 2012

The "John Lewis economy": What to make of today's speech by Nick Clegg?

Regular readers will know that I worry about how little from political speeches are shown on prime-time television news programmes these days – as compared with interviews.

In the discussion after my UK Speechwriters' Guild Christmas lecture last month, someone made the interesting point that it's no longer necessary for TV companies to do this in the internet age, because keen anoraks can watch as many speeches as they like online.

Another innovation is the close coordination of "on message" speeches and interviews, as was demonstrated rather skilfully over the weekend by Ed Balls.

But does anyone watch the speeches?

One problem with some of the speeches that appear online is that they are so earnest or uninspiring (or both) that it's difficult to imagine prime-time news programmes – even in the glory days of the past – managing to select suitable quotable quotes for transmission to a wider audience.

One such example was Nick Clegg's speech at the Mansion House earlier today. It seems to have generated two main sound bites:

1)   a John Lewis economy

2)   The 1980s was the decade of share ownership. I want this to be the decade of employee share ownership.

But what he actually meant by either of these (not to mention the rest of the speech) was a question being widely asked on Twitter during the day.

As I've noted before, Clegg's communication skills continue to interest me – and this video and transcript look like promising data for closer analysis – comments and suggestions welcome ...

Excerpt from the speech:

" ... we don't believe our problem is too much capitalism: we think it's that too few people have capital. We need more individuals to have a real stake in their firms.

More of a John Lewis economy, if you like.

And, what many people don't realise about employee ownership is that it is a hugely underused tool in unlocking growth.

I don't value employee ownership because I somehow believe it's it's "nicer" – a more pleasant alternative to the rest of the corporate world. Those are lazy stereotypes. Firms that have engaged employees, who own a chunk of their company, are just as dynamic, just as savvy, as their competitors. In fact, they often perform better: lower absenteeism, lower staff turnover, lower production costs. In general, higher productivity and higher wages. They even weathered the economic downturn better than other companies."

Is employee ownership a panacea? No. Does it guarantee a company will thrive? No of course not. But the evidence and success stories cannot be ignored, and we have to tap this well if we are serious about growth. The 1980s was the decade of share ownership. I want this to be the decade of employee share ownership.

17th January 2012

Is it wise for Ed Miliband to play snakes and ladders with Jon Snow?

I'm grateful to Neill Harvey-Smith (@nhs999) for drawing my attention to a fascinating video clip via Twitter, where he tweeted "From the Ed Miliband treasure trove, media training lesson #24: don't do this."

The board had already been set up for the game by Shadow Chancellor Ed Balls with his Fabian Society speech and related interviews over the weekend and now, three days later, his leader lands on this whopping snake – posted on YouTube very soon after the end of the Channel 4 News on which it appeared.

It vividly demonstrates the risks faced by an inexperienced interviewee when trying to hold his own against an old hand like Jon Snow and I suspect that Mr Miliband and the Labour Party must be very glad that Channel 4 News doesn't reach a mass audience.

I also think that a more technical analysis of Mr Miliband's performance may well reveal some of the reasons why he's so far failed have a more positive impact on the wider public.

Jon Snow turned out to be one of several top political journalists who had been queuing up to take it in turns to interview Ed Miliband yesterday – all, judging from the background on the BBC, ITN, *Sky News* and Channel 4 News, in the same room.

ITN was able to edit out Tom Bradby's questions from the version posted on YouTube – which would hardly have been possible with the frequency of Jon Snow's interruptions on Channel 4 News.

In the absence of any such things to irritate or distract Mr Miliband, he was able to produce a performance that came across as a good deal more articulate, coherent and assured than in his joust with Jon Snow.

YouTube scorecard so far:

Channel 4 News version: 3,865 viewers (9 Sept 2014)
ITN version: 285 viewers (9 Sept 2014)

Obama's State of the Union speech: Behind the scenes with the speechwriters

Few British political speechwriters though there may be, anyone who writes any kind of speech is likely to be interested not only in this film (search for *Behind The Scenes: Writing the 2012 State of the Union Address* on YouTube) but also by the fact that it had nearly 400,000 views on YouTube within 24 hours of being posted there.

A cunning part of team Obama's communication strategy perhaps, but there's something very refreshing about a top politician openly admitting that he gets help with his speeches and being willing to give a public platform to those who help him.

So far, I've only watched it once and found the most annoying part was the awful background musak – but the producers of the film maybe know something that I don't about how distracting noises can enhance the impact of such propaganda.

The State of the Union address itself seemed to go down pretty well. But the video posted by the White House had another major distraction.

25th January 2012

Obama's State of the Union speech: Enhanced by PowerPoint?

When I first started watching the version of President Obama's State of the Union speech posted on YouTube by the White House, I wondered what the blue rectangle on the right hand side was for.

But all quickly became clear: it was for PowerPoint style slides and they, presumably, were what transformed it into an "enhanced version".

So we got to see a picture and the words MORE THAN 1 MILLION AMERICAN TROOPS SERVED IN IRAQ BETWEEN 2003-2011

Then a wanted poster for Osama bin Laden with a big red cross through it.

Then more pictures of US troops followed numbers of how many of them had fought in various wars.

And so on and on and on, through pictures, bar charts, graphs, diagrams lists of bullet points, on the US economy, education, etc., etc., etc.

Enhancement or distraction?

Watching this, I was left gasping, wondering who on earth in team Obama believes that his speeches are actually enhanced by such distractions, unless it was the same person who thought that background musak "enhanced" the film of his speechwriters preparing the speech.

Does it mean we can now expect President Obama to take a slide projector along with him during the forthcoming presidential campaign?

I think not – for the obvious reason that he's a good enough communicator to know that the words in his speeches and the way he delivers them are enough on their own to get his messages across.

What's more, I very much hope that this White House model of an "enhanced presentation" doesn't give other lesser speakers (e.g. most British politicians) the idea that this is the way to improve their own speeches "going forward".

If you haven't seen it yet, it's well worth watching all the way through – and coming to your own conclusion as to whether the visual aids enhance or distract from what he said.

26th January 2012

Speaking of the moon: Gingrich v. Kennedy

Republican presidential hopeful Newt Gingrich has told us that, by the end of his second term, there would be Americans living on the moon. With enough of them there, they'd even be able to become a state of the USA. And why not? After all, in 1961, President Kennedy had made the first of two famous speeches about American plans to send a man to the moon. The first was to Congress, followed up a year later by his "We choose to go to the moon" speech at Rice University.

So if Kennedy could get away with such an ambitious goal, why not Gingrich?

Er, at least 3 reasons:

1. Kennedy had already been president for more than a year when he went public with his proposal.

2. Before that, he'd already had time to consult with the relevant experts and no doubt had a pretty good idea that a man on the moon within a decade was entirely possible.

3. Kennedy never made any colonial claims on the moon. Nor, though he may have left a US flag there, did Neil Armstrong – or anyone else.

24th February 2012

To read or not to read? That is the question for speechwriters – or is it?

Yesterday's conference of the UK Speechwriters' Guild was another stimulating treat, for which founder Brian Jenner deserves the thanks of all of us who were lucky enough to attend. As with the last one, he'd pulled yet more rabbits out of the hat, including speakers from Russia and the Netherlands, rounding it off with a memorable double act starring Graham Davies and Phil Collins (even if it was an extended plug for a forthcoming book that might eventually compete with mine!). But, had there been more time, an interesting argument might have developed between some of us who were there and some of the speakers.

Authenticity?

For me, the most worrying buzzword of the day was "authenticity". Although several speakers had it high on their agendas, I doubt if I'm alone in remaining unclear about what exactly it's supposed to mean – other than different things to different people.

It was certainly curious (and vaguely challenging) for an audience of speechwriters to be told that it's not a good idea to write speeches at all. Nor was it particularly encouraging for people who make a living by writing speeches to be told that it's not a good idea to let your clients read scripts either – whether from pieces of paper or a teleprompter.

So what were they on about?

As far as I could tell, the prophets of doom were giving voice to some rather misconceived and misleading concerns about some well-known facts about the experience of public speakers and audiences.

1.   The language of the written word often sounds stilted and conceals the personality of the speaker in a cloak of formality when read aloud – i.e. they don't come across as themselves (sincere, passionate, etc.).

2.   Reading from a script can sometimes (though by no means always) result in an unacceptable loss of eye contact and rapport with your audience.

3.   The answer to these problems is not to use a script or notes.

To which my reactions are:

1.   True (but easy to remedy)
2.   True (but easy to remedy).
3.   False.

There's obviously no point in my trying to substantiate these by reproducing the sections from *Lend Me Your Ears* that deal with these issues (Chapters 1-3: 'The Language of Public Speaking' – on how the languages of everyday conversation, the written word and the publicly spoken word differ).

But a few famous examples (and thousands of not so famous ones that I've seen over the years) might help to reassure any colleagues whose confidence might have been dented by yesterday's claims that writing a speech will inevitably lead you (and your unfortunate clients) down the road to inauthenticity.

Freedom from scripts?

I don't deny, of course, that there are a few business and political speakers (e.g. Tom Peters, Steve Jobs, Tony Benn and David Cameron) who have impressed a lot of audiences with their apparent ability to speak without referring to notes or scripts. Nor do I deny that this might be a worthwhile objective for speakers to aim for.

But for most people, it's safer to regard it as a longer term goal, not least because it depends on their having enough time to work on the techniques for doing it effectively – which most don't have.

Exceptions that prove the rule?

Although Steve Jobs may have excelled at ex-temporising when speaking at Apple product launches, he was quite open about reading out his brilliant Stanford Commencement Address – which would hardly have attracted more than 15 million YouTube viewers had he dismally failed to be authentic and/or "come across as himself".

Seen & Heard

The point is that, if you get the language of public speaking right, it works. Some extreme cases from my own experience even suggest that, if you get the script right, your client has to be virtualy dyslexic to fail.

And if the timing of looking up and down from a script is roughly equivalent to the way gaze works in everyday conversation (where eye-contact is spasmodic rather than continuous), audiences hardly even notice it.

Nor, in the hundreds of courses I have run, would the vast majority of delegates have found that they feel more comfortable and easier to "come across as themselves" when using notes than when they were pretending not to have any (while trying to ad-lib from headings on PowerPoint slides).

And, if being seen to use notes were such a terrible sin, how, in later life, would former UK prime minister Harold Macmillan have captivated so many of his audiences at after dinner speeches by pretending to use notes on cards that were in fact completely blank (and when he was, in any case, almost blind)?

Writers: keep on writing

As Martin Shovel (@MartinShovel) pointed out in one of the discussions, if speechwriting were such a waste of time, how had Barack Obama and his team of writers got away with it?

And how were so many of those at yesterday's conference managing to make a reasonable living by pursuing such a pointless exercise as writing speeches?

The answer is as simple as it is obvious: it isn't pointless.

Nor should anyone seriously believe that the problem of authenticity is an insurmountable one for writers or speakers. It might be so if the world were populated by brilliant actors, all of whom were equipped with the technical skills to act out parts that were different from themselves.

Fortunately for all of us (and I don't just mean professional speechwriters), that isn't the case either.

News broadcast of a speech read out in full for 3 minutes: too much & too inauthentic?

Something very unusual happened today.

Presenter Eddie Mair told us on BBC Radio 4's early evening news programme PM that they were going to play the whole of Charlotte Church's statement after she and her family had settled their case for phone-hacking damages against News International's now defunct *News of the World*.

It lasted about three minutes – far longer than most clips from political speeches replayed on radio and television news broadcasts these days.

Regular readers will know that the British broadcasters' reluctance to play extended excerpts from political speeches and their preference for having their reporters tell us what speakers are saying is something I've been complaining about for quite a while.

They'll also know that I don't believe that reading a written-speech aloud always means that the speaker is doomed to come across as "inauthentic".

Charlotte Church may not be a politician, but the unusually long clip (you can view it on my blog) gives us a chance to check on both these issues at the same time. Was it too long for listeners and did she sound inauthentic? I first heard the clip on the car radio, so you'll have to close your eyes or look away to experience it in more or less the same way as I did (though without the added bonus of the beautiful Somerset countryside).

For what it's worth, I thought she made rather a good job of it – even though I could tell that she was reading from a text). Nor did my attentiveness to what she was saying lapse for a moment – even though we're all supposed to have such short attention spans that we're incapable of listening to a speech for anything like as long as three minutes.

So I'm still wondering why it is that our broadcasters no longer allow us to listen to excerpts from speeches by politicians that last as long as this ...

P.S. Fellow anoraks won't be surprised to know that the sound bite singled out for the headlines was a simple contrast: "They're not sorry, they're just sorry they got caught" (e.g. http://t.co/PjUzYQYQ) – which reminded me of my sons' Sinclair Spectrum computer chess game, which used to say after you'd played an obvious move: "I expected that!"

9th April 2012

Rowan Williams: Emperor, Archbishop or Cambridge academic with no clothes?

Regular readers will know that I've found the communication skills of the Archbishop of Canterbury an occasional source of bewilderment and amusement. Now he's decided to pack the job in to become master of a Cambridge college, you might think that he'd see his final Easter sermon as a wonderful chance to go out with a bang and/or leave a lasting mark on the Anglican communion.

But it was not to be either of these.

Archbishop Rowan apparently saw it as a golden opportunity to demonstrate his academic credentials to his eagerly awaiting colleagues in Cambridge and to show off his intellectual superiority over the ignorant masses (including any potential converts who might have been trying to make sense of his carefully chosen words for the day).

He may not have matched his record of a 147 word sentence, but he did manage one that went on for 87 words and averaged 45 words per sentence in this early paragraph from the sermon (the full text of which is reproduced below):

"Two new books on the economic crisis, one by the American Michael Sandel, the other by Robert and Edward Skidelsky, both rather surprisingly float the idea that without some input from religious thinking our ludicrous and destructive economic habits are more likely to go unchecked (45 words).

"And, notoriously, Alain de Botton's recent book on how to hold on to the best bits of religion without the embarrassing beliefs that go with it created quite a public stir (31 words).

"If it doesn't exactly amount to a religious revival, it does suggest that a tide may be turning in how serious and liberal-minded commentators think about faith: no longer seen as a brainless and oppressive enemy, it is recognized as a potential ally in challenging a model of human activity and social existence that increasingly feels insane, a model in which unlimited material growth and individual acquisition still seem to trump every other argument about social coherence, international justice and realism in the face of limited resources (87 words).

"We may groan in spirit at the reports of how few young people in our country know the Lord's Prayer, but there is plenty to suggest that younger people, while still statistically deeply unlikely to be churchgoers, don't have the hostility to faith that one might expect, but at least share some of the Sandel/Skidelsky/de Botton sense that there is something here to take seriously – when they have a chance to learn about it (75 words).

"It is about the worst possible moment to downgrade the status and professional excellence of religious education in secondary schools – but that's another sermon ... " (25 words).

Leaving aside the fact that the average length of sentence in speeches by effective speakers is 16 words, one has to ask whatever happened to the first step in preparing any speech or presentation (or sermon), namely analyse your audience (*Lend Me Your Ears*, pp. 280-86).

Just who did he think was out there in the congregation at Canterbury cathedral yesterday, let alone among the millions who might have caught a glimpse of him on television?

What was the key message he was trying to get across to such a huge audience on the most important day in the calendar of his church?

Has anyone the faintest idea what he was talking about or what nugget he wanted us to take away from it?

Papal plot revisited?

The more I've seen of Williams in action, the more I'm drawn to two theories about him. One came from a friend of mine, on which I've blogged before:

' ... it was no coincidence that Tony Blair was thinking about converting to Roman Catholicism when he elevated Rowan Williams to the top Anglican job, and that his selection of such a hopeless communicator was proof that Blair was serving as a secret agent for the Pope with a view to bringing the Church of England into disrepute.

'At the time, I thought it rather a good joke, but the more I've seen of the Archbishop's communication skills since then, the more I'm beginning to wonder whether there might be more than a grain of truth to the theory.'

'The emperor has no clothes'

Having once been a fellow of an Oxford college, I'm depressingly aware that the Cambridge college that's taken the risk of giving him a job will provide a very safe and comfortable haven for Dr Williams.

He reminds me of certain dons I knew in Oxford who, whether writing or speaking, specialised in inarticulate obscurantism. Whenever I dared to confess to colleagues that I couldn't understand a word they said or wrote, the standard reply was "Nor do I, but he really is terribly bright you know."

How they knew was a mystery to me and will, I suspect, remain a mystery to the fellows of Magdalene College, Cambridge who have, for reasons best known to themselves, elected the outgoing Archbishop to be their Master.

12th April 2012

Militant verb-avoidance in Miliband's latest speech

In the internet age, we can often can read a speech, free from any "embargo", before it's actually been given – as with one we'll be hearing from Ed Miliband later today (posted on *Politics Home* at 9.53 a.m. this morning).

One thing that struck me about it was that there were rather a lot of sequences without any verbs, a practice pioneered in some of Tony Blair's early leader's speeches to the Labour Party conference. But I'm no more convinced by it now than I was then.

Reading Miliband's forthcoming speech also reminded me that verblessnes is not something I recommend in my speechwriting courses either.

It also made me realise that I'm not quite sure why I don't and wonder whether I should.

Maybe it's because all these verbless phrases and isolated participles come across as disembodied lists that make it sound like the speaker's reading out the blobs/bullet points on a PowerPoint slide.

Or maybe I'm just an old fogey who's too preoccupied with the conventions of grammar to have noticed that the language of public speaking has changed.

If it has, I'd welcome your advice on whether you think it's a change for the better.

In the following sequences from the speech, the few sentences with verbs in them are singled out in italics:

> *"Nobody will be in any doubt that change is necessary for our country.*
> Unemployment rising.
> 1 million young people out of work.
> Living standards squeezed for all but a few at the top.
> Irresponsibility still being rewarded in huge pay rises and bank bonuses.

And there are problems that go beyond one government.

Long hours.

Wages not going up.

Costs rising.

Strains on families.

Worries about the future.

An economy not working for working people.

I have changed where we stand.

Equality of sacrifice and fairness of reward matter.

To me.

To Labour.

To Britain.

For too many years, some of the most powerful in society thought no-one could stand up to them even if they were ripping people off.

Energy companies.

Train companies.

Banks.

Even media companies.

I have changed where we stand.

No company is too powerful to challenge.

Standing with people in tough times is what counts.

To me.

To Labour.

To Britain.

That we are the party for the tougher times not just the easier times.

I have changed where we stand.

Changing our economy with:

Better quality jobs.

A living wage.

Making sure that businesses can get the money they need to grow.

This matters.

To me.

To Labour.

To Britain.

And I am proud to lead a party affiliated to three million working people through our link to the trade unions:

The nurses who look after the sick.

The teaching assistants who teach our kids.

The shopworkers, the engineers, the bus drivers.

But I know we can do more.

We do it by making promises we know we can keep.

Not image over substance.

Not fake change.

But by offering a different direction for the country

That is where I stand.

That is where Labour stands.

With you, on your side in these tough times.

That's what we're fighting for in these local elections."

24th April 2012

The language "surfacing" from James Murdoch at today's Leveson Inquiry

At about 1.00 p.m. today, I was asked by a leading Scottish newspaper to write a 400 word piece on James Murdoch's performance at today's Leveson Inquiry – deadline 6.00 p.m.

Tight though this was compared with the usual deadlines I work to, I agreed. Then, at about 4.30 p.m. just as I'd finished the first draft, another phone call from them: the revelations about Alex Salmond's involvement with the Murdoch family had wiped everything off tomorrows front pages so they wouldn't be able to use my contribution after all.

Not unusual in my experience with the media but, with a blog where I can post unfinished stuff, not much of a disaster either:

As one who spends most of his working life helping business people to communicate more effectively, I should have known better than to tune in to James Murdoch's evidence to the Leveson Inquiry today. But I can never resist the chance to collect examples of how and how not to do it.

Having heard Mr Murdoch in action before, I knew that he had a tendency to use management-speak to get his points across. What I now know is that he's one of the most extreme cases I've ever come across.

He spoke about "negotiating some of the detail going forward", an "undertaking in lieu", of someone who had "gotten what they'd professed to want", about "a case about whether or not there was an insufficiency with respect to…"; he "recalled concurring with that view" and "believed (he) would have appreciated assurances that the process would be handled objectively in the future."

He had much to say about "our rationale for the transaction and our analysis of the plurality concerns" and even threatened to "take plurality off the table."

"Nothing (he) said to Mr Osborne would have been inconsistent with our public advocacy on the subject."

And he was lucky enough to have "a management board where senior executives … had ample opportunity to be able to discuss these issues and surface them."

As his flat mid-Atlantic drawl droned on, it was like listening to paint dry. As for what it all meant to your average native speaker of English, much of it was anyone's guess. And that, presumably, is the point. Why else would so many business people become so addicted to the language of jargon and management-speak.

After all, the more long words of Latin origin you use, the more obscure your message is likely to be. Better still, saying that you "concur with that view" rather than "agreeing with it" implies a degree of neutrality and detachment. As an added bonus, if your audience is trying to work out what your words actually meant while, at the same time, trying to listen to whatever you say next, they're less likely to be able to understand that either.

Anyone in search of data for a treatise on the obscurantism of contemporary business language need look no further than James Murdoch – who also provides us with a variation on a famous quotation from George Bernard Shaw: "he who can communicate communicates; he who can't owns the media of communication".

8th May 2012

Relaunching the coalition and the cost of Etonian English?

About a month ago, I blogged about a speech by the leader of the Labour Party in which Ed Miliband used quite a lot of verbless sentences.

Today, I'm grateful to Stefan Stern for alerting me via Twitter (@stefanstern) to an article by David Cameron in today's *Daily Telegraph*, presumably written as part of the coalition's "relaunch" after Tory and LibDem losses in the recent local elections.

For Mr Stern, it (rightly) reminded him of the "content-free" political speech by the late Peter Sellers.

Miliband was making a speech, but Cameron was writing an article

In the case of Ed Miliband's speech, one of the comments on my blog pointed out that had the full stops been commas, the verbless sentences would no longer have been verbless and could have served as useful stage directions to help the speaker to deliver his messages in nice short chunks.

I can see (but don't agree) that some speechwriters might want to make a case for verbless sentences when writing for clients speaking in our sound bite hungry world.

But I cannot see any justification (or excuse) whatsoever for leaving out verbs when writing an article that is explicitly intended to be read by readers (of a supposedly "quality" newspaper), as in the following two paragraphs, purportedly penned by the Prime Minister – which, apart from the first sentences, degenerate into verbless lists:

"This is painstaking work.
"Seeing through the reductions to government spending.
"Cutting regulation and business tax to help the private sector.
"Helping start-up firms, investing in apprenticeships and boosting trade to

help rebalance our economy in favour of enterprise, manufacturing, technology and exports.

"And repairing our wrecked financial system so that we can have confidence in our banks and they can lend properly again.".…

"I'm proud of the battles we've fought in the first two years of this Government.

"Battles that we won in education, so that schools toughen up on exams, insist on discipline, and have the freedom to do what teachers and parents want.

"Battles that we won against the teeth of Labour opposition on immigration control and welfare reform, too."

If this is the kind of English you end up writing after being educated at Eton, I'd be asking them for my money back. Or, if it were a ghost-writer who actually wrote this stuff for Cameron, s/he should be sacked forthwith and sent off for intensive private tuition with Mr Gove. I'd also quite like to know who pays for such illiterate scribes to work in Downing Street – tax-payers or the Conservative Party?

27th June 2012

Treasury lamb to the Paxman slaughter

Just occasionally, from the plethora of forgettable TV and radio interviews that punctuates our day in this age of 24 hour news coverage, one will stand out as being so memorable as to be worth watching again.

As I've noted in other blogposts, they never work in favour of the the politician being interviewed. And, when they appear on programmes with very small audiences (like *Newsnight* on BBC 2) we may never get to see them unless someone, as in this case, has bothered to upload it to YouTube.

This particular specimen was to be seen last night when Jeremy Paxman tried to find out when a junior treasury minister had actually heard about the government's latest U turn on the budget, namely the decision to defer the increase in fuel duty for a few months (visit my blog to see what happened, you'll have to scroll in just over 6 minutes).

Free ammunition for pundits

If you sit through the first 6 minutes, you'll no doubt be amazed at HM Treasury's willingness to provide yet more data for the likes of Messrs Mason and Nelson to pontificate on how it all proves that the government has lost its way.

Free ammunition for Paxo

Then, after 6 minutes, we get to the finale, as a young and inexperienced minister is left to mercy of an old and highly experienced interviewer. As you watch Ms Smith struggling to fend off Paxo's onslaught, you may well find yourself asking just who at the Treasury had taken the decision to leave it to so junior a minister to field such awkward barrage of questions from the master of awkward questions? Who at the Treasury (if anyone) is in charge of briefing and coaching ministers before they go on air – or do they just not bother? Or is someone in the higher reaches of the Treasury or Tory Party out to destroy Chloe Smith's career before it's really got off the ground?

3rd September 2012

Mitt Romney's US = Unbearable Smugness

On the day of President Obama's inaugural speech in 2009, I blogged about a line I didn't want to hear in his speech:

> "If there's one thing that irks me about speeches by American presidents,
> it's their tendency to overstate the case for their country being the first,
> finest or only example of freedom and democracy in the world."

And, to be fair, he obliged by avoiding any such extremes of smugness. But there will, I fear, be no such luck if Mitt Romney makes it to the White House. Having watched his acceptance speech a couple of times, I'm finding it difficult to decide which of the following I find more annoying: the fact that he uttered these lines at all, or the rapturous response they triggered from the audience:

> "like all Americans who went to bed that night knowing that we lived in
> the greatest country in the history of the world."
> "When the world needs someone to do the really big stuff, you need an
> American."

13th September 2012

B – for the Duchess of Cambridge's second speech (and/or her PR team)

After the Duchess of Cambridge's first speech, one of the comments on YouTube said: "Extremely annoying how she reads the script every 2 seconds, that was most likely written by her PR team."

But the overall consensus was that, for a first effort, it wasn't too bad at all.

Second effort though this one may have been, the rather carping comment above seems even more appropriate than last time – or at least raised a number of questions.

• Had she rehearsed the speech and, if so, how many times?

• How was the speech laid out on the two pages she was using?

• Why hadn't the height of the microphone been fixed before she started to speak?

• Had the sign in the background been properly secured?

• Why was there a gap on the left of the sign that allowed a police woman disguised as Princess Anne (and various other people) to peer out and distract the wider audience?

Or, to put it more bluntly, with the resources available to the royal households, why on earth don't they bother to get the basics right?

18th September 2012

Does Mitt Romney's mouth move faster than his brain?

I've not studied Mitt Romney's style of speaking in much detail, but there may be a clue in his latest gaffe as to why I'd felt there was something a bit odd about him.

It's the sheer speed at which he speaks.

Speeches by effective public speakers are delivered at about 120 words per minute, which is much slower than the 180 words per minute found in conversations between native speakers of English (see my books).

But in the sequence that got him into so much trouble, Mr Romney manages about 200 words per minute – i.e. 20 words per minute quicker than conversation.

Apart from the fact that this is abnormally fast for a conversation (let alone a speech) it raises two intriguing questions:

1. Is he speaking too quickly for his brain to be able to produce carefully considered and/or "elegantly stated" opinions?

2. How, in American culture, is "fast-speaking" likely to be regarded by the wider public?

For what it's worth, to my British ears, "fast-speaking" tends to have mainly negative connotations ...

19th September 2012

A neat contrast wins applause for Obama's talk show point about Romney

I may have been rather critical of President Obama's rather uninspiring (for him) acceptance speech at the Democratic National Convention, but was rather more impressed by his performance on the *David Letterman Show* last night, prompting as it did an interruptive burst of applause – just after he'd used a nice simple contrast:

> "My expectation is that, if you want to be President,
> you got to work for everyone, not just for some, [Applause starts]
> and thee uh--"[Applause continues]

As noted elsewhere on this blog (and in my books), the contrast is one of the most important rhetorical devices for triggering applause in political speeches. And, as is evident from this example, it can work in the same way in other settings too (e.g. TV interviews).

26th September 2012

A generous audience for Clegg – but why on earth draw attention to it?

In previous years, I've criticised Nick Clegg (and/or those advising him) for the decision to go for the management guru style of delivery in his leader's speech – i.e. wandering around the stage pretending that he's not using a teleprompter.

So the big plus this year was to see the Deputy Prime Minister looking rather more statesmanlike than usual by the simple device of staying firmly at the lectern.

But there's another important lesson he still has to learn: if a particular line goes down well with your audience, don't comment on it or otherwise draw attention to it.

This particular joke (about the Conservative's "Green" credentials – "to make blue go green, you have to add yellow") was, perhaps predictably, the first sound bite from the speech to be tweeted by BBC television's @daily_politics shoe – and will probably make it on to some of tonight's prime-time news programmes.

It was so successful that it triggered a massive 23 seconds of applause (i.e. 15 seconds more than the standard 8 seconds burst).

But surely it's far better to leave the audience to draw their own (positive) conclusions about what they've just seen and heard than to comment on the difference between what you'd expected and what had happened. All that achieves is to highlight the scripted calculated nature of the line in question – and perhaps also gives away that there'd been a good deal of discussion about it beforehand with your aides:

> "I thought you'd groan rather than clap at that one, but anyway [slight laughter] what a generous audience."

It reminded me of a line Mrs Thatcher once used in the early 1980s, when she based her commendation of her foreign secretary, Lord Carrington, on a television beer advertisement of the day: "Yes, he really is the peer that reaches parts that other peers can't reach."

This prompted much laughter and applause, during which she could be seen (and just heard) saying "Oh, it did work, then ... "

In this particular case, Nick Clegg's good luck is that, in order to include the unfortunate line, the the television news shows would have to play the whole 23 seconds of applause that comes before it – so it's unlikely to be seen by anyone other than anoraks like me (and/or readers of blogs like this one).

1st October 2012

Ed Balls may be a better speaker than he was, but ...

James Forsyth's assessment of Ed Balls as "a vastly improved platform speaker" (*Spectator*) was quite widely echoed by other journalists today on Twitter.

Michael Crick of Channel 4 News (@MichaelLCrick) told us that Mr Balls had "rehearsed his speech in his hotel room with an ironing board" – adding, rather unkindly: "which may explain why, in the end, it was a bit flat."

Looking on a brighter side, I think it's quite impressive these days to hear that our politicians take the trouble to rehearse their speeches at all, especially when they've taken the apparently daring decision to use a hard copy script rather than read from an Autocue.

But there were two things about this particular speech that puzzled me:

• First, quite a few tweets on Twitter noticed and commented on the Labour Party's unexplained decision to abandon a red background completely in favour of making it look as though they'd stolen the Conservative's erstwhile monopoly on blue.

• Second, although I can see why today's Labour hierarchy prefer saying "conference" to "comrades" (as in the past) was it really necessary for Mr Balls to repeat the word 33 times during his speech – especially when both words draw attention to the fact that he has trouble saying his 'r's and pronounces the words as "confwence" and "comwades"?

For me, at least, I found the excessive, and in my view pointless, repetition of "confwence" so distracting and annoying that I stopped watching the speech when he was only about half way through – which is presumably not what he hopes for from his audiences.

Ed Miliband's tour de force

It's not often that a party leader's conference speech gets as widespread a thumbs-up as Ed Miliband enjoyed yesterday – even though what seems to have impressed the media most is his new-found ability to speak so fluently (and for so long) without any apparent reference to a script.

Could it be, I began to wonder, that our broadcast media are themselves so dependent on scripts and teleprompters that they're all too easily impressed by a style of speaking that they rather wish they could master for themselves?

Cameronesque?

Or did David Cameron really set a new standard when he won his party leadership by speaking without notes at a "beauty parade" in 2005, underlining the power of an unscripted conference speech two years later by deterring Gordon Brown from holding a general election at a time when Labour would almost certainly have won?

Subsequent attempts by others, like Nick Clegg and Gordon Brown, to emulate David Cameron's skill at speaking without a script have not met with anything like as favourable a media response as Ed Miliband attracted yesterday.

Scriptlessness or better than expected?

It's not clear to me whether this was mainly the result of scriptlessness, a more relaxed delivery than usual or, perhaps most likely (?) because Miliband's previous performances had set such low media expectations.

The trouble now is that he runs the risk, if he reverts to using scripts again, of being denounced for not speaking from the heart and/or having employed someone else to write his speeches for him.

Other quibbles

Regular readers of this blog will know that I'm still not convinced by this walkabout management guru style of delivery for political speeches. Other quibbles include:

- Glum-looking backdrop: I still don't see the point of having part of the audience behind the speaker. Although reasonably well-behaved, this particular group looked very glum for much of the time and were, on occasions, rather slow to join in the applause.

- Too youthful a sample*: Some viewers (e.g. me) were quite shocked by how very young a sample of voters they represented, with no one much over 45 anywhere to be seen among those behind him.

- Hands: Finally, if you're going to wander about the stage, what to do with your hands and how to respond to applause can pose problems for a speaker. On the whole, Mr Miliband coped quite well on both these fronts. However, he might like to note that there were some on Twitter who took exception to the fact that he spoke for quite long periods with one hand in his pocket. If it's any comfort to him, the complainants probably went to a public school where you weren't allowed to put your hands in your pockets until you reached the sixth form ...

1st November 2012

Clegg's reply to the Tory rebels weakened by lack of rehearsal

As a former MEP who has worked for an EU commissioner, Nick Clegg is obviously better informed about Europe than most of our MPs.

Given yesterday's anti-EU vote in the House of Commons, it was therefore quite fortunate that he was booked to speak this morning at the Chatham House think-tank on international affairs – even if there wasn't much time to write much of a critique in time for today.

What a pity, then, that the Deputy Prime Minister didn't allow more time to rehearse what he wanted to say a few times before he said it. Had he done so, he wouldn't have had to spend so much time looking down at his script and might even have managed a rather livelier and less "wooden" delivery ...

20th November 2012

Parliament Week trailer: Ashdown & Atkinson in conversation

Tomorrow evening, Paddy Ashdown and I have been invited to an event organised by the UK Speechwriters' Guild as part of Parliament Week 2012. It's given me an excuse to rummage through some ancient video clips, and it occurred to me that those who won't be there tomorrow might like to hear about them (you can also view them on my blog).

A promising newcomer?

The first one dates from 1981, when Paddy Ashdown was still the prospective parliamentary candidate for Yeovil, and John Heritage and I were in the process of recording all the televised output from that year's three main political party conferences.

At this stage, Paddy wasn't really aware of how rhetoric works and had to break off when his three-part list prompted a burst of applause – looking vaguely surprised that it had brought so positive a response from the audience. Nor had he given much thought to wearing a jacket and tie – and maybe he'll be able to tell us tomorrow night whether the lectern was hiding sandals.

1987 General Election

After becoming an MP in 1983, Paddy was transport spokesman for the Liberals and had been lent a copy of my book *Our Masters' Voices* (1984) by a mutual friend (now Lord Bradshaw) who introduced us with a view to my helping the new MP with his speeches.

By the time of the 1987 General Election, Paddy had become the education spokesman for the SDP Liberal Alliance, which meant that he would have to speak when they launched their campaign at the Barbican.

So this was the first speech that we worked on together to be televised. A puzzle with an alliterative three-part solution was among the lines that got the desired response. And one of these "Rs" came from a Scrabble dictionary, which can be a useful resource for searching lists of words quickly and without being deflected by definitions.

Although *Our Masters' Voices* had quite a lot to say about rhetorical devices like contrasts and three-part lists, it said little about the importance of imagery and story telling as ways of getting your message across. However, having by this stage become more involved in coaching people to make speeches and presentations, I'd become much more aware of how effective metaphors, similes, analogies and anecdotes could be.

Liberal Party merger debate, 1988

Having fought the 1987 general election as two parties in an alliance, the Liberals and SDP turned to the question of whether they should become a single party. Paddy was keen that they should, and planned to speak in support of merger at the special assembly early in 1988. I wrote a speech but did not go to the conference. On the train to the venue, one of his other advisors persuaded him to leave out every sentence I'd written – except for one.

To my great delight, it was the "Tower of Babel/tower of strength" contrast that was the only line that was selected as a sound bite on prime-time news programmes. One of the commentators even claimed it was a "clear statement" of Ashdown's intention to run for the leadership if a new party were formed (which it wasn't).

Leadership campaign, 1988

Once Paddy had decided to run for the leadership of the new party, we spent weeks working with him on the speech in which he would announce his candidacy – not realising at the time that, for the next three weeks, he would need at least one new speech per day.

Amidst the ongoing panic that followed, I remember getting a note from one of the other writers saying "My price is a peerage, what's yours?" – but, for some strange reason, neither of us has (yet) been elevated to the House of Lords.

But I was quite pleased that a widely played sound bite from the speech was a simple three-part list in which yesterday, today and tomorrow were used as metaphors for past, present and future:

The new leader

A few days before the result was announced, it became clear that our candidate was going to win. By then, the gains of the two parties at the 1987 election had been largely whittled away, and Paddy was well aware of the need to remind the public that the Alliance was still going strong (?) in a different form.

Reflecting on my brief to cook up some lines to get this across, I was stuck in one of those traffic jams on the M6 where there's so little movement that you have to turn the car engine off.

Reaching for my pen and pad I started trying different possibilities and came up with a contrast between being "not only back in business, but mean business", which BBC political editor John Cole seem to think good enough to headline his introduction to live footage – of yet another three-part list.

Who's helping?

I've often likened speechwriting as an occupation to being rather like robbing banks, in that you can't go around advertising your wares by boasting which speeches you wrote for whom. Nor, usually, can you expect a client to tell all his friends that he'd got someone else to help him.

But on this, Paddy had a different and refreshingly open approach. During his leadership campaign, he asked me if I would mind if he told the media who'd been helping him with his speeches.

Initially, I wasn't convinced that this would be a good idea from his point of view, as my involvement in coaching someone to win a standing ovation at the 1984 SDP conference had earned me the name "Dr Claptrap" in some quarters. But his line was that it was as rational to consult an "expert" on speechmaking and rhetoric as it was to consult "experts" on IT or any other field he felt he needed help with.

At around that time, the director of communications of a large multi-national company told me it wouldn't do my business any good if it became known that I was associated with such losers as the Liberal Democrats.

Ten years later, I was still in business, Ashdown had more than doubled the number of Liberal Democrat MPs but the company of the director of communications had gone into liquidation a few years earlier.

As for why I got involved, I had been a keen supporter of the SDP and believed then (as I still believe now) that, if Ashdown didn't win the leadership of the new party, it would be the end of three party politics in the UK for at least a generation.

How much?

Party members who worry about how much I was paid by the Lib Dems during the twelve years I worked with Paddy will be relieved to know that it was a grand total of £0.00. In fact, given that I never charged for travel costs, it was actually a substantial minus figure – not least because, in those early years, all the Sainsbury cash had stayed with David Owen's rump SDP (before being diverted to "New Labour").

For those of us whose journey to the Liberal Democrats was via the SDP, the Blair years were arguably pretty much what the gang of four had been hoping for all those years ago ...

18th December 2012

One = Three religious questions in Obama's Connecticut speech

For students of rhetoric and oratory, there's always a silver lining to the horrific mass shootings that have become such a regular feature of American life – because one thing that's certain is that we'll get to hear yet another example of President Obama making a masterful speech that catches the mood of the nation.

The full video and transcript of what he said at the interfaith Prayer Vigil in Newtown, Connecticuton on Sunday can be seen on my blog. But one line that particularly intrigued me was this one, in which he set up "a simple question" that turned out to be three questions:

> "All the world's religions — so many of them represented here today —
> start with a simple question: Why are we here? What gives our life
> meaning? What gives our acts purpose?"

Nor has the fact that no one seems to have noticed or raised any queries about this apparent inconsistency surprised me. As I noted four years ago, his speech in Chicago on winning the presidency for the first time contained 29 three-part lists in just over ten minutes. Nobody noticed that either, nor did it stop people from being impressed by the "quality" of the speech.

Much the same, it seems, applies to this speech, even to the extent that some commentators have been hailing it as his "Gettysburg Address".

Seen & Heard

18th January 2013

Lance Armstrong's "straight" answers to Oprah's Yes/No questions

Having never previously seen any Oprah Winfrey interviews, I've no idea whether her interviewees have to agree beforehand to answer any "Yes/No" questions she might ask with a straight "Yes" or "No".

But that's what disgraced cyclist Lance Armstrong did in his interview with her.

Whether or not it was not the way she had expected him to confess, as she'd said in her trailers for the show, I do not know. I do know, however, that to my English ears, such apparently straight answers to a series of "Yes/No" questions definitely qualifies it for a place my collection of unusual TV interviews.

23th January 2013

Cameron on Europe: a press release thinly disguised as a speech

Finding out when and where David Cameron's much-trailed speech on Europe was taking place today posed at least as much of a challenge as working out what the point of it all was.

What I eventually discovered was that both the when and the where of the speech were quite unusual – unless it's suddenly become fashionable for our politicians to deliver major speeches at 8:00 a.m. in the morning on the off chance that the American news agency in central London (where the speech was being given) would be able to drum up an audience at a moment's notice to listen to it – or, to be more precise, to prepare reports on what he said for the rest of the day's news programmes.

Who was there?

From the above, there's very little evidence that anyone was there at all: no coughing or sneezing and not so much as a hint of applause at the end of the speech.

Yet there were, of course plenty of people there, not supporters who might have cheered or clapped, but representatives of the media busily writing notes on what he was saying – while he was saying it (which keen "listeners" could follow live, as the words came out of his mouth, on the BBC website.

Speech or press release?

So does this really count as a political "speech" delivered by a leading politician, or was it merely a case of a leading politician taking the trouble to read out a press release – on the grounds that no one would take any notice of it unless it were disguised, however thinly, as "a speech"?

And are we going to have to put up with more and more such non-speeches as the stock-in-trade of contemporary political communication?

4th February 2013

Another extended press release disguised as a speech – and does it matter?

Hardly ten days on from seeing David Cameron reading an extended press release on Europe as if it were "a speech" to an audience and we have Chancellor of the Exchequer, George Osborne, doing much the same thing at the offices of JP Morgan in Bournemouth earlier today. As with the PM's speech, the absence of any coughing, sneezing or applause left me wondering whether there was an audience there at all and whether this is yet another example of a politician reading out a long-winded press release as if it were a speech.

So what? My blog on this after Cameron's Europe speech prompted an interesting comment on Twitter from speechwriter Sam Coates (@SamuelCoates):

> "re: Cameron speech lacking non-media audience, are you in danger of being too purist? Better a speech than press conf/release?"

To which I admitted that perhaps I was being rather too purist and asked, "but are you conceding that it was a press release?"

"No" he tweeted "a well-articulated speech seen live by many not in the room. But admittedly not one that had to worry about claptraps etc!"

Speeches as press releases – and does it matter?

From this, it seems that Mr Coates is rather more relaxed about this trend than I am – which gets me wondering whether my unease about politicians reading out what are, in effect, extended press releases to non-partisan audiences is a further reflection of my advanced years (and the relative youthfulness of Mr Coates).

As I asked in my last blog on the subject, "are we going to have to put up with more and more such non-speeches as the stock-in-trade of contemporary political communication?" – to which I'd add "does it matter?"

13th February 2013

Water-bottle gate: a reminder about drinking and speaking from Senator Marco Rubio

Since Senator Marco Rubio, an early favourite for the 2016 Republican presidential nomination according to some newspapers responded to President Obama's State of the Union address a few hours ago, he's attracted a good deal of flack on Twitter for the way he grasped for a bottle of water during his speech (about 23 seconds in) – in a sequence that's apparently going viral.

Yet all of us who do any public speaking at all know that a glass (rather than a bottle) of water close at hand (rather than a few feet away and nearly out of reach) is an essential part of your backup equipment.

The awkward, even shifty, way in which Rubio reached for his water may not have been very elegant or well-timed. But it came nowhere close to the disaster I saw some years ago at a Labour Party annual conference.

The speaker was making a long and boring speech about a long and boring composite motion that he was proposing. A cutaway shot of the audience showed that some were reading newspapers, some were audibly chatting to each other and very few were paying attention.

So when the speaker paused for a drink of water, the audience must have thought he'd finished and promptly started clapping.

But he hadn't finished and thanked them for the applause – before droning on for several more minutes.

13th February 2013

State of the Union Address, 2013: surfing applause to bring about better gun control?

One of the things that impressed me when writing *Our Masters' Voices* (1984) was former Labour cabinet minister Tony Benn's technical ability to carry on speaking after his audience had started to applaud. It created the impression that he had not been attempting to trigger applause and that he was now having trouble making himself heard because what he'd just said had gone down so well with the audience that they couldn't wait any longer to show their approval.

It's a technique referred to in American English as "surfing applause", a phrase that sums it up so well that I wish I'd known it when I first started writing about it. When done well, the audience reaction comes across as unequivocally positive, with speaker and listeners sounding as though they are on exactly the same wavelength.

It was therefore fascinating to see where President Obama took to surfing the applause during this year's State of the Union address – at the point when he starts to identify groups of people and individuals who have suffered from gun violence and who "deserve a vote".

Although it would be nice to think that the president's technical skill at rhetoric and oratory might be enough to get the job of gun control done, I fear that this will never happen – and will be thwarted by the peculiar (and peculiarly) American obsession with "the right to bear arms".

25th March 2013

Boris Johnson's Sunday morning meeting with Eddie Mair

On several occasions, I've asked whether interviews are ever capable of delivering good news for politicians and wondered why our political leaders appear content with the deal that appears to have been done with the media – in which news interviews have more or less taken over from speeches as the main means of political communication in Britain.

Vivid evidence of the damage a politician can do to himself was provided yesterday morning on a TV show in which interviews play a major part, and where the producers' best hope is that an interviewee will say something – or, better still, say some things – that will attract much wider media attention than the show normally enjoys.

This time, the interviewee was Mayor of London Boris Johnson, for whom at least three of Eddie Mair's questions caused problems: was he fired from *The Times* for inventing a story, had he told former leader of the Conservative Party Michael Howard a "bare-faced lie" and had he talked to a friend on the phone about having someone beaten. A curious feature of this story was the way in which it didn't become a story on the BBC, whose news broadcasts later in the day carried on as if the Mair-Johnson interview wasn't news at all, even though other media outlets thought differently.

The interesting question now is whether these few moments from a Sunday morning TV show will have any more lasting impact on Mr Johnson's reputation and political career.

If nothing else, I suspect that I won't be alone in watching tonight's Michael Cockerell documentary that prompted Eddie Mair's questions.

13th May 2013

More nails in the coffin of political speech-making in Britain?

In earlier blogs, I've suggested that a major change in the past 25 years has been the replacement of political speeches by broadcast interviews as the main form of political communication in Britain – even though interviews hardly ever result in anything other than bad news about the politicians themselves. As a result, effective political speech-making has become a dying art, in which there appears to be a curious collaboration between the media and politicians to continue relegating the coverage of speeches in favour of the broadcast interview.

At the same time, the politicians are also doing their bit to eliminate much of the passion and liveliness that were once a normal part of political rallies – by speaking in rather strange venues to audiences with little or no interest in politics, and certainly no motivation to applaud or boo anything they might hear.

The big questions I'd like to hear answers to from people in politics and/or the media is what the point of such strange venues is and whose idea it was to "neutralise" the political speech - politicians, their advisors or the media?

I'd also quite like to know why a supermarket chain (Morrisons) has become the venue of choice for leading Conservative politicians.

You can view the clips on the blog. They are intended to illustrate the trend by comparing leading politicians from 30 Years ago with leading politicians of today.

Classic examples from the 1980s

Note that in each example the speakers deliver the key points with passion and that audience responses are very evident for all to see and hear.

Not so classic examples from 2010-2013

Note that all three leaders speak with their backs to a window, through which distractions are clearly visible (e.g. people walking about, cars and lorries driving by, boat on the river, etc.). Little effort goes into conveying much in the way of passion – which is hardly surprising given that it's not at all clear who is actually in the audience. Nor is their any evidence of what impact, if any, they might be having on those in audience (who remain completely silent and, for the most part, invisible).

Morrisons?

Last week, David Cameron followed George Osborne's curious example a month earlier by making a speech at a supermarket distribution centre (Morrisons). Evidence of audience attentiveness and or approval (or disapproval) is fairly thin on the ground and their wandering about becomes something of a distraction.

Cameron's speech on Europe

When this much heralded speech had to be rescheduled, I tried to find out exactly when and where it was happening. After more than an hour's search on the internet, I came up with the extraordinary finding that it had already taken place – at 8.30 a.m. in the morning – at the London headquarters of an American company (Bloomberg).

There was no applause, booing or cries of "Here. here". And, as it was in February, the complete absence of coughing, sneezing and nose-blowing got me wondering whether there was anyone there in the audience at all. But of course there were, if no one else, plenty of journalists present.

David Cameron's performance left much to be desired, even though he's one of our best contemporary political orators – and one was left wondering whether he'd bothered to rehearse what was supposed to be such a very important speech.

3rd June 2013

Latest press release by Ed Balls disguised as a speech to Thomson Reuters

While top Tories like David Cameron and George Osborne have recently read out their press releases at Morrisons' distribution warehouses, today opposition shadow chancellor Ed Balls read out his latest announcements at Thomson Reuters in London.

Whether or not this was a subtle Labour wheeze to move up-market from Messrs Cameron and Osborne is anyone's guess.

But, judging from the amount of noise from the Twitterati and elsewhere on the internet, the venue was a good enough choice for plenty of journalists to have made the effort to turn up, even if no one else was there.

So Mr Balls didn't have to worry too much about how he delivered his "speech" (if it really was a speech), or whether the audience responded with any applause, booing or heckling – of which I heard none.

The unfortunate public can now look forward to more video clips of Mr Balls in action (action?) for the rest of the day on 24 hour and prime-time TV news programmes. Whether any of it will inspire any of us enough to be able to remember anything from it, I very much doubt.

29th August 2013

British students' first encounter with segregation in 1963

British students of today will no doubt be appalled to know that, by the end of our first year at university, my girlfriend and I had saved enough money from our grants to book tickets on a London to New York charter flight – for £50 return.

As it was a last minute decision to go, we hadn't much of a plan about what to do when we got there, other than to visit relations who had emigrated to North America in the early 1900s. We'd also been too late (and too short of cash) to buy the then amazing Greyhound Bus deal of unlimited travel for 99 days for $99 – so we had little choice but to hitch-hike

An early stop was in Portsmouth, Virginia, to stay with my girlfriend's great uncle Willie. Then in his 80s, he had emigrated to the USA as a young man and had developed into a typical white Southerner, a first hint of which were the numerous Confederate flags arrayed both inside and outside his house.

We'd heard about racial segregation in the Southern states of America, but had no idea that it was practised so widely or to such an extreme extent. Three examples stood out from the many:

1. To get to a local swimming pool, much needed to survive in levels of humidity we'd never before experienced, we had to walk through an area populated by black Americans. Everyone at the pool was white, which Uncle Willie explained by telling us "they have their own pool elsewhere."

2. One Sunday, we were taken to the local Baptist church, where every face was also white. "They have their own church elsewhere", explained Uncle Willie.

3. On another day, we went to Virginia Beach armed with details supplied by Uncle Willie of bus times for getting there and back. At Virginia Beach, the only people on the beach were white, also predictably explained by Uncle Willie: "They have their own beach further along the shore."

On the way back, we realised that there was actually an earlier bus home than the one that Uncle Willie had suggested. All the other passengers in it were black, and seemed vaguely surprised when we got in – and even more surprised when we headed for and sat in the back seat.

When we told Uncle Willie about our day out, he was furious, telling us that we'd taken the wrong bus. That one was for blacks only and we should have waited for the later one for whites. What's more, as whites, we should certainly not have sat anywhere near the back seat.

A lesson we quickly learnt was that it was quite impossible to argue rationally with Uncle Willie (or any other white Southerner we met). After all, everyone knew and accepted that black people liked having their own swimming pools, churches, beaches and buses, and that the arrangements suited both blacks and whites.

Any comparison with South Africa was dismissed out of hand – not least because they didn't seem to know where it was, let alone about the kind of society the apartheid regime was running in those days (when many of us in the UK were already boycotting South African fruit and wine).

I now realise that it was only a matter of weeks before there would be a march on Washington where a black Baptist minister would be making a speech with a few relevant points about what we had just seen. Planning for the march must have been in full swing, but we never heard anyone make any mention of it.

Uncle Willie and his friends obviously had no plans for making the short journey to Washington in August, 1963 – and were no doubt greatly underwhelmed when Martin Luther King went banging on about having a dream.

9rd September 2013

George Osborne speaks into thin air at a building site somewhere in London

Readers will know that I've been mystified by the locations at which the Prime Minister and Chancellor of the Exchequer have delivered some rather important recent speeches.

Finding out exactly where, when and to whom George Osborne made his speech on the economy this morning has been quite a challenge.

The *Daily Express* tells us that he was at a building site in East London and, according to *Sky News*, he was "addressing an audience of academics, think tanks and businesses in London".

As usual at such events, there was no hint of a response from anyone in the audience, if indeed anyone was there at all.

Also as usual, there's a weird backdrop of a blank window with a bar chart to the left that looks like a rather creative use of scaffolding – unless, of course, it's the latest in templates from PowerPoint.

24th September 2013

How well does English really work as a "common language" of communication?

The following is a script of my presentation at last week's European Speechwriters Conference.

This talk has been prompted by a number of experiences running courses on speechwriting and presentation in various parts of Europe.

Like some of my previous presentations at UK Speechwriters' Guild conferences, it poses more questions than it answers. But at least it may open a discussion of possible interest and relevance to many of you here today.

All the courses on speechwriting were conducted in English. None of those attending was a native-speaker of English.

But *all* of them had the job of writing speeches in English, to be given by other non-native speakers of English to audiences of yet more non-native speakers of English.

We who have been native speakers of English since acquiring language in the first place (and who have little need to develop a command of any other language) cannot help being full of admiration for the fact that they can do it at all. But the challenge they face brings three true stories to mind, and raises at least three questions worth discussing.

Speaking to non-native speakers

The first time I ever spoke to an audience of non-native speakers of English was more than three decades ago at an academic conference in the Council of Europe chamber in Strasbourg.

It was long before I'd developed a technical interest in how audiences react to public speaking, when my main experience had been listening to academics read out papers at other academic conferences.

I was to present a 30 page academic paper, for which I had been allocated 5 minutes. So I decided (very unwisely) to read it aloud as quickly as possible and see how far I got – which wasn't very far. After about half a minute, the chairman interrupted me. The simultaneous interpreters had complained that they couldn't keep up with me speaking at such a pace, so he asked me to slow down.

Later on, at another academic conference at the University of Konstanz, I could tell that my audience was looking increasingly puzzled by what I was saying.

By then, I had become a bit more sensitive to the needs of my audience and came up with what might have been a suitable strategy: simplify, simplify, simplify.

Suitable strategy it might have been if only I hadn't use more colloquialisms and slang to "simplify" my points. And that, of course, was no solution at all, as it made my talk even more unintelligible to the audience than it had been in the first place.

In the third example, I wasn't actually speaking but was in an audience of mixed, nationalities, mainly from Europe, at a conference in Urbino.

It was a memorable lecture analysing a letter by Pliny the Younger by the well-known semiologist and author, Umberto Eco – though memorable more for what happened than for what he said.

He had just started his lecture when a group of locals demanded to know why he was speaking English in an Italian university. His response was impressively democratic and he asked the audience:

"How many of you can only speak English?"

I was one of the tiny minority of 5 or 6 native speakers of British and American English who raised their hands.

In response to which Eco quickly rephrased his question:

"For how many of you is English the only foreign language you can understand?"

The vast majority of hands now went up, to which Eco turned to his compatriots and said:

"As my lecture was advertised to be in English and the only language most people here understand is English, I shall give my lecture in English" – at which point, the rebellious Italian minority walked out.

Lingua Anglica

So, although English may have become Europe's new Lingua Franca its dominance is not always without its problems.

Speaking more quickly and simplifying via colloquialisms and slang are obviously no solution.

And there is quite a lot of good news. For one thing, the same rhetorical techniques are just as effective in getting messages across in any particular language – and have been for at least 2,000 years since the classical Greeks began teaching and writing about rhetoric.

For example, I remember when writing *Our Masters Voices*, Francois Mitterrand had just been elected President of France – and the one line that was widely quoted in the British media was a poetic contrast with alliteration.

In English his aim was translated as: "My aim will be to convince, not to conquer."

The original French version must have arguably sounded even more poetic, with its simple rhyme: "á convaincre, pas á vaincre."

Stories and imagery

Nor is it just rhetorical techniques like contrasts and three-part lists that work effectively to get messages across in any language. The same is true of using stories or anecdotes to illustrate your key points. Other forms of imagery can also work effectively in any language, but metaphors do sometimes need handling with care, especially in the case of sporting metaphors.

As a native speaker of British English, I often find myself bemoaning the fact that we have imported so many baseball metaphors from American English, even though it's not a game that's played or understood by most British adults. But that doesn't stop us having to listen to fellow British presenters telling us about "Stepping up to the plate" or "getting past first base".

Cricketing metaphors may be fine for speakers of English in Australasia, the Caribbean or the Indian sub-continent, but they're not much use in the USA, or indeed in the rest of Europe.

All of which brings me to some rather obvious questions, about which I'm curious, but to which I have no obvious answers. Although English is so widely spoken around the world, how well is it actually understood? Or, going back to my opening comments, how effectively are non-native speakers of English who give speeches written by other non-native speakers of English to audiences of yet more non-native speakers of English?

I used to do quite a lot of work with the director of communications at a British company that had recently been taken over by a Dutch company. When I made some remark about how lucky they were that the Netherlands was part of the English-speaking world, he replied:

"Yes, their English is very impressive – but there are times when we're not quite sure whether they've really got the point."

The crunch question

It was a similar story from a Japanese student in Oxford who was studying for a PhD. As she had spent many of her teenage years growing up in the USA, she was fluent in Japanese and English, which enabled her to pay for her studies by doing simultaneous translation at high level business meetings. After one such meeting between Japanese and British motor manufacturers, I asked her how it had gone – to which she replied:

"OK as far as it went, but I do think that they should pay me for an extra hour after the meetings so I could tell them what I think they really meant."

Her point, of course, was that the simultaneous literal translation was all very well, but she was also noticing and interpreting a good deal more than the words that were actually coming out of the Japanese mouths. And what she thought they really meant was a potentially valuable asset in the negotiating process.

Three questions

Many of you in this audience will have had first hand experience of such issues, so I'll end with three questions in search of an answer. How important do you think the problem of translating what speakers really mean is? Does the use of English as a common language mean that there's something unavoidably cloudy about the way the countries of Europe – and the wider world – are communicating with each other? And if listeners are not quite understanding what a speaker really means, how much does it matter?

Lincoln the movie: "too many words" and "too American" for British ears?

Last night we went to watch the film Lincoln in our local village hall – and, as something of a speech and communications nerd, it was something I had been looking forward to for quite a while. But, from a few minutes in, I found it increasingly difficult to get two rather negative thoughts out of my mind.

One was a memorable line from the film Amadeus, when Mozart is confronted by the complaint that his latest composition suffered from having had "too many notes." From discussions afterwards, I know that I wasn't the only person in the audience who thought that Lincoln suffered from having "far too many words".

Among other things, this had the effect, of making the film too long. For example, when individual members of Congress started to vote on the crucial amendment one by one, I wondered just how many hundreds of these we were going to have to sit through.

I'll admit that our village hall film shows do have a problem with the sound quality, so it was also a relief to learn afterwards that I hadn't been to only one there who had trouble hearing the dialogue. Leaving that to one side, however, there was something else that was difficult to get out of my mind – that I'd implicitly touched on in a recent presentation on on "How well does English work as a common language?"

This was the fact that differences between American and British culture may have ensured that Lincoln was unlikely to impress British audiences as much it had apparently impressed audiences on the other side of the Atlantic.

Before the film started, another member of the audience had already said to me "I don't know much about American history and I've really only come because I felt I ought to – I might learn something."

Too Ethnocentric for a British audience?

And here lies the rub. We Brits really know very little about the history of the USA, let alone its constitution or how it works.

We do know that they had the audacity to declare their independence from us, that they had a civil war that led to the end of slavery – though not the end of segregation – and that they had opted to have a president rather than a monarchy. But most of us know very little about the separation of powers between the legislative and executive arms of government, nor about the differences between the individual constituent states of the USA and the federal government – or the machinations between them that this gives rise to. So for us, some of the basic assumptions at the heart of the film were at best culturally strange and at worst, completely foreign to us.

Vices & virtue as drama?

Apart from the characters of Lincoln and his family, it was never really made clear who everyone else was and we were left guessing who they were and which side they were on, whether in the ongoing debate or the civil war itself. All too often conversations sounded more like a succession of speeches or soliloquies, as when Mrs Lincoln had a row with her husband.

But, however unrealistic, unclear or plain boring the script might have been to British-English ears, the superb acting of Daniel Day Lewis not only deserved all the acclaim and awards that he received for it but was main thing that made it worth seeing at all.

Now we've had an Anglo-Irish actor making such an excellent job of playing a US president so soon after an American actress (Meryl Streep) apparently played a British prime minister (Margaret Thatcher) rather well, we may even be witnessing a promising trend that might actually bring our two cultures a bit closer together.

But that may depend on whether screen-script writers on each side of the Atlantic take note of the famous line that's widely attributed to George Bernard Shaw – England and America are two countries divided by a common language – but which he apparently never said ...

3rd October 2013

Cameron's speech: who thinks he should be seen pretending not to use a script?

It is very well-known that technology can have a marked impact on how effectively speakers come across to an audience – as anyone who's ever been at a PowerPoint presentation knows only too well. So a matter, if not *the* matter, arising from this year's party conference season is just how effectively do speakers come across when they pretend not to use a script?

Three "scriptless" leaders

Because this year, we saw Ed Miliband repeating the feat of memory that worked so well for him last year, while Nick Clegg and David Cameron relied on huge teleprompter screens that were hidden towards the back of the audience – as did George Osborne, Jeremy Hunt and no doubt a few others.

Of the party leaders, Miliband showed us that he could indeed do it again and Clegg showed us (as I've long suspected) that standing at a lectern works better for him than wandering about the stage like a management guru.

But Cameron was more disappointing than usual, not least because he's a talented enough public speaker, whether speaking from a script or from memory, not to have to rely on such gadgets. You don't have to watch very far into the speech to notice that his head and eyes don't always move in time together: his head sometimes turns slightly while his eyes stay firmly glued to the screen directly in front of him – rather like some of Margaret Thatcher's problems when she spoke from Autocue screens.

Where is the advice coming from and what's the evidence for it?

As has often concerned me about the BBC's obsession with PowerPoint style news and current affairs coverage, what gave them the idea that audiences like it and can they point to any research that actually supports such a claim.

So for Messrs Miliband, Clegg and Cameron (and their aides), I have a similar question or two.

Who has advised you that it's a good idea to be seen to be pretending not to have a script and have they shown you any empirical evidence that supports their claim. If so, what is it and where can I see it?

If not, why on earth are you taking any notice of their advice?

(P.S. And some questions for Mr Miliband: who thinks it's a good idea to have some of the audience behind you and do they have any evidence to support their claim? If so, what is it and where can I see it? If not, why are you taking any notice of their advice?)

23rd October 2013

Majorspeak revisited?

Regular readers will realise why, given my regular posts on the peculiar times and places selected by today's politicians, I was greatly frustrated by yesterday's news headlines being dominated by a former Conservative prime minister making what *The Daily Mail* described as a "wide ranging and passionate speech" to a real audience in a suitable location – without any media camera crews being present. So you can't see it on YouTube or anywhere else, and, for once, all we can do is look at are those parts of it that were quoted in the media.

Improved mastery of rhetoric and imagery?

Compared with what I wrote in 1993 ("Majorspeak: observations on the prime minister's style of speaking"), some of which is touched on in the video clip on my blog, there was some evidence that his command of rhetoric and imagery has improved – probably because of his experience on the lucrative US speaker circuit in the years since he left office.

There were, for example, some impressive contrasts:

"Governments should exist to protect people, not institutions"

The Conservative Party "is at its best when it is tolerant and it is open and at its worst when it's hectoring and censorious"

He said it was wrong that so many families would have to choose between keeping warm and eating this winter.

There was at least one three-part list in which the third item contrasted with the first two:

"and it is very easy, criminally easy, to overlook these silent citizens, they don't demonstrate, they don't make a fuss, they just get in with their lives."

There was a puzzle with a three-part list in the solution:

"How do I know about these people? Because I grew up with them. they were my neighbours, the silent have-nots."

He also made some interesting use of imagery:

"If we Tories only navel gaze and only pander to our comfort zone, we will never win general elections. All the core delivers is the wooden spoon."

Majorspeak revisited?

An observation at the time of the 1992 general election was John Major's tendency to speak very "formally" (See Chapter 19, *Political Communications: The General Election Campaign of 1992*, Crew & Gosschalk, 1995). This was evidenced partly by his choice of words that are rarely, if ever, heard in everyday conversation (e.g. "whomsoever", "wayside inn", "on the morrow", "badinage", etc.) and partly by his reluctance ever to use the elided forms for negatives and certain tense constructions (e.g. he was more likely to say "we do not" than "we don't", "we had" rather than "we'd" etc.

In yesterday's speech, "hectoring" and "censorious" suggest that his preference for obscure words lives on. But the fact that he said "they don't" twice in quick succession is perhaps evidence that he has started to break away from his former preference for using the full forms.

The bad news is that, without the video-taped evidence, we may never know.

24th January 2014

Capturing details in a speech: a musical reminder of failure

Yesterday, I had my first piano lesson for 55+ years, which reminded me of something I gave up on when starting the research into political speeches that eventually resulted in *Our Masters' Voices* in 1984.

It was easy enough to collect tapes of political speeches, but many of the most significant findings from conversation analysis had come from detailed transciptions of recordings of actual conversations (for more on the methodology of which, see *Structures of Social Action*, J. Maxwell Atkinson, John Heritage 1984).

So the first challenge was how to transcribe the lines spoken just before bursts of applause in the speeches. Variations in intonation clearly mattered, not least because the way speakers talked in speeches featured more (and longer) pauses and much more marked tonal shifts upwards and downwards than is typically found in everyday conversation.

I started by trying to capture such details by trying to transcribe syllables, words, sentences and phrases on the different lines and spaces in the staves of blank musical manuscript paper. But two obstacles stood in my way.

One was that it was far more time-consuming than doing the transcripts in *Our Masters' Voices* – which took well over an hour to transcribe each 10 seconds of speech.

The second one, as I realised again yesterday, was that I was never much good at sight-reading music anyway, so my attempts to capture details of the beat, timing and positioning of words on the lines and spaces of a stave were doomed to failure.

I'm hoping that it may not be too late to improve my sight-reading of music – but have no illusions about my chances of ever being able to write music, let alone to transcribe speeches, on manuscript paper.

3rd February 2014

Metaphors from the flooded Somerset Levels playing field

The *Sky News* website has been reporting some linguistically interesting comments on the floods on the Somerset Levels. According to Gavin Sadler, a member of campaign group Flooding on the Levels Action Group (FLAG): "We were *in the same boat* last year and were told it was a one in a 100-year flood – now it's happened again."

Meanwhile, shadow environment secretary Maria Eagle told *Sky's* Murnaghan programme "The Environment Secretary appears to me to be *out of his depth*. He's just not taking it seriously".

"Triggered metaphors" are close relations of "triggered puns", on which I've blogged previously from time to time. Needless to say, contributions of similar examples are always welcome.

26th August 2014

What if "energised" Salmond wins???

The Independent newspaper described Alex Salmond's performance in last night's leader's debate as "energised" - which is surely bad news for Alistair Darling and the Labour Party.

One of the big questions about the debate to me is why did David Cameron and the Tories allow an experienced former Labour cabinet minister lead the *Better Together* campaign – when the loss of Scotland, legally complicated though it would be, would mean that Labour might never again form the government of the residual UK. In fact, why are the Conseratives opposing Salmond & Co. at all, I wonder?

Then there's the question of what the long term point of a Scottish National party would be if they actually win the referendum on independence?

I'm not too keen on the idea of an independent Scotland, in spite of my Scottish ancestry, but I do wish someone would answer some of these rather obvious questions.

About the Author

Max Atkinson was a fellow of Wolfson College, Oxford and previously taught at the universities of Essex, Lancaster and Manchester. He was also a visiting professor at the Henley Management College and various universities in Europe and the USA, after which he formed a consultancy specialising in public speaking and presentation skills.

In 1985, he ran a seminar on speech writing in the Reagan White House and, from 1987 to 1999, was a close advisor to Paddy Ashdown, former leader of the Liberal Democrats.

Visit his website: www.speaking.co.uk

And read the blog this book was based on: maxatkinson.blogspot.co.uk

Notes

Index

Seen & Heard

Seen & Heard

SUNMAKERS

Publish your expertise

 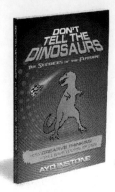 

 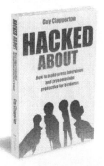 

www.sunmakers.co.uk

Printed in Great Britain
by Amazon.co.uk, Ltd.,
Marston Gate.